Preston Sturges'
Vision of America

M000217174

Preston Sturges's Vision of America

Critical Analyses of Fourteen Films

JAY ROZGONYI

McFarland & Company, Inc., Publishers

Jefferson, North Carolina

The present work is a reprint of the library bound edition of
Preston Sturges's Vision of America: Critical Analyses of
Fourteen Films, first published in 1995 by McFarland.

LIBRARY OF CONGRESS CATALOGUING-IN-PUBLICATION DATA

Rozgonyi, Jay, 1960–
    Preston Sturges's vision of America : critical analyses of
fourteen films / Jay Rozgonyi.
        p.   cm.
    Filmography : p.
    Includes bibliographical references and index.

    ISBN 978-0-7864-9371-5
    softcover : acid free paper ∞

    1. Sturges, Preston—Criticism and interpretation.
I. Title.
PN1988.3.S78R68 2014
791.43'0233'092—dc20   94-24196

BRITISH LIBRARY CATALOGUING DATA ARE AVAILABLE

© 1995 Jay Rozgonyi. All rights reserved

No part of this book may be reproduced or transmitted in any form
or by any means, electronic or mechanical, including photocopying
or recording, or by any information storage and retrieval system,
without permission in writing from the publisher.

On the cover: Betty Hutton and Preston Sturges on set
of *The Miracle of Morgan's Creek* (1944), directed by
Preston Sturges (Paramount Pictures/Photofest)

Manufactured in the United States of America

McFarland & Company, Inc., Publishers
    Box 611, Jefferson, North Carolina 28640
    www.mcfarlandpub.com

Contents

Acknowledgments

In trying to write acknowledgments for a film book I feel somewhat like an Academy Award winner struggling to thank all the right people without boring the audience. As the cliché goes, there are so many people who have helped me, and I do not want to forget any of them.

I first have to thank two people without whose assistance this book would never have gotten into print. The late Martin Williams, a talented writer as well as an editor at Smithsonian Institution Press, was generous with his time. He encouraged me to write the book that *I* wanted to write. Similarly helpful with advice was James Robert Parish.

A major debt is also owed to all my colleagues at Nyselius Library at Fairfield University, who have suffered through nearly two years of hearing about this project. In particular, I am grateful to Nancy van Vlissingen, who turned up even the most obscure books and articles on interlibrary loan; Veronica Kenausis, a wonderful friend, who provided research assistance and moral support; Margaret Schneider, my assistant in the Media Department, and all my student workers, who kept after me to finish this book so that they could buy copies and have them autographed. A very special thank-you goes to Betsy Hoagg, the former head of the Nyselius Reference Department. Not only did she allow her staff to assist me, she also gave me encouragement, reassurance, and even a bit of prodding.

Others whose words and actions helped me include Richard Allee, who came through with a tape and an article at a crucial moment, and my sister-in-law, Jeannie Solensky, who was always ready to listen.

Finally, there are three people for whom mere thanks are not enough. My father, James Rozgonyi, who did not live to see the publication of this book: He may not have loved movies the way I do, but I know that he would have been very proud to hold this volume in his hands. Don Coonley: Everything I think and write about film and media continues to be influenced by all that I learned from his classes more than ten years ago. And Suzanne, my wife: She watched every movie, discussed every idea, and edited every word, but more importantly, she provided the love and support that made it possible for me to even attempt this challenge.

Introduction

Of the thousands of people who toiled behind Hollywood's cameras from the 1920s through the 1950s, only a handful were able to take their five-day-a-week, studio-assigned projects and, over the span of an entire career, put their own personal stamp on the films they created. The ones who were able to do it—Alfred Hitchcock, Frank Capra, and John Ford, for example—possessed not only a rare artistic talent that wasn't stifled by the studio system, but also an extraordinary level of control in terms of producing and even writing their own projects.

Few would argue against the suggestion that Preston Sturges falls squarely in the company of the Hitchcocks, Capras, and Fords, rather than with the talented craftsmen who handled most of the studio output. From the time he first came to Hollywood as a highly regarded New York playwright, his writing was accorded a measure of respect that few studio writers enjoyed. Later, Sturges was the first contract writer—before Billy Wilder or John Huston—to be given the opportunity to direct his own screenplays, and during his years at Paramount he was hailed as a genius in studio publicity and recognized as an eccentric visionary by the general public. By the time Sturges reached 20th Century–Fox in 1948, he was producing his own films as well.

That independence was probably at least partially responsible for the unique filmmaking style that Sturges developed. His razor-sharp dialogue, wild plot turns, and wondrously original secondary characters gave life to a remarkable set of movies that could never be mistaken for the work of another director. But Sturges's inclusion in the ranks of the auteurs is based on more than just a style that can be traced from one film to the next; his real accomplishment was in using his relative power within the studio system, as well as his significant talent, to inject into his movies a reasonably consistent vision of life in America.

Because film, at least during Sturges's time, was primarily a commercial medium, the driving force behind his work was entertainment rather than art. Still, I think it can be argued that in film after film he returned to a handful of basic themes and treated them with more depth than is

1

usually given to simple diversions. Obviously, not all of his movies cover the same topics or do so in a similar way; after all, Sturges was not creating a filmic dissertation, with each new movie constituting a separate chapter of theory and analysis. But if we take into account the circumstances under which he worked, finding fourteen films in his fewer than twenty major works that *do* explore the same area makes a strong argument for an artistic vision.

These fourteen films share a similar characteristic: they deflate many of the ideas that Americans embrace about society and themselves. For the most part, these tend to be vague concepts that form something of a collective mythology: America and its citizens are special and somehow above the common shortcomings of others; America has an equitable, classless system that allows people to accrue wealth and achieve success solely on the basis of their own hard work; most people are ethical and well-intentioned, and honesty always pays off while dishonesty is invariably punished; and all citizens are treated justly and equally under the law, no matter what their economic status may be.

While there are undoubtedly many insightful works that analyze this kind of American self-image and mythology, I've chosen not to include them in my discussions for one main reason: for anyone who has grown up in the United States, the ideas mentioned above need no more official corroboration than does the story of George Washington and the cherry tree. They are part of a fund of knowledge that Americans all share, concepts and values that are instilled in us from the earliest years onward. Moreover, Sturges's characters clearly share this knowledge as well; some may wholeheartedly believe in the myths, while others may take advantage of someone else's belief, but they are all aware of the role these ideas play in forming the popular view of life in America.

My basic plan for this book was to identify Preston Sturges's major works and then analyze each film separately for the way in which he addressed these general themes. Although determining what constitutes a director's major efforts can be somewhat subjective, in Sturges's case the process was not particularly difficult. Of the movies that he did not direct, I chose to look only at those that, according to his biographers, he was clearly responsible for shaping through his screenplays.* Of the six films I found, only two — *The Good Fairy* and *If I Were King* — are not discussed in the book, simply because their settings are not the United States. Of the twelve films Sturges did direct, ten are included here. His final work, *The French They Are a Funny Race*, is not discussed both because it is set abroad and because it is so poor and uncharacteristic of Sturges that it is simply

<hr />

*James Curtis, Between Flops; Donald Spoto, Madcap; and Diane Jacobs, Christmas in July. Sturges's autobiography, Preston Sturges by Preston Sturges, was also consulted.

better forgotten. *Unfaithfully Yours*, on the other hand, is an excellent film, but was left out simply because it sets its sights on other themes.

As with any critical study, it was necessary for me to establish a set of guidelines for my analysis. Since I always intended this to be a study of only one aspect of Sturges's art, and since Sturges was first and foremost a writer, I decided that it was logical to limit my discussion to ideas that stemmed directly from his writing and not to consider (except in a few obvious cases) his directorial techniques. For that reason, the chapters often contain lengthy examples of dialogue, all of which were transcribed as accurately as possible from the movies themselves. In a few cases I was able to consult published versions of screenplays, and when something has been drawn from one of these sources I have made that clear in the text or in a footnote. In addition, because a reader may not always have seen a particular film within recent memory, I have included a detailed plot synopsis at the beginning of every chapter.

The other major decision I made was to limit the ideas in this book to my own and not to try to respond to the interpretations of other scholars and critics. As a longtime fan of movies, I have always found it rewarding to watch a film and then read one person's considered analysis of what that work has to say. It does not matter whether I agree or disagree with the author's ideas, as long as the writing causes me to think about the movie. It was with that goal in mind that I set out to write this book. As much as I respect rigorous academic scholarship, I never intended this work to refer to every published source or incorporate everyone else's theories; instead, I would like any serious film fan to be able to pick up the book, read any single chapter, and come away with some clearly stated, thought-provoking ideas.

I have no illusions that the view of America presented by Preston Sturges in one film exactly conforms to that presented in any of his other films. *Remember the Night*, for instance, offers a very positive vision of families and small-town values, while *The Miracle of Morgan's Creek* is full of feuding households and hypocritical townspeople. But the important point is that in film after film, Sturges did deal with the same basic issues, and although the emphasis of this book is to analyze each movie on its own, I have added a fairly lengthy conclusion in which I attempt to show that, for the most part, his perspective was remarkably consistent throughout his career.

After completing this volume I have come to appreciate more than ever that critiquing movies can be a dangerous activity. As we have come to consider filmmakers as artists, we seem to want more and more to categorize them, to account for each and every movie they have made, and to wrap up into a neat package the ideas they have presented and the themes they have explored. That is hard enough to do with any artist, but with a writer/director who worked in the Hollywood studio system, it is just about impossible. Luckily for us, Preston Sturges's primary aim was not to make a scholarly assessment of our society, but rather to entertain, and he did that magnificently well. Now, after the couple of hundred hours I have spent watching his films, and the thousands of hours I have spent thinking and writing about them, I can honestly say that the Wienie King, the Ale and Quail Club, and Ignatz Ratzkiwatzki of Camp Smum are still as funny to me as they were the first time I saw them. And *that*, more than anything else, is for me the proof of Preston Sturges's genius.

ONE

The Power and the Glory

Produced by Jesse L. Lasky; Directed by William K. Howard; Screenplay by Preston Sturges; Photography: James Wong Howe; Edited by Paul Weatherwax; Art Direction: Max Parker; Music: Louis DeFrancesco, J. S. Zamencik, and Peter Brunelli. Released by Fox Film Corporation, 1933.

Cast: Spencer Tracy (Tom Garner); Colleen Moore (Sally); Ralph Morgan (Henry); Helen Vinson (Eve); Sarah Padden (Henry's Wife); Clifford Jones (Tom Jr.); Henry Kolker (Mr. Borden).

Synopsis: In a large, fully packed church, a funeral mass is being held for Thomas Garner, the president of the greatest railroad in America. The solemn mourners listen intently as the minister eulogizes Garner as a great and kindly man, but for Henry, Tom's secretary and lifelong friend, the service is too much to take. He quietly gets up and makes his way to Tom's office at the Southwestern Railroad. There he meets the elevator operator, who offers a completely different opinion of Tom, saying that he is better off dead. Henry chastises the man, then enters Tom's office, silently looks about the familiar surroundings, and pockets a picture of Tom and his young son before leaving.

At home that evening, Henry's wife claims that Tom was a good-for-nothing who kicked his wife out and was hated by everyone. Henry declares that that is not an accurate picture—that people simply did not understand Tom—and in a flashback scene he begins to recount the story of Tom's life from his own firsthand experience. As a child, Henry meets the older and bigger Tom at the local swimming hole, where Tom tries to convince a frightened Henry to swim. Afraid to take the risk, Henry is pulled into the water by Tom, which makes Henry so mad that he starts a fight with the much stronger boy. This feistiness earns Tom's respect; later, after Tom dives into the water and nearly drowns, Henry's concern and help cement their newfound friendship.

Henry then jumps ahead many years in his story. A middle-aged Tom has been the president of the Southwestern Railroad for years, and Henry is his devoted secretary and right-hand man. After working out an unspecified deal over the phone, Tom enters a board meeting and tries to convince the directors to back him in purchasing the Santa Clara Railroad. Although they are all dead set against the move, Tom keeps pushing them until they agree. He thanks the board for finally seeing it his way, then informs them that he has already made the deal and bought the railroad.

As the tale turns to Tom's wife, Sally, Henry goes back to the time when Tom was twenty. As a trackwalker with the railroad he is a happy man; one day, on receiving a letter from Henry, Tom takes it to Sally, the local schoolteacher, and tries to get her to read it to him without letting on that he cannot read or write. Despite his efforts, Sally detects Tom's lack of education and offers to tutor him at night. Eventually the two fall in love, and Tom nervously proposes to her during an arduous mountainside walk.

The story of Tom's first months with Sally prompts Henry to relate a parallel tale. The scene changes to the time of the Santa Clara deal, when the railroad's president arrives to find out whether Tom intends to let him retain his position. While Tom keeps the rival executive waiting out of spite, Henry sees the man and his daughter, Eve, whispering in the outer office. When the two railroad presidents finally meet, they decide to go out to lunch along with Eve; by the time Tom returns from lunch hours later, his hatred for his rival has turned to respect and amiability, and all he can talk about is how pretty and nice Eve is. Shortly thereafter Tom's son comes to see him at the office. Since Tom Jr. has been expelled from Yale for drunkenness and poor behavior, Tom decides to punish him by giving him an entry-level job at the railroad and making him live on his wages alone. At home that evening, when Sally protests against Tom's action, the couple argue and Tom leaves to spend a few nights at his club.

The time frame then reverts to the early days of Tom and Sally's marriage. At Sally's instigation, she and Tom discuss his future, but they disagree about what he should do. Tom is happy to be a trackwalker and to eschew the worry and effort of moving up in the railroad organization, but Sally is anxious for him to be a success. She outlines a plan to get all the material things she would like: while Tom goes to engineering school she will take over his trackwalking job. Although Tom is reluctant, there's not much he can do. All the arrangements have already been made with his boss, and in the end he agrees to "try to be somebody." Tom heads off to Chicago, where he takes both day and evening classes, while Sally stays at home and struggles to do the difficult job that will keep them going.

The story of Tom and Eve is picked up again with a scene of the couple at a restaurant. Although he affirms his love for Eve, Tom says that he simply cannot divorce Sally. When Tom is back at his office Sally comes to see him and tells him what he has already realized—that their relationship has deteriorated. She takes the blame, admitting that she forced him to work hard and to pursue a career when he was content to be a simple trackwalker. In turn, Tom confesses his attraction to Eve, but says that he will leave her and devote himself to his wife. Sally won't hear of it, though, because she thinks that Tom deserves some fun for once in his life; as she leaves the building, she commits suicide by throwing herself in front of a streetcar.

At Henry's house, back on the day of the funeral, Henry's wife claims that Sally was never happy with Tom. Henry counters with an example of their joy early in their marriage. On the same day that Tom comes home to announce that he has been put in charge of his first bridge construction, Sally breaks the news that she is pregnant.

Following the birth of Tom Jr., Henry's story moves forward to the time shortly after Sally's suicide. Tom tells Tom Jr. that he will be marrying Eve and that he will no longer require his son to work as an entry-level bookkeeper. Tom and Eve are married in a small, private wedding, but almost immediately Tom is called away by a strike of railroad workers that he has been trying for months to prevent. Forcing his way into a large workers' meeting, Tom declares that he will not stand for a strike by his employees. Although Eve wants her new husband to be with her, Tom stays away for six weeks, until the strike ends in violence and the deaths of more than 400 men.

In another brief scene at Henry's home, Henry's wife claims that Tom killed himself because he felt guilty over the hundreds of men whose deaths he had caused. Henry disagrees, however, and his narrative shifts to Tom's last day. It is his wedding anniversary, and he leaves the office to bring a present to Eve and their infant son. On entering the house Tom overhears Eve telling a caller on the telephone that her baby looks just like him. Tom returns to the office for a board meeting, but he cannot get the incident out of his mind. On the verge of collapse, he returns home with Henry and questions Eve. She cannot bring herself to tell him who the real father is—the implication is that it's Tom Jr.—and Tom, muttering that she deserves to have some fun in her life, makes his way to his bedroom, takes out a gun, and shoots himself. The last word he speaks is "Sally."

•

Over the years *The Power and the Glory* has generated much more attention than would seem likely for a film that did not do very well at the box office and that hasn't been revived very often or released on videocassette. Discussion of the film usually centers on one of two items: the influence its story and structure had on *Citizen Kane,* or the deal Preston Sturges made when selling the script to Fox Studios (he received a percentage based on gross receipts, as a playwright would).

Sturges might have been happier, however, if he had sold the script outright. The deal did give his work a level of respect previously unheard of in Hollywood, and even though he was not the movie's director, barely a word was changed from his final script to the completed film. In addition, the movie may not have generated much in box-office revenue, but Sturges did earn a fair amount of money from it (if his own explanation in a letter to the *Hollywood Reporter* was correct, he must have gotten approximately $42,000).* But he also incurred the wrath of many Hollywood executives, who controlled the film industry's purse strings. By prompting Sturges to try to construct similar arrangements elsewhere, the deal also caused a setback to his ultimate goal of writing and directing his own scripts.

But while film industry historians may be concerned with royalties and Hollywood power plays, it is the *Citizen Kane* connection that today draws most film fans and critics to *The Power and the Glory*. People who are in the business of bashing Orson Welles use Sturges's 1933 drama as one of the prime weapons in their arsenal. Pauline Kael, in her notorious *Citizen Kane Book*, implies that Sturges's film greatly influenced his "friend and drinking companion" Herman Mankiewicz (the "true" author of *Kane*),† while others have spoken of a more direct influence on Welles himself. There is no doubt that Sturges's unorthodox narrative, which features a wealthy industrialist as the main character, bears a striking resemblance to *Citizen Kane*, but that neither accounts for their major differences nor takes away from the greatness of Welles's masterpiece.

In this book, however, *The Power and the Glory* is important for the way in which Sturges uses the story to comment on the American Dream. Like many Sturges films that came later, this one deals with the American myths that the opinions of the masses (read "democracy") are almost always right and that there's a direct correlation between wealth and happiness. Perhaps because this was one of Sturges's earliest scripts, or perhaps because he had yet to settle on his own role as satirist and cynical commentator, *The Power and the Glory* is somewhat less successful at skewering these myths than the later comedies would be. Still, the ideas that would come to fruition in later years were already present in this story.

Mass Opinion and the Truth

Even the most cursory viewing of *The Power and the Glory* reveals that Preston Sturges's primary concern in the film is how the public perceives

---

*James Curtis, Between Flops, *p. 83.*
†*Pauline Kael, "Raising Kane," in* The Citizen Kane Book, *pp. 50–51.*

those who are "successful." His innovative narrative structure sets the stage before we ever see Tom Garner or learn the truth about him: we are given the generally accepted view that he was a ruthless and powerful businessman and a rotten human being who was more or less despised by everyone. (It is just one more ironic touch on Sturges's part that such a hated man would have so many people turn out for his funeral.) The comments made by the elevator operator Henry meets ("I knew him a long time, too. I'm glad he croaked . . .") and by Henry's wife ("It's a good thing he did kill himself . . . he was a good-for-nothing") present the established opinion. Henry's wife further tells us that Tom killed more than 400 men and mistreated his wife before kicking her out for a woman young enough to be his daughter. By having Henry's wife say, "I did understand him, and so did everyone else," Sturges makes a connection between her comments and the feelings of the masses. But, as in so many of his films, Sturges wants us to know that people can easily be misled or misread the situation. In this case he uses the nonchronological flashback structure to reveal just how wrong their simple perception is.

Sturges has Henry begin his story of Tom's life with what is perhaps the most humanizing incident we see: the childhood meeting of the two lifelong friends. Although Henry describes Tom as older and bigger, his perception seems to be based more on Tom's attitude and personality than on his physical traits. Henry's reminiscence of how he gained Tom's respect by standing up to the older boy hardly portrays Tom as ruthless or insensitive. Instead, he appears to be a rather typical youngster, challenging another to do what seems reasonable but also admiring him for doing it and for taking a stand. Similarly, when Tom injures himself diving, he displays a genuine appreciation to Henry for his attention and concern.

Sturges continues his debunking of the accepted view of Tom by moving to the period when he makes the deal to acquire the Santa Clara Railroad. Although it could be argued that Tom comes across as less than praiseworthy by settling a deal without informing his board of directors and then steamrolling through a formal consent, Sturges stacks the cards in favor of Tom. The directors are depicted as weak and cowardly, speaking harshly against Tom and his plan when he is not in the room and then failing to do anything but acquiesce to his wishes when he confronts them. Their only reason for not wanting to acquire the railroad is, as Tom puts it, "economy." We get a further reason to feel kindly toward Tom as the scene ends, when he insists, against Henry's wishes, that his friend buy some stock in the new railroad company; it is this purchase, Henry's voice-over informs us, that allowed him to buy the house we have just seen.

It is quite some time, in fact, before Sturges shows us anything that we can construe as detrimental in Tom's character. The next sequence in the film introduces Sally, develops her relationship with Tom as she teaches

is left speechless. She simply stands up, touches Henry on the shoulder, and leaves the room, silenced by the truth that Tom was neither a saint nor a devil, but something in-between. Her silence is an acknowledgment that the accepted opinion—which in a democracy represents truth—can often be wrong.

Success and Happiness

In the title he chose for his script, Sturges immediately makes it clear that he intends to treat Tom Garner's success with irony. We are told that Tom is a noted businessman, but the story we see of him is almost entirely a personal one. No real work incidents are shown, with the exceptions of the purchase of the Santa Clara and the strike—and even these have strong personal elements to them. The railroad acquisition introduces Tom to Eve and also allows him to set Henry up with a bit of financial security, and the strike is portrayed as the breaking point in Tom's second marriage, since it drives his wife into the arms of his son. We cannot judge Tom's power or glory in the business world as completely as we might like, but he certainly has little of either in his personal life.

The issue of Tom's happiness arises numerous times in the film, both through spoken references and through scenes and images that can be sorted into categories of "happy" and "unhappy." Although the unique narrative structure offers glimpses of Tom at various points in his life, a regrouping of the scenes into chronological order reveals that there are only two major time periods shown: (1) the period from the time Tom is twenty through the birth of his son, certainly no more than ten years and probably less; and (2) the last few years of Tom's life, from the Santa Clara deal to his death, about five years at most.* The two periods are separated by roughly twenty years, a time about which we know essentially nothing.

In the first group we are shown three episodes: Sally's tutoring of Tom and their courtship and eventual engagement; the early days of their marriage and the beginnings of Tom's struggle to go to school and succeed; and the promotion of Tom to head his first construction project and the birth of the couple's son. All these sequences, which clearly come before Tom's success, can only be characterized as happy, and the images of a young couple who are obviously deeply in love are reinforced by Henry's voice-over. "They stayed happy a good, long time," he says as the engagement sequence ends, and he adds, "maybe Tom would be a trackwalker yet—happy and satisfied," as the scene changes to the first days of their

---

The only incident that falls outside of these periods is the swimming hole scene in which Tom and Henry first meet as boys.

marriage. In the scenes of their early life together, then, there is no indication that Tom and Sally were anything less than happy.

Contrasted with this are the five episodes that clearly fall after Tom has made it: the purchase of the Santa Clara; his first meeting with Eve; his declaration of love for Eve, the disclosure of his affair to Sally, and Sally's suicide; his remarriage and neglect of his honeymoon because of the strike; and his betrayal by Eve and his subsequent suicide. Unlike the earlier sequences, these can hardly be described as happy visions of Tom's life. At best, the sequences surrounding the purchase of the Santa Clara and Tom's first lunch with Eve are neutral (although Tom's susceptibility to Eve's flirtations can also be read as an indication that his marriage to Sally has deteriorated). The other three sequences, however, combine to offer an unmistakable portrait of a miserable life. In the restaurant Tom proclaims his love for Eve, but considers it a horrible yet unavoidable mistake; his attempt to be honest about it with Sally only drives her to suicide. Following his remarriage he is forced to abandon his honeymoon to attend to the strike; the outcome this time is an infuriated wife and 406 dead employees. And finally, after taking time off from work to bring Eve an anniversary gift, he discovers not only that his wife is having an affair and that his child is not his own, but presumably that his own son is the child's father. The result for Tom, as for Sally earlier, is suicide.

As Sturges portrays it, the break between Tom's happy life and his unhappy one is obvious. The scene in which Tom Jr. is born is the last we see of Tom's happy period, in both chronological order and in the order in which the scenes are presented in the film. Tom has begun moving up the ladder of success, as he's been put in charge of a construction project for the first time, but he and Sally are still in love with each other and leading a humble life. Their house is only slightly better looking than the ramshackle cottage they first occupied, and it is nothing like the fancy penthouse apartment in which Tom will reside years later. The couple is obviously happy and in love, but Tom greets the news that he is going to be a father with a telling remark: "I'll make so much money for you and that kid that we'll buy the Southwestern and give it to him to play with." To hammer the point home—that this is the end of Tom's contentment and the beginning of his misery—Sturges has Tom recite a portion of the Lord's Prayer after his son is born, then follows it with Henry's comment, "The power and the glory—what they can do to a man." The implication is clear: for Tom Garner, the power and the glory ruined his life.

On just how Tom attained that power and glory, however, Sturges has much less to say. For one of the few times in a Sturges movie the method seems to have been hard work. In later films, such as *Christmas in July*, *The Palm Beach Story*, and *The Sin of Harold Diddlebock*, success, position, and wealth would be systematically denied to characters who were hardworking

Tom Garner (Spencer Tracy) and his wife, Sally (Colleen Moore), in the earlier—and happier—days of their marriage.

and honest. In *The Power and the Glory*, Sturges may be suggesting that perhaps it is not prudent for certain people to be successful.* All indications are that Tom was perfectly satisfied to walk the tracks, which he characterizes as easy work that also lets him "get a lot of good fishing in on the side."

**As James Curtis puts it in* Between Flops, *when he discusses C. W. Post, Sturges's inspiration for the film, "maybe he bolted from the place he was meant to hold in life and was punished for his temerity" (p. 79).*

He decides to go to school and to work his way up the career ladder solely because Sally wants to have "good clothes and a better house, and maybe even a horse and carriage." Even Henry states after Tom's death that he might be a happy trackwalker yet if it had not been for Sally's insistence that he make something of himself. And before her suicide, Sally herself tells Tom, "I wanted the money and the power, and you just wanted to go fishing." About the only time Tom expresses any interest in money and power is when he vows to buy the Southwestern for Tom Jr.—a desire for success that is directed entirely toward another person.

In *The Power and the Glory*, Sturges clearly meant to say that despite what the American Dream may tell us, money and power do not equal happiness and sometimes the simpler things in life are more valuable. (Ironically, the second idea is one that Sturges would satirize nine years later in *The Palm Beach Story*.) But while there are a number of rich people who enjoy their wealth in other Sturges films, in *The Power and the Glory* no one has both money *and* happiness. Tom and Sally are clearly content when they are first married, even though they are poor, but as Sally tells Tom at the end of her life, "You've built so many miles of railroad, and every mile has taken you farther away from me." Mr. Borden certainly has money, but he ends up losing his wealth (the Santa Clara Railroad). When Eve later states that his railroad never interfered with his personal life, Sturges's point becomes clear: Borden's insistence on maintaining a private life prevented him from keeping his railroad, for pleasure and wealth cannot exist side by side. And none of the other rich characters— Sally; Eve, after her marriage to Tom; or Tom Jr., whose life is more or less ruined by money and privilege—can in any way be called fulfilled.

The only contrast to Tom's unhappiness, then, is his own early years with Sally and the brief scenes of Henry and his wife, a devoted couple who have little more than their love for each other. Neither of these couples needs money to be happy, but only one of them was smart enough to realize that. Tom's success ultimately results in misery on the outside—he is hated and reviled by the general public—and misery on the inside—his personal life includes betrayal, suicide, and possibly even the murder of hundreds of men. And all his money can never compensate for that kind of unhappiness.

TWO

Diamond Jim

Produced by Edmund Grainger; Directed by A. Edward Sutherland; Based on the book by Parker Morrell; Screenplay by Preston Sturges; Adaptation by Doris Malloy and Harry Clork; Photography: George Robinson; Photographic Effects: John P. Fulton; Edited by Daniel Mandell; Art Direction: Charles D. Hall; Sound: Gilbert Kurlaw; Musical Score: Franz Waxman. Released by Universal, 1935.

Cast: Edward Arnold (Diamond Jim Brady); Jean Arthur (Emma/ Jane Matthews); Binnie Barnes (Lillian Russell); Cesar Romero (Jerry Richardson); Eric Blore (Sampson Fox); Hugh O'Connell (Charles Horsley); George Sidney (Pawnbroker); Robert McWade (A. E. Moore); William Demarest (Harry Hill); Bill Hoolahahn (John L. Sullivan); Charles Sellon (Station Agent); Purnell Pratt (Physician).

Synopsis: In 1856, on the day that James Buchanan is elected president of the United States, a baby boy is born to a saloon keeper and his wife. In honor of the new president they name their child James Buchanan Brady, promising him a life of love and opportunity. By the time he is ten years old, however, both his parents have died and Jim is forced to live with his aunt and uncle. With children of their own and not much money, the couple have no choice but to send Jim out to work, and before he turns thirty he has been a bellhop, a baggage carrier, and even a tramp. In 1886 Jim is working as a baggage master at a small railroad station when he spots a newspaper ad for a railroad supplies salesman. Convinced that he can get the job even though he has no experience, he "borrows" some money from the cash drawer, rents a set of clothes and a diamond, and hurries down to the offices of A. E. Moore & Company. Presenting himself as a customer rather than a job seeker, Jim does an end run around all the other applicants, walks into Moore's office, demonstrates his knowledge of railroad equipment, and gets the job. Just as he promises, his success as a salesman is almost immediate.

During his travels Jim meets Sampson Fox, an Englishman who is trying, with no luck at all, to market a new type of railroad undertruck. Jim is intrigued by the product and agrees to sell it for Fox at a substantial commission. His interest wanes after he discovers that the woman he loves is going to marry another man, but when the prospect of a big deal arises he throws himself into his work. On the very day of his romantic rejection he gets Charles Horsley to order 500 trucks by plying the railroad magnate with liquor and burlesque girls. When a more sober Horsley balks at the transaction the next morning, Jim agrees to let him off the hook — because, he claims, one of Horsley's competitors had already committed to buying that production run of undertrucks. Unwilling to be outdone by a business rival, Horsley insists on taking the trucks, giving Jim the leverage he needs to sell another set to Horsley's competitor. After creating a demand for the product, Jim takes the next logical step and sets up a factory in the United States to build the undertrucks. In a short time the operation grows to enormous proportions, and Jim becomes fabulously wealthy.

He takes to showering himself with flamboyant, custom-made diamond jewelry, frequenting nightclubs and restaurants, and satisfying his immense appetite with gargantuan gourmet meals. It is at one of his nightclub stops where Jim first sees a singer named Nell Leonard, with whom he is completely taken. Jim helps set Nell up as a legitimate theatrical performer under the name Lillian Russell, and the two become deeply devoted friends. Jim also develops a close friendship with Nell's boyfriend, Jerry Richardson, and when Jim meets Jane Matthews, seemingly the exact double of the woman he nearly married, the two couples begin spending a great deal of time together. His interest in love renewed, Jim proposes to Jane, and she accepts. Just before the wedding, however, Nell tells Jim that Jane has been another man's mistress, and he leaves his fiancée standing at the altar. Jim soon realizes how much he truly loves Jane, and from that point on he keeps pursuing her. Jane resists his repeated proposals, though, partly because she still resents having been jilted the first time, but mostly because she has gradually fallen in love with Jerry Richardson.

In the meantime the country's economy has worsened, and the stock market begins to drop on a daily basis. Everyone starts to sell railroad stock, feeding the downward spiral, but Jim refuses to give in to the panic. Insisting that railroads are the backbone of the United States, he buys more and more of the stock; unfortunately, his purchases are not enough to save the market from total collapse. Wiped out financially, Jim is forced to go back to where he started: selling railroad supplies for A. E. Moore & Company.

After a fateful railroad trip Jim comes up with the plan that he is convinced will make him wealthy again. While on his sales rounds he is aboard a train that derails and in moments is engulfed in flames. From that experience Jim gets the revolutionary idea of building railroad cars of steel, and he persuades Moore to set up a manufacturing facility. To prove the safety of his invention, Jim arranges to have one of the steel cars crashed into an old wooden one—while he is riding in the new car. Despite Jane's last-minute attempt to stop the stunt, it goes as planned, but while disembarking to the cheers of the crowd Jim collapses and nearly dies. The years of abuse he has inflicted on his stomach have taken their toll, and he recovers only after major surgery and a year of hospitalization. When Jim is finally released, the doctor warns him that he must drastically change his eating habits or face certain death.

On his discharge from the hospital Jim finds that his scheme has paid off and he is once again a rich man. To celebrate, he plans a grand tour of Europe for himself, Jane, Nell, and Jerry, but before the group can leave, Jane and Jerry finally inform him of their love affair. Devastated, Jim goes to break the news to Nell. He tries to convince her that the two of them should go ahead with the trip anyway, and maybe even marry each other, but it is clear that the enthusiasm is gone for both of them. Unable to live with having his heart broken a second time, Jim returns home, spends some time going through his personal papers and photographs, and asks his cook to prepare one final culinary feast for him. Knowing full well what the result will be, Jim gives himself over to the one thing that has never disappointed him.

◉

Although Preston Sturges was only the last of a number of writers to work on *Diamond Jim*, the film still bears his unmistakable stamp. He had been hired to polish a script that three other writers had worked on, but rather than doing a simple rewrite, he tossed the entire screenplay and started again from scratch.* In so doing he created the framework for a movie that was not unlike his earlier original work *The Power and the Glory*. In both films Sturges developed a larger-than-life character who goes from poverty to immense wealth by way of the railroad industry, who gains all the material things that any person could want, and who ultimately finds his life lacking despite all his money and possessions. Though the men are much different in temperament—Tom Garner is less likable and more of a no-nonsense businessman, while Jim Brady is a genial philanthropist with care and concern for all—they both end up taking their own lives, unable to bear the burden of their disappointments.

Where *Diamond Jim* and *The Power and the Glory* are similar is in their portrayals of men who live out the American Dream, only to find that the

---

Diane Jacobs, Christmas in July, p. 160.

rewards they have been promised are not really as fulfilling as they have been led to believe. The men differ greatly, however, in the means each uses to achieve success. While Tom Garner improves himself through hard work and formal education, Jim Brady attains his position in anything but a traditional way. As in so many Sturges films, Brady cannot count on living out a Horatio Alger story; he succeeds precisely by going against the dictates of education, hard work, honesty, and frugality. Furthermore, on the one occasion when he does profess a belief in the foundations of the American Dream, he is rewarded with his worst failure. The scene comes near the middle of the film, when the bottom begins to fall out of the stock market. At a restaurant filled with investors and railroad barons, Jim moves through the crowd and overhears one man after another expressing his lack of faith in America and the railroad industry. Outraged that they are ready to give up on railroads and sell everything they have, Jim launches into a rousing speech that could easily have fit into a Frank Capra film:

> If I ever saw a bunch of white-livered, yellow-bellied cowards I'm looking at 'em right now. When things are going good, you go around and slap each other on the back, telling yourselves how smart you are. The minute the market makes a little turn, you . . . quit like a bunch of rats jumping off a sinking ship. The only trouble with this country is you fellows. It was built up by a bunch of guys who had guts, and believed in what they were doing. I said guts. The man just said here that in six months the railroad business will be in bankruptcy. I want to go on record as saying the railroads aren't begun to be built yet. Have you ever seen the standing wheat in Nebraska, or the corn in Kansas, or the fruit crop of Oregon, or the cotton growing so thick down South it looks like snow? Why, you ain't never seen nothing but ticker tape. Why, this is the richest country in the world, and now is the time to buy and not to sell.

In a Capra film, of course, such a speech would have been greeted with thunderous applause. All the investors would have changed their minds, and because of their newfound convictions, the market decline would have been completely reversed. In *Diamond Jim*, however, the speech does absolutely no good, even though Jim is right on target. He continues to follow the path he knows is right, buying and investing in railroads, and ends up losing everything he owns. In a later film Sturges might have made more out of such a scene, for it fits in perfectly with his recurring notion that the public can easily cause major shifts in events, largely through a collective lack of forethought. Here he just lets the moment pass, though, as a mere indication that Jim's steadfast belief in America and its greatness will get him nowhere.

It is in Brady's original rise to financial heights and in the manner in which he regains his position after the stock market crash that Sturges offers a picture of the real means of attaining success in America. As he

would do so often in his directorial efforts, Sturges makes it clear that the
traditional way of getting to the top—working hard, being honest, playing
by the rules—simply does not work. For all its romantic appeal, the Horatio Alger myth does not hold much water in Sturges's America; in Diamond Jim's rise, though, we see just how things really work.

Success and Its Rewards

In *Diamond Jim*, Sturges provides three examples of the way in which
Jim Brady becomes a success in the railroad business. The first two come
early in the movie, as Jim initially tries to move up from station baggage
master and then as he attempts to make a sale that will immediately net
him personal profits and great professional status and influence. The third
example comes after Jim has lost his fortune, as he concocts the scheme
that he hopes will earn his money and position back for him. In all three
cases the means that Jim uses go against the traditional notions of honesty,
hard work, and even, to some extent, providing a better product. But in
all three cases Brady's technique also pays off.

Brady starts on the road to success in the very first scene that portrays
him as an adult. As the baggage master at a small railroad station, he
catches a glimpse of a newspaper ad seeking an experienced salesman for
the A. E. Moore railroad supply company. Without a moment's hesitation
he announces to a fellow employee that he has found the opportunity he
has been waiting for. When the friend expresses doubt over Jim's qualifica-
tions, Brady counters:

> Oh, I know all it says in the book. How to get 'em, how to clinch an argu-
> ment . . . jokes a salesman should know. Everything like that. . . . I'm
> gonna get that job. I've got the grip, I've got the approach with the laugh,
> and I got the final persuader [makes a threatening fist]. I've been a
> bellhop, and I've been a tramp, and I've been a baggage smasher. . . .
> Well, I ain't gonna stop there.

The friend remains skeptical, but Jim obviously knows what it takes to get
ahead. He promptly "borrows" $20 of the railroad company's money, goes
to a pawn and consignment shop, and rents a suit of clothes. "I'm looking
for a job," he says to the owner. "I gotta look good." The owner tells Jim
that he needs a diamond, because "to make money you got to look like
money." Taking the pawnbroker's advice, a well-dressed and diamond-
clad Brady arrives at the A. E. Moore & Company offices. When he finds
the line of job seekers winding out the door and into the hallway, he simply
enters the door intended for customers. Although he never specifically tells
Moore that he is a customer, Jim also does not bother to correct the
misconception until he has had the chance to prove that he really knows

railroad equipment. When Moore finds out that he has been deceived, he's furious.

> *Moore*: Why didn't you come in through that door?
> *Brady*: Because it looked kind of crowded.
> *Moore*: Now get out of here. Of all the...
> *Brady*: All right. Now you listen to me a minute. You're making the biggest mistake you ever made in your life and you know it. I can sell railroad supplies because I know what I'm talking about. I'm a railroad man. And if I don't sell yours it will be somebody else's, and if it ain't this year it will be next year. And now you remember that. Good day!
> *Moore* [running after the departing Brady]: Wait a minute. Can you really sell?
> *Brady*: I sold you, didn't I?

Brady's unconventional, deceptive means get him the job, of course, while all the experienced salesmen wait patiently in line to see Moore. The approach is soon enough placed in contrast to the method by which conventional salesmen work. When Jim meets Sampson Fox on one of his trips, Fox is trying to sell a new railroad undertruck that is manufactured in England. He has traveled all over the United States and has not made one sale—at least not until he agrees to let Jim help. For a one-third commission Jim tells Fox that he will sell the trucks, and within a day of their agreement he does exactly that. This second example of Jim's mode of operation contains an even heavier dose of deception than did his scheme to get the Moore job.

When Brady and Fox encounter Charles Horsley, the owner of a major railroad, in a local bar, Jim goes into action. He has Fox go down to the local burlesque house and bring back four women; then he proceeds to get Horsley drunk on liquor and female attention. As instructed, the women cajole Horsley into signing a contract to buy the trucks; when one of them later expresses her dismay to Jim he tells her, "His railroad needs those trucks, [and it] doesn't make a bit of difference how he gets them."

The next morning Horsley tries to get out of the contract, but Jim is ready for him.

> *Brady*: You mean you're not going to hold us to it? You want to call the deal off? ... You see, everyone was pretty drunk last night, ... and we up and sold you part of a shipment that was already sold to the Wheeling and South Carolina.... That's what we came to see you about. We was in a terrible fix, Mr. Horsley. [He tears up the contract.] That makes me feel better.
> *Horsley*: What do you mean by tearing up that contract? Haven't we got as much right to this ... this ... whatever it is ... as our competitor, the measly little Wheeling and South Carolina? ... I bought those things and you're going to deliver them.

Although Horsley agrees to buy 500 undertrucks, even an order of that size is not enough for Jim. Along with Fox he then goes to the Wheeling and South Carolina Railroad, informs the owner that his competitor purchased 500 of the trucks, and promptly sells another 600. The Wheeling's owner places the order not because his railroad needs the trucks or because they are a better apparatus, but solely because he does not want the Wheeling and South Carolina, "the leading railroad in the South," to be outdone.*

The final example of Jim's method of achieving success, which occurs after his financial fall, entails little deception but lots of audacity. Having been involved in a train wreck and subsequent fire, he becomes convinced that what the industry needs is a steel car. After prevailing upon A. E. Moore, for whom he is now working again, to build the new vehicle, Jim agrees to risk his own name—and his life—in advertising its introduction. He invites thousands of people, including the presidents of major railroads, to a rural stretch of train tracks, where he has arranged to have an old wooden car and a new steel car propelled toward each other and crashed while he is riding inside the steel car. It is the kind of stunt that may not prove very much, but that, because of its novelty and spectacle, attracts enormous attention. A hundred years later such an event would be called an advertising gimmick or pure hype, but clearly the concept is not new to our time. To Preston Sturges, selling something based only on the publicity surrounding it was already very much a part of the American way of doing things.

Brady does not restrict his glitz and hype to his professional life, though. He has the nickname Diamond Jim because he likes to surround himself and others with the jewels that he views as a symbol of his success. The first time we see Jim using jewels as part of his image is when he is preparing to interview for the sales position. Although he at first wants to rent only a suit, the pawnbroker convinces him to wear a diamond as well. Jim decides he so needs the diamond to appear successful that he agrees to take the pawnbroker along on the interview with him, for the man refuses to rent his diamond without accompanying it. Later, as Jim earns more and more money, he turns increasingly to diamonds to let the world know of his status.

After his manufacturing facility for undertrucks makes him wealthy,

---

*The issue of whether the undertruck is actually any good is not initially clear. As part of his spiel Fox claims that it is lighter, faster, and all-around superior, but Jim does not pay much attention at first. After selling 1100 trucks to the two railroads, Jim tells Fox that they might make lots of money manufacturing them in the United States. "If they're half as good as you say they are, there might be something to it," he says. Of course, since Jim eventually makes his fortune on the trucks they apparently are good, but at the time of the first two sales he has no way of knowing about the quality of his product.

for instance, he shows up at a jeweler's shop to buy some diamonds. Although the jeweler shows him the most expensive items he has, Jim still is not pleased.

> *Brady*: Trouble with this stuff is, well, everybody's got it. It ain't got no ... well, everybody's got it. It's like silk hats. I got a silk hat, my secretary's got a silk hat, my valet's got a silk hat, and my cook's got a silk hat. See?
> *Jeweler*: But not like yours, Mister.
> *Brady*: Well, they're silk hats anyway. Now, I want some jewelry so people will know it's me, and not my cook. I want something elegant. I don't care how much it costs.... You see, I'm in the railroad business. I ain't ashamed of it! Now you can make me a locomotive wheel ring, and maybe a caboose and cuff links.... It doesn't have to be small ... I ain't ashamed of it. Listen, brother, where I come from, them that has 'em, wears 'em!

Jim also flaunts his riches by giving elaborate gifts. When he holds a huge party to celebrate the opening of Nell's latest show, he gives each of the guests a diamond designed especially for that guest. The pawnbroker, for example, receives a diamond pin in the shape of the three-ball symbol of a pawnshop, while Sampson Fox is given a miniature replica of his original railroad undertruck. Even the racehorse Jim owns gets diamonds—embedded right in its hooves. Such ostentation, while certainly not unique to the United States, does undoubtedly fit with a society that equates money with success. In *Diamond Jim* Sturges does not harshly criticize such behavior, but his own formative years in Europe would surely have made him aware of how unsophisticated and garish it might seem to many other people.

In *Diamond Jim*, Sturges treats success—as exemplified in Jim Brady—more positively than he does in almost any of his other films. The script includes a number of Sturges's major themes—the need to use unconventional means, the importance of luck, the influence that an uninformed or fickle group of outsiders can have—but the overall tone is far less cynical or satirical than the tone in later works. Where *Diamond Jim* is much more downbeat, though, is in its portrayal of the effect that success has on Jim and the other characters. Just as Tom Garner discovered in *The Power and the Glory*, Jim Brady finds that achieving the American Dream does not necessarily make for a happy life.

Success and Its Disappointments

In the first few minutes of *Diamond Jim*, there is a brief scene of Mrs. Brady lying in bed and talking to her newborn son. "You got the blood of kings in your veins," she tells him. "You can do anything you want in life."

It is an important moment that echoes throughout the entire movie, for as much as her words set the tone for Jim's professional accomplishments, they comment ironically on his attempts to achieve personal happiness. Without making a direct correlation between those two parts of Brady's life, Sturges nonetheless shows that Jim's great professional success brings almost no true personal fulfillment.

Time after time in *Diamond Jim*, various characters wish someone else happiness, but their wishes never really come true. In fact, happiness for one character usually comes only at the expense of another. Jim wants Emma, his first great love, to be happy, even though she is making him miserable by marrying another. Later, when Jim tells Nell that he has finally found someone else he can love, she first responds, "I want you to be the happiest man in the world," then promptly makes him one of the unhappiest by divulging that Jane's past is not as immaculate as he thought. (Learning this, he becomes, in his own words, "the man whose heart [Jane] broke.") Even Jane, who can have her own fulfillment in her love for Jerry, cannot bring herself to tell Jim about her affair because she does not want to hurt him.

Jim even goes so far as to try to buy happiness with his money by giving gifts that may seem thoughtful but that verge on the obsessive. After his initial failure to follow through on his wedding to Jane, Jim repeatedly attempts to get her to marry him. When she keeps refusing he thinks that perhaps she just needs to be plied some more. First he sets up a lavish, surprise ceremony at his house, complete with minister, organ, and sumptuous decorations, only to see Jane break down in tears. He continues to give her gifts of diamonds, however, in the hope of winning her over.

> *Brady*: Nothing means nothing without you. Nothing! Why, there ain't a day goes by that I don't stop to think about you, wondering what I can do to make you happy. [He gives her yet another gift of diamonds.]
>
> *Jane*: Jim, I don't want you to give me these things anymore. Don't you see what I'm trying to tell you? Oh, it isn't as if you didn't have anything else. You have everything in the world, and you really don't need me.

Of course, Jim has only material things, but not Jane, whom he needs as much as he needed Emma. The emptiness he feels without them comes to be filled by yet another symbol of success: food. Sturges does not show us Jim's gargantuan appetite and gourmet taste until after he is a success. Only after he becomes wealthy from manufacturing do we see his penchant for flamboyant diamonds and meals of epic proportions. As the film progresses, Jim increasingly comes to see happiness in terms of food, especially as personal fulfillment (in the form of love) gets further and

Jim Brady (Edward Arnold, *left*) is introduced to Jane Matthews (Jean Arthur) for the first time.

further beyond his reach. As his meals become bigger and more expensive, they seem to consume more and more of his thoughts.

> *Jane*: Are you happy, Jim?
> *Brady* [feeding candies into his mouth]: Sure. Say, this candy is great!
> *Jane*: Oh, I didn't mean that. You have everything in the world you want, haven't you?
> *Brady*: I haven't got you.

By the time Jim collapses from years of abusing his body by overeating, it is clear that food has become his happiness. Just before he is discharged from the hospital after a one-year stay, he describes to the doctor the mammoth meal he is going to have as soon as he gets back to New York. The doctor, however, has other ideas.

> *Doctor*: You're not going to eat [oysters] again, Jim. They're deadly poison to you. And so are lobsters, and rich gravy, and game, and all of those things. . . . That doesn't mean you can't go on for a long time, and live happily.
> *Brady*: You might as well be dead if you can't go on living.

For Jim, living has come to be equated with eating, and although he can make do for a while with his new diet of lettuce and eggs and a little chicken, only the hope of Jane's love keeps him going at all. Once she reveals to him the truth about her feelings for Jerry, Jim has nothing left but his professional achievements and his money. They clearly are not enough. As in *The Power and the Glory*, the money, power, and status that are supposed to satisfy instead leave an emptiness that cannot be filled at all.

It is quite appropriate that Sturges ended his screenplay on a wholly fictional note. Although there is no indication that the real Jim Brady ate himself to death, the finale that Sturges concocted fits in well with the theme of the entire film. At home on the evening of Jane's great revelation, Jim goes through some of his personal effects for one last time: Fox's original model of the undertruck, a series of IOUs for many thousands of dollars, and an inscribed photograph of his mother. Crumpling up the IOUs, which signify the financial aspect of his life—and his great success— Jim tosses them into the fireplace. But he slips the photograph of his mother into his coat pocket, next to his heart. All his money and all his outward triumphs mean nothing now, and he symbolically leaves them behind when he throws the notes into the flames. As he moves into the dining room to consume his final meal, however, he takes with him the photo of his mother, for it represents the enduring love he never found. As a child he lost his mother and as an adult he lost the two women he loved, and with them the hope of any personal fulfillment. With the photo in his pocket and the words "I'm ready" on his lips, Jim turns instead to the thing that had always served as the substitute for that love: food.

THREE

Easy Living

Produced by Arthur Hornblow, Jr.; Directed by Mitchell Leisen; Based on a story by Vera Caspary; Screenplay by Preston Sturges; Photography: Ted Tetzlaff; Special Photographic Effects: Farciot Edouart; Edited by Doane Harrison; Art Direction: Hans Dreier and Ernst Fegte; Set Decoration: A. E. Freudeman; Sound: Earl Hayman and William Thayer; Musical Direction: Boris Morros. Released by Paramount, 1937.

Cast: Jean Arthur (Mary Smith); Edward Arnold (J. B. Ball); Ray Milland (John Ball, Jr.); Luis Alberni (Louis Louis); Mary Nash (Mrs. Ball); Franklin Pangborn (Van Buren); Barlowe Borland (Mr. Gurney); William Demarest (Wallace Whistling); Andrew Tombes (E. F. Hulgar); Esther Dale (Lillian); Harlan Briggs (Higgenbottom); William B. Davidson (Mr. Hyde); Nora Cecil (Miss Swerf); Robert Greig (Butler).

Synopsis: J. B. Ball, one of the most powerful bankers in the United States, rises early one morning for breakfast in his luxurious New York City apartment. He is just sitting down to eat when he is besieged by his butler, who has bills for him to pay, and by his son, John, who wants money for another new car. Furious at how his family and servants are wasting his hard-earned money, Ball lashes out at them, which causes his son to vow to get a job and make it on his own. Ball then turns his anger to his wife and her new $58,000 sable coat, which he wrests away from her and throws off the balcony of their penthouse. The coat lands on the head of Mary Smith, who is riding on the top level of a double-decker bus. When she tries to return the coat to Ball, he not only refuses to take it but insists on buying her a new hat to replace the one smashed by the falling coat.

After a visit to a dress shop, Ball, who still has not told Mary who he is, drops her off at work: the editorial offices of *The Boy's Constant Companion* magazine. Annoyed at her lateness and suspicious of her expensive coat and hat, Mary's boss calls her into his office. When she cannot explain to his satisfaction how she got the coat, she is fired for lying and betraying the sanctity of American boyhood. In the meantime, the dress shop manager, Van Buren, has begun making phone calls to tell people that J. B. Ball was in his store that morning buying expensive gifts for his beautiful young mistress.

When Ball arrives at work he discovers that his wife has left him to go to Florida. Still upset over his family problems, he carries on with his business for the day. In a meeting with Louis Louis, the owner of a Park Avenue hotel that Ball financed, Ball announces his intention to foreclose on the troubled establishment. Louis convinces the banker to give him one more week to make his payments, but he leaves Ball's office uncertain of how he will find the money. When he meets up with Van Buren and hears about Ball and his "mistress," though, Louis sees a way out of his plight.

That evening he tracks Mary down and sends her a note asking her to come to the hotel. He sets her up in the lavish penthouse suite, charging her no more than the rent she had been paying for one room. In return, he simply asks that she tell "that certain party" that she loves the hotel and will not move out. Baffled, but on the verge of eviction, Mary agrees, then heads out to the Automat to buy food with her last few pennies. There she meets John Ball Jr., who has just begun work as a busboy. Although he is caught trying to sneak a meal to her, his struggle to get away starts a near riot that allows the couple to escape to Mary's new apartment.

With his wife and son gone, J. B. Ball decides to leave his empty house and spend the night at the Hotel Louis. On arriving at the hotel he briefly encounters Mary in the lobby. Gossip columnist Wallace Whistling, who has been tipped off by Louis, observes the two and immediately phones his paper with the item. After the morning edition hits the streets, the hotel lobby quickly becomes packed with customers who want to stay in the same establishment honored by J. B. Ball's presence. An avalanche of phone callers and visitors also descends on Mary, with offers of clothes, jewelry, cars, and so on, all because of her presumed relationship with J. B. Ball. When a stockbroker arrives at the apartment wanting to know Mr. Ball's opinion on the future of steel, Mary asks the only Ball she knows—John Jr.—and tells the man that the price of steel is going down. In reality, J. B. Ball is frantically buying steel because he thinks the price is going up. Once the stockbroker gets word to his clients, everyone in the country begins dumping steel stock. Ball sees his entire fortune going down the drain, a realization that is only made worse when he learns that his wife, after reading about Mary in the paper, is divorcing him.

Soon enough the news hits the streets that J. B. Ball is on the brink of failure. John Jr. catches a glimpse of a newspaper and leaves Mary to rush to his father's office, where he is joined by his mother, who has also heard about the financial disaster. Before long, the Ball family figures out exactly what has happened to drive steel prices down, and they hope to turn the market around by getting Mary to call the stockbroker and tell him that the price of steel is going up. While they are anxiously searching for her, she shows up at the office on her own. Although she is mad at John Jr. for not having told her who he was, she makes the phone call and watches as the stock market returns the Balls to solvency. Once they all explain things and iron out their differences, Mr. and Mrs. Ball are happily reunited, John and Mary are about to be engaged, and John will soon go to work for his father, who congratulates him on using his business skills to solve the family's dilemma.

❂

Although *Easy Living* was made three years before Sturges's directorial debut and was directed by a man (Mitchell Leisen) whom Sturges considered unqualified, the film bears many similarities to Sturges's later efforts behind the camera. In particular, its blend of verbal acumen and broad slapstick (especially in the Automat scene) looks forward to such films as *The Miracle of Morgan's Creek* and *The Sin of Harold Diddlebock*. Sturges's first major work at Paramount, *Easy Living* takes advantage of the studio's great roster of supporting players, including Franklin Pangborn and William Demarest, whom Sturges would use so effectively in his own films.

Despite its obvious resemblances to his later works, however, *Easy Living* cannot be called a fully developed Sturges comedy. In films such as *The Palm Beach Story*, Sturges would so mold the comedic conventions to his own original vision as to give the viewer the feeling of watching an entirely new genre. In *Easy Living*, however, he provides a creative take on an established genre, a traditional screwball comedy filtered through a unique mind. The themes are those he explores in his later films, but the comedy and the message are never as fully integrated as they would be in his directorial efforts.

Where *Easy Living* parallels Sturges's later works most closely is in its use of fate, or, more specifically, instant success, as the device that sets the plot in motion.

It is an idea that Sturges had worked with before, most significantly in the unproduced play that would become 1940's *Christmas in July*. Both films present struggling office workers who suddenly have success fall into their laps and as a result are treated like royalty and besieged by people seeking their favor and their riches. In both cases Sturges uses the situation to offer interesting comments on success in America and on the shifting opinions of people—observations that help to define his view of American society.

The Nature of Success

As he would do in *Christmas in July*, Sturges comments on the traditional notion that hard work equals success by providing glimpses of a variety of people, some of whom are successful and some of whom are not. J. B. Ball, for example, is one of the three or four most powerful bankers in the country, a rich, respected, and even feared businessman. But, as in most Sturges films, we find out that he did not earn any of his wealth and status himself; instead, he inherited them from his father, also an influential banker. In fact, his attempt to lecture John Jr. in the film's first scene is cut short when the senior Ball lets slip that when he was John's age, he was just as lazy and did just as much partying as John does now.

With the character of John Jr., Sturges continues his examination of success. Although John has a college education, which is traditionally considered one of the ways to rise to the top, it means little when he heads out on his own to try to support himself. He quickly loses his job as a busboy at the Automat but says to Mary that he does not care, because "you slave for twenty years and you're still behind the nut salad." Later, John tells Mary that he is not trained to do anything but wile away time, and even though he scours the papers looking for work he cannot come up with anything he could even consider doing. In the end, of course, John will wind up with a handsome job with his father's bank, ensuring him of just as much success as J. B. Ball has achieved, and with just as little effort.

For Louis Louis, the owner of the Hotel Louis, it is obvious that hard work will get him nowhere. A renowned chef, he took a chance by building a luxury hotel to capitalize on his name, but despite his efforts the establishment is on the brink of foreclosure as the film opens. During the course of *Easy Living*, Louis moves out of certain bankruptcy, but only because he deliberately spreads gossip and provides the name of his most notorious guest to anyone who asks. With plain, honest labor, the Hotel Louis would have been closed down; with a relaxing of ethical standards and a few simple phone calls, it becomes the hottest place in town.

Mary is another character for whom hard work and honesty seem pointless. As the film begins she is one week behind in her rent, with only the one dime she needs to ride the bus to work that day and almost no savings except for a few cents. Although she attempts to be honest with her boss about being late and owning a fur coat, she is fired from *The Boy's Constant Companion*. Sturges even suggests that she may be better off without a job there. The frighteningly staid and provincial office is staffed by old, dried-up men and women who believe that integrity and industriousness equal success, but have nothing to show for it. Supervised by Mr. Higgenbottom, a pompous and hypocritical man, the office of *The Boy's*

The staff members of *The Boy's Constant Companion* are not quite convinced by the explanation offered by Mary Smith (Jean Arthur, *right*) for her new fur coat.

Constant Companion is a place where people in their right minds would never want to be.*

Mary makes the transition from unemployment and near poverty to affluence and security without doing any hard work, but also without being aware of just what is happening around her. Her inability to tell the truth about her benefactor's identity (though it is through no fault of her own) makes her an almost instant success when people read her vague remarks as tactful. She suddenly has a fur coat, a beautiful penthouse suite, the companionship of a handsome young man, and the dresses, jewelry, and cars of any number of merchants who are all vying for the attention of J. B. Ball. By the end of the film her success will be complete: she will keep all material items, marry John Jr. (who is similarly rewarded, although he, too, does not understand the situation), and live in a penthouse suite at least as nice as the one at the Hotel Louis. Sturges's message could not be

---

Sturges emphasizes the hypocrisy when he shows Mary in Higgenbottom's office trying to explain away the existence of the fur coat. Glancing up at a portrait of George Washington, she finds that she cannot tell a lie. But when she truthfully says she received the coat from an unknown benefactor, Higgenbottom refuses to believe her and fires her for lying.

clearer: buy into the American success myth and the only thing you will get is a job at *The Boy's Constant Companion.*

The Value of Public Opinion

In *Easy Living,* Sturges also takes aim at the masses, faulting them for being unable to hold an opinion or think critically as well as for wanting to act in whatever manner will benefit them personally.

The first theme can be seen in several of the film's characters, who seem to exhibit a lack of critical judgment. Louis Louis, for example, only hears what he wants to hear when Mary tries to tell him, both directly and through her actions, that she does not know J. B. Ball. Even when Ball himself says that he has no real connection to Mary, the hotel owner chuckles to himself and marvels at Ball's diplomacy. Similarly, both John Ball Jr. and Mary never question all that is happening around them. Mary just accepts the fact that a luxurious apartment and expensive gifts would be given to her for doing nothing, while John, who knows that Louis mentioned a Mr. Ball to Mary, never puts two and two together when someone shows up at the hotel asking for Mr. Ball's opinion on the steel market.

The tendency for most people to avoid thinking for themselves, though, extends beyond the main characters in the film. The rush on the Hotel Louis occurs when people are told that J. B. Ball keeps his mistress there; his stamp of approval is enough to bring them flocking to a place that was nearly empty before. Even the frenzy to sell steel stocks takes place when thousands of people leap to act on a single, very tenuous piece of information.

The most obvious example of this unthinking attitude is found in the character of E. F. Hulgar, the man whom J. B. Ball describes as one of the leading stockbrokers in the country. When Hulgar arrives at Mary's door looking for Ball's opinion on stocks, Mary suggests that he use his own judgment, to which Hulgar replies, "That's the one thing in the world I don't want to use!" In spite of his professional status, Hulgar is like so many other prosperous people in Sturges's America: unable to think for himself. If success is based not on knowledge and astuteness, but on sheer luck in stumbling upon the opinions of others, there is not much reason to admire those who are successful.

But despite the fact that people are eager to act on the judgment of others, no one in the movie has much respect for anyone else. When Mary tries to be honest with her boss, she ends up losing her job. So we see that even *The Boy's Constant Companion,* an avowed purveyor of high moral values, is staffed by people whose minds immediately leap to the worst. If the protector of "the ideal American boy" cannot be counted on to be open-minded, who can?

Certainly not most of the other characters in *Easy Living*. Everywhere we turn, Sturges shows us people willing to look for the worst in others. Mrs. Ball, despite her years of marriage, believes the gossip column allegations about her husband and Mary Smith. In the dress shop, Van Buren not only jumps to the conclusion that Ball is outfitting his mistress (rather than thinking that Mary is his daughter-in-law or niece), but immediately destroys Ball's privacy by broadcasting the news. And Van Buren's small-mindedness is matched by Louis Louis, who thinks it only natural that a man in Ball's position would have a beautiful young mistress.

Compounding this lack of respect is the characters' general affinity for looking out for their own interests, even if it means ruining others or breaking the law. When Louis Louis sees an opportunity to blackmail his banker into keeping the hotel open, he does not hesitate over the ethics of the matter. Similarly, when John is interested in impressing Mary, he has no qualms about giving away the Automat's food. Wallace Whistling, the gossip columnist hot on the trail of a scoop, does not look for any verification of the rumor about Ball's mistress. And even Mary accepts all kinds of gifts without trying to discover why she might deserve them.

But it is the character of E. F. Hulgar who takes self-serving behavior to the extreme. His attempts to snoop out stock market tips from Mr. Ball are clearly illegal, not to mention unethical. Hulgar has undoubtedly done the same thing before, since he does not want to use his own judgment. He is a successful man who operates without the sense of morality and the desire for fair play and honest competition that are supposedly the foundation of American business and society. Even when Hulgar is defeated and steel prices start to go up again, it is not because he has been beaten by an honest opponent; rather, someone else has been more clever at illegally manipulating the market. Hard work and virtue are left for *The Boy's Constant Companion*; riches remain with the selfish.

When taken to a logical conclusion, the randomness of success and the unreliability of the opinions and ethics of the public come together to cause the very events that nearly ruin and then save J. B. Ball. For if people have no convictions and can easily be led to frequent a particular hotel or buy a particular stock, stability—and any certain rewards for hard work— disappears. The flippant remark of young John Ball can almost bankrupt one of the most powerful businessmen in America, Van Buren's lewd mind can make a wealthy mistress out of a penniless Mary, an erroneous gossip column can turn a foundering hotel into a hot spot, and a simple fur coat can create all this upheaval and more. If even the stock market, the very basis of our economy, is ruled by chance, and people's lives can shift direction at a moment's notice, then how much faith can one have in truthfulness and justice? For Sturges, all it takes is one ordinary office worker to show how feeble our treasured myths really are.

FOUR

Remember the Night

Produced and Directed by Mitchell Leisen; Screenplay by Preston
Sturges; Photography: Ted Tetzlaff; Edited by Doane Harrison;
Art Direction: Hans Dreier and Roland Anderson; Set Decora-
tion: A. E. Freudeman; Sound: Earl Hayman and Walter Oberst;
Musical Score: Frederick Hollander. Released by Paramount,
1940.

Cast: Barbara Stanwyck (Lee Leander); Fred MacMurray (John
Sargent); Beulah Bondi (Mrs. Sargent); Elizabeth Patterson
(Aunt Emma); Sterling Holloway (Willie); Francis X. O'Leary
(Willard Robertson); Charles Waldron (Judge in New York);
Charley Arnt (Tom); Tom Kennedy (Fat Mike); Georgia Caine
(Lee's mother); Snowflake (Rufus).

Synopsis: It is Christmas time in New York City and Lee Leander is
trying on a bracelet at a Fifth Avenue jeweler's shop. Not completely satisfied with the way it looks, she asks the jeweler to show her another one.
When he bends down and puts his head in the display case, though, Lee
makes off with the original bracelet and disappears into the crowd of
Christmas shoppers. A few minutes later she turns up at a pawnshop a few
blocks away to complete the scam, but the owner is wise to her and locks
the door and calls the police.

At the district attorney's office, the case against Lee looks open-and-
shut, but the D.A. makes sure of winning by assigning it to John Sargent,
a prosecutor who is especially good at getting convictions against women.
In court, Lee's lawyer claims that the brilliance of the jewels in the bracelet
hypnotized his client and that she did not know what she was doing.
Realizing that this wild story, along with the jury's goodwill during the
holiday season, is about to get Lee acquitted, John asks for a continuance
until after Christmas so that an expert psychiatrist can be called to testify.
After the judge grants the request and orders Lee taken back to jail, John
feels bad about her being in prison over the holidays and arranges for her
bail to be paid.

34

Back at his apartment, John is preparing for the 750-mile car trip to Indiana to spend Christmas with his mother. Before he can leave, though, Lee arrives at his door in the company of the bail bondsman, who thought that John's motive in having her released was less noble. After clearing up the misunderstanding, John finds that Lee has nowhere to go for the holidays, and he decides to buy her dinner while they figure out a place for her to stay. During their conversation John discovers that Lee is also from a small town in Indiana, only about an hour away from his home. When she tells him that she has never been back there, he suggests that he drop her off at her mother's house and pick her up on his way back.

The pair set out for Indiana that night, but make a wrong turn and get lost in Pennsylvania. Stuck in a farmer's pasture, they are forced to spend the night sleeping in the car, only to be greeted the next morning by the shotgun-toting farmer himself. He brings them to the local judge on all sorts of criminal charges, and the two are about to be hauled off to jail when Lee deliberately starts a fire in the judge's wastebasket. As the judge and the farmer scramble to put the fire out, John and Lee race to the car and make their escape from the state.

Finally reaching Indiana, they head first to Lee's childhood home, but rather than getting a loving reception Lee is criticized and condemned by her hateful and unforgiving mother. Deeply shaken, she turns to John for help, and he offers to put her up at his mother's house. John's family—his mother, his Aunt Emma, and Willie, the live-in farmhand—greet Lee warmly. Even though John tells his mother the truth about Lee's situation, she is still accepted as one of the family. On Christmas morning there are even gifts for her from Mrs. Sargent and Aunt Emma, as well as one from John that his mother prepared without his knowledge.

Over the next few days Lee helps out with the church rummage sale, learns to make popovers, and goes to an old-fashioned barn dance. During the week, John and Lee begin to fall in love, almost without being aware of it, but Mrs. Sargent picks up on their feelings for each other. Before her son leaves she pleads with Lee to give John up so he will not lose everything that he has worked so hard to attain.

On their way back to New York, as they drive through Canada to avoid the Pennsylvania authorities, John confesses his love for Lee and begs her to remain out of the country where she cannot be prosecuted. She insists that she must go back and stand trial—that it is the right thing to do. In the courtroom John reveals his own plan for keeping Lee out of jail: he begins bullying her on the stand, knowing full well that the jury will always sympathize with a woman who is being treated roughly. When she realizes what he is doing, Lee immediately asks to change her plea to guilty and is sent back to jail until a sentence can be handed down. At the jail, Lee refuses John's request to marry right away. Declaring that she must pay for her mistake first, Lee says that marriage will have to wait until she gets out; if she loses John in the meantime, it will be the cost for a lifetime of misdeeds.

●

Remember the Night begins in classic Preston Sturges style, with the entire first sequence, from the opening shot to the end of the courtroom scene, having much the same feeling as the initial scenes of *The Palm Beach Story* and *The Miracle of Morgan's Creek*. In all three we are thrown right into the story, without an establishing shot or scene to set the stage and without an introduction, direct or indirect, to any of the important characters. In *Remember the Night*, the first image we see is a close-up of a woman's forearm and hand moving back and forth with a bracelet on the wrist. The dialogue gives us the barest of details: she is looking to buy a piece of jewelry but is not quite satisfied with this one. Sturges and director Mitchell Leisen hold the camera as the scene continues, giving us an upside-down view of the clerk reaching into the display case for another item. But by the time he finds what he is looking for, the arm is gone and we have had the setup—a modest jewel heist—hurled in our faces. The sequence plays itself out without dialogue: we watch from a high camera angle as the thief loses her pursuers in a crowd of Christmas shoppers, turns up at a pawnshop across town, and is captured when the owner recognizes her (or her scam).

From there the film turns unquestionably comic. The trial scene begins with the introduction of John Sargent and his sidekick Rufus, the black valet (a humorous character in the context of the time); establishes the light interplay between John and his assistant in court, particularly as they discuss ways to manipulate a jury; and reaches its peak with the story that Lee's lawyer fabricates to get his client acquitted. Although the humor in the defense comes largely from the dialogue and its delivery, the tale itself is completely absurd; in essence the story is as follows:

> Miss Leander removed the bracelet in a temporary loss of will and consciousness known as hypnotism. A salesman showed her the bracelet, urged her to put it on her arm and examine it under a stronger light, then removed himself. Staring at the stones, shimmering blindingly in her eyes, she was transfixed, and when next she realized it, she was on Fifth Avenue, blocks away from the jeweler's, with the bracelet still on her wrist. Dazed and confused, she made her way back to the shop, but found it closed for the day. She sought out a phone book, determined that the shop owner lived in Roslyn, Long Island, and resolved to take a train there to return the bracelet personally. But without any money, she did

the only thing she could to secure the train fare: she pawned the bracelet. In trying to do so she was recognized and captured for the robbery.

The story is important because it repeats a message that Sturges expressed in previous films, such as *The Power and the Glory* and *Easy Living*. The details of the defense, as well as the overblown manner in which they are delivered, have the predictably ludicrous effect: they are swallowed hook, line, and sinker by the fools in the jury box. Not only does Sturges once again show us people who are inconceivably gullible, but this time they are also jurors, those who perhaps more than any others represent the ideals of democracy and justice. The point may be a minor one in its context, but when taken alongside similar scenes in other Sturges films, it has to be seen as yet another jab at the sanctity of America's political and social fabric.

The scene matters more, however, in creating the expectation among the audience that *Remember the Night* is going to be a broad farcical movie. Up to the end of the lawyer's argument, Sturges has been increasing the laughs from one scene to the next; with the defense, however, the comedy reaches its peak, and Sturges begins an amazing transition from a frenzied comic tale to a warm and moving examination of love and redemption. There is still humor after the courtroom scene: Fat Mike, misunderstanding John's intentions, brings Lee to John's apartment; Rufus provides more low-level comic relief; and John and Lee get stuck in a farmer's field and have trouble milking a cow. But by the time the action shifts to Indiana, the only humor we get is in the form of endearing characters and their traits, such as Willie and his Austrian cap or Aunt Emma and her ambivalent feelings about love and marriage. As the story moves toward its resolution, with John and Lee returning to New York, the film becomes completely serious and ultimately as involving and powerful as any drama. This shift in style and mood, which Sturges handles brilliantly, contributes enormously to the impact of the ending. What seems to begin as an out-and-out comedy turns thoughtful and reflective, and much to the viewer's pleasant surprise, two characters who appear to be self-centered movie "types" become fully developed, sympathetic people.

What finally emerges from *Remember the Night* is something a little different for Preston Sturges: a touching tale of the formative power of love and the tragedies that occur when it is missing. Sturges, however, may later have tried to deny that that was his message. In his autobiography, *Preston Sturges by Preston Sturges*, he claims that he had trouble putting pizzazz into the story. At first he tried plot lines that had John Sargent taking Lee into the mountains because he wanted to reform her, because his conscience bothered him, and because of the Yuletide spirit; Sturges claims that he dispensed with those and ultimately settled on giving John a less chivalrous

motivation. The result, he writes, was that "love reformed her and corrupted him, which gave us the finely balanced moral that one man's meat
is another man's poison. . . ."* In reality there is absolutely no indication
in the film that John has any illicit acts in mind, and while it is clear that
Lee has been reformed at the end, it is debatable whether or not John has
been corrupted.

What does seem certain about *Remember the Night*, according to two
of Sturges's biographers, is that it was a product of Sturges's recent marriage to Louise Sargent. Donald Spoto writes that "at first . . . Preston and
Louise were a blissfully happy married couple," and that "*Remember the
Night* has the benevolence and security that came from this happy early
period . . . . The film has a prevalent romantic glow and its dialogue expresses a directness about love that could come only from a man close to
that experience."† And James Curtis agrees with Spoto's assessment when
he claims that Sturges "was involved in a great love affair—his courtship
and marriage to Louise. And his mind was naturally filled with romantic
ideas."§ Curtis also notes that Louise was consulted on virtually every
aspect of the script, and that if she thought something did not ring true,
Preston would immediately set to work making changes.**

Preston's relationship with Louise, however, turned sour and eventually resulted in divorce. Since the comments in his memoirs were written
after the divorce (their actual date is uncertain), Sturges might have
wanted to distance himself from the film and its association with Louise.
It is also possible that Sturges later denied the poignancy and sentiment
of *Remember the Night* simply because its optimistic, emotional tone
seemed out of keeping with his other work. In any case, the film's primary
theme is the power of love, its ability to create a strong person, and its
unlimited potential to redeem those who have been deprived of it. Along
with this redemption comes a clearer knowledge of right and wrong, of a
moral imperative that goes beyond mere written law.

The Road Not Taken

To set up his study of the effects of love, Sturges places his two main
characters on the same road, leads them up to a fork, and then allows each
to go in a different direction. As we gradually discover through the course
of the film, John and Lee have strikingly similar backgrounds. Both were
born and raised in Indiana, both led poor, difficult lives because they lost

*Preston Sturges by Preston Sturges, *p. 288.*
†*Donald Spoto,* Madcap: The Life of Preston Sturges, *pp. 146, 148.*
§*James Curtis,* Between Flops, *p. 123.*
**Curtis, *p. 124.*

their fathers, and both ended up in New York, enmeshed in the legal system. In their starting circumstances they closely matched each other, but the paths they took caused them to develop in completely opposite ways.

Sturges illustrates this idea by providing a number of specific parallel situations throughout the film and showing how the two characters would or did react differently. When John and Lee are having dinner before leaving for Indiana, for instance, their conversation turns to the issue of right versus wrong.

> *Lee*: Right or wrong is the same for everybody, but the rights and wrongs aren't the same.... Supposing you were starving to death, and you didn't have any food and you didn't have any money, and you didn't have anyplace to get anything. And there were some loaves of bread out in front of a market. Now remember, you're starving to death. And the man's back was turned. Would you swipe one?
> *John*: You bet I would.
> *Lee*: That's because you're honest. You see, I'd have a six-course dinner at the tavern across the street and then say I'd forgotten my purse. Get the difference?
> *John*: Yeah. Your way's smarter.

The difference in approaches to solving the hypothetical problem says a lot about John's and Lee's respective characters. John's solution could hardly be called anything but sheer human survival; in the circumstances described it is what even the most moral people would do, and they could not readily be condemned for it. Lee's action, on the other hand, would be far more calculated and deceitful and therefore less easily defensible. The fact that her mind moves to such a plan shows that she is accustomed to thinking in devious ways. Even with his legal savvy and knowledge of criminals, John still reacts in a far more justifiable way; it wouldn't enter his mind to follow Lee's route. In fact, when he tells her that he gets the difference and that her way is smarter, the look on his face and the tone of his voice suggest that he does not really understand at all.

Once the couple arrives in Indiana, Sturges provides another comparison in the way John and Lee are treated by their mothers. Lee's mother, who resides in a dark, dingy old house, comes to the door with a snarl on her face. She invites Lee and her guest in, but does not have a single nice word for them and does not even care to be introduced to John. She ends up driving her daughter away, unwilling to forgive her for an adolescent indiscretion for which Lee has apologized on numerous occasions.

In contrast, John and Lee are greeted at the Sargent house with open arms. John's mother is thrilled to see her son and accepts the unannounced guest with genuine pleasure. Even when John tries to tell his mother that Lee is a criminal, Mrs. Sargent refuses to judge the woman on anything but the fine character traits she displays. Mrs. Sargent is nothing less than a warm, friendly, and loving mother—exactly the opposite of what Lee has experienced.

Undoubtedly the most important contrast between John and Lee comes in similar incidents from their childhoods. In Lee's case, the episode is described when Lee asks her mother if she is glad to see her.

> *Mother:* Glad? Why should I be glad? Good riddance to bad rubbish, I said the day she left. . . . Just like her father she was. Always laughing at serious things she was. Never doing what she was told till she winds up stealing as I always said she would. Stealing my mission money that I put by with the sweat of my brow.
>
> *Lee:* I didn't steal it! I've told you a thousand times, I only borrowed it. I was going to pay you back out of what I earned.
>
> *Mother:* But you didn't pay me back, did you? And you never paid me back. And you never paid anybody else back.
>
> *Lee:* How could I after you called me a thief in front of the whole town? You think anybody would let me work for them after that?
>
> *Mother:* We weren't good enough for her here. A decent home and a hard-working mother with a crook for a daughter.

Later that night, after John and Lee share a pleasant evening with his family, John explains to his mother why he brought Lee with him and that she is not a "nice" girl. Mrs. Sargent is not so sure, though.

> *Mrs. Sargent:* She probably didn't get enough love as a child. Do you remember how bad—well, you weren't really bad—but do you remember when you took my egg money I was going to buy a new dress with, and then how hard you worked to pay it back, when you did understand?
>
> *John:* You made me understand.
>
> *Mrs. Sargent:* No, dear. It was love that made you understand.

With these similar incidents and their dissimilar outcomes, Sturges points to the obvious conclusion: the love that John Sargent received as a child instilled in him a moral compass that would always lead him in the right direction, while the lack of affection between Lee and her mother left her without a clear sense of how to act honorably.

Tradition and the Source of Values

At first glance, *Remember the Night* appears to be a film set up to draw direct comparisons between the lifestyles and values of city dwellers and those of small-town residents. The two main characters were born and raised in the country, moved on to the city, and in the course of the film travel from the urban to the rural sphere and back again, while they both change significantly along the way. Since Preston Sturges later wove entire films, such as *Hail the Conquering Hero*, around the eccentricity and foolishness of small-town life, the assumption would seem clear: *Remember the Night* is a study of the relative value of two types of places, with small towns coming out on the bottom.

But the truth is not quite that simple. Of course Sturges cannot resist making *some* comparisons and poking fun at a few people. Too much of a cynic to come down completely on one side, he does offer a few knocks at the effects of city life. The portrait he paints of the jury, for instance, caught up in the defense attorney's implausible story, is one of his many examples of mass gullibility. From the moment we see them it is impossible for us to have respect for this jury; and once we learn of the common sense and genuine insight of the characters at the Sargent farmhouse, we cannot help but conclude that the city must have been responsible at least to some extent for the jury's lack of skepticism.*

To reinforce this negative view of the city, we get the farmer's view of New Yorkers after he catches John and Lee in his field.

> You New Yorkers think you can trespass on people's property, break down their fences, fool around with their cows, spend the night in their fields with ... [pauses and looks at Lee] I don't know what kind of a ...

It is true that Sturges does not enthusiastically support the farmer and his small town: he is foolishly obsessed with the idea of people trespassing on his land and he lives in a place that is not as comforting as John's town is. Nonetheless, Sturges's message here cannot be totally ignored: people from the city just do not have the same values that other folks have.

Still, Sturges is concerned less with describing those moral values than in showing just how they are instilled in people, and geographic background alone cannot provide the answer. Despite the fact that John lives in the city and appears to function quite well there, he is still a principled person. Just as he wouldn't pull Lee's restaurant scam rather than steal a loaf of bread, he does not think of devious or immoral angles to many things. He may ask Fat Mike to arrange for Lee's bail, but it never occurs to him what some people might think he is doing it for. Similarly, when the judge happens upon the table that John and Lee are sharing at the restaurant and displays his strong disapproval, John is honestly surprised. ("Gee, you're sweet," Lee tells John. "You never think of anything wrong, do you?") And when the fugitive pair make their escape from the judge's

---

*When John and Lee are back in Indiana, both Mrs. Sargent and Aunt Emma figure out that John and Lee are in love long before they themselves recognize the fact. There's no one in the city—including the judge, the symbol of wisdom—who is as perceptive about human nature as the two women from the farm.

house in Pennsylvania, John wonders aloud how the fire got started in the wastebasket.

Where all of these incidents lead, literally as well as figuratively, is right back to the home of Mrs. Sargent. From the moment John and Lee arrive there, the tone of the film changes and it becomes clear that we have found the source of John's values. Everything about the setting, from the warm reception the pair enjoy to the comforting feeling of the house and its activities, suggests a place suffused with love. Unlike the house where Lee grew up, which is dark and unwelcoming, the Sargent house is brightly lit and beaming with life.

One of the most interesting connections Sturges makes is the link between the love that builds values and the simple traditions that strengthen and renew them. When John and Lee arrive at the farmhouse, the contrast is so great that they could easily have been sent back in time seventy-five years. There is no electricity; light is generated by oil lamps and candles. The house has no central heating; the rooms are warmed by fireplaces. The old-fashioned stove in the kitchen sits within the room's fireplace and uses wood to cook the family's food. And even though the film takes place around 1940, there is no sign of a radio or phonograph in the house.

The activities of the holiday week also reflect the return to a simpler time and simpler values. After dinner on the night of John and Lee's arrival, the family makes popcorn to string for decorating the Christmas tree. As they sit in the living room, they listen to John play the piano and then join in singing when Willie and Lee take over (the song they sing is "The End of a Perfect Day"). On Christmas morning, all of the gifts given by Mrs. Sargent and Aunt Emma are homemade items, such as socks and sweaters. And the events of the following days are all decidedly old-fashioned: baking popovers, working at the church rummage sale, bobbing for apples, and attending a New Year's Eve barn dance.

By being exposed to this way of life, Lee becomes a new person. Although she falls in love with John, she agrees not to pursue her feelings because she does not want to hurt him—a significant personal sacrifice that she would not have made back in New York. In a sense Lee is allowed to relive her childhood during the holiday week, to experience the love she was denied, and to perceive the subtle shadings between right and wrong that she needs to know in order to act in a moral way.

Understanding the Nature of Right and Wrong

Just as Sturges contrasts Lee's childhood with John's, he also provides a comparison throughout the film of their understanding of morality. The two characters frequently debate the proper thing to do, and the position Lee takes changes as the film moves to its climax, representing her development into a moral person.

From left to right, **Lee Leander (Barbara Stanwyck), Mrs. Sargent (Beulah Bondi), John Sargent (Fred MacMurray), and Aunt Emma (Elizabeth Patterson) open Christmas presents at the Sargent farmhouse.**

The scene in which John and Lee discuss how they would get food if they were starving is one example. John seems to be taking a position of greater moral right: stealing a loaf of bread would be against written law, but allowing a human being to starve to death is a greater moral wrong. There is little defense for Lee's solution, however; it achieves the same result—keeping a person from starving—but does so in a much more calculated and immoral manner.

The incident in Pennsylvania, from which John and Lee are able to escape because of Lee's pyrotechnics, offers another opportunity for examining this issue. After the couple crosses the border into Ohio, Lee informs a stunned John that she started the fire on purpose.

> *Lee:* Look, it's better than going to jail, isn't it? I told you my mind worked differently.
> *John:* Do you realize that house is probably in flames a mile high?
> *Lee:* I hope it is.
> *John:* Well, so do I, but what's that got to do with the morals of the case?
> *Lee:* What has morals got to do with it?

Once again, Sturges presents a situation in which the written law and the moral law are at odds, but Lee is unable to recognize that. We know that even though they did violate the *written* law (trespassing and milking a cow they did not own), they really did nothing wrong in the larger sense; they ended up in the field because a detour was not clearly marked, and they wanted to get just a little milk to drink before starting out again. Although John realizes this (his gut reaction is to hope the house burned down), he still feels that the situation should be resolved honestly—he did offer to pay for damages—and knows it is wrong to have escaped as they did. Lee, however, thinks of nothing but expediency, and she takes the first opportunity she gets to flee.

By the time Lee's stay in Indiana is over, though, she has come to appreciate what it means to make a moral choice, and she is the one who speaks up for doing so on the trip back to New York. As John and Lee discuss how to handle the remainder of her trial, we find something of a reversal in their arguments. John contends that Lee ought to remain in Canada, where she is out of U.S. jurisdiction.

> *John*: You know I love you, don't you?
> *Lee*: Don't say that.
> *John*: Why shouldn't I say it? Because some chiseling jeweler claims you swiped one of his bracelets?
> *Lee*: I did swipe it.
> *John*: The jury will tell you whether you took it or not. He got it back, didn't he? What you did yesterday and what you do today are two different things. All the state wants you to do is lay off other people's property; it doesn't care how that condition is arrived at.

But while John may appear to be practicing the same disdain for legality that prompted Lee to start the fire in the judge's home, he is in fact acting on a higher moral obligation. For just as Mrs. Sargent knew on the first day she met Lee ("she's as honest as all outdoors"), John realizes that Lee is not really a criminal. She has simply been denied love and was homeless and starving when she took the bracelet. What is more, as he explains to Lee on their return trip, he feels responsible for her current plight.

> *Lee*: You know it's funny that of all the people in the courtroom, you were the only one that seemed to have a heart. You think you'd be the last one.
> *John*: Don't give me any credit. I played a fairly dirty trick on you and I felt a little bad about it, that's all.
> *Lee*: How did you play me a dirty trick?
> *John*: By having your case put over until after the holiday, when I saw that the jury was going to acquit you for Christmas.
> *Lee*: Why, you dog. That was pretty smart of you, all right.... Then when that fat slob got me out, it was because your conscience was bothering you.
> *John*: A little.

John's attempt to circumvent the legal system and to ensure Lee's release, then, is not really immoral or illegal. Rather, he hopes to make up for his previous indiscretion: blocking the court from doing its job. By first urging Lee to remain in Canada and then bullying her on the stand to obtain her acquittal, he of course implies that he loves her. More importantly, he acknowledges that his moral failing (denying "justice" by getting the trial postponed, which he felt guilty about right from the start) has wrongfully put Lee in danger of going to prison. Knowing that she should not be convicted—both because she would not have been if he had not interfered initially and because her theft of the jewels was little different from a starving person's theft of bread—he makes every effort to secure her rightful release, even if that release is strictly "against the law."

For Lee, however, there is a larger issue, which goes beyond the actual stealing of the bracelet and its appropriate punishment. For the first time in her life she understands the higher moral values of right and wrong that John has known all along. Finally realizing that the life she was living was unethical, she wants to act on her new moral sense and make up for her misdeeds. As soon as she grasps what John is trying to do in the courtroom to ensure her acquittal, she speaks up to confess her crime. Later, in jail, she tells John why she did so.

> *Lee*: How long will I get?
> *John*: How do I know? Maybe you won't get very long, but if you'd kept your trap shut, you wouldn't have to go at all.
> *Lee*: There wasn't anything else to do.

For Lee, going to jail is not merely a way to pay for the jewel theft; it is a way to pay for an entire life of expediency—stealing bracelets, sneaking dinners, and starting fires. Like John when he stole his mother's egg money, Lee has to work hard to repay what she owes, now that she understands. And just as it was with John, love has made her understand.

FIVE

The Great McGinty

Produced by Paul Jones; Written and Directed by Preston Sturges;
Photography: William C. Mellor; Edited by Hugh Bennett; Art
Direction: Hans Dreier and Earl Hedrick; Set Decoration: A. E.
Freudeman; Sound: Earl Hayman and Walter Oberst; Musical
Score: Frederick Holland. Released by Paramount, 1940.

Cast: Brian Donlevy (Dan McGinty); Muriel Angelus (Catherine
McGinty); Akim Tamiroff (The Boss); Allyn Joslyn (George);
William Demarest (The Politician); Louis Jean Heydt (Thompson); Harry Rosenthal (Louie, the Bodyguard); Arthur Hoyt (Mayor
Tillinghast); Libby Taylor (Bessie); Steffi Duna (The Girl);
Esther Howard (Madame LaJolla); Frank Moran (The Boss's
Chauffeur); Jimmy Conlin (The Lookout); Dewey Robinson
(Benny Pelgman).

Synopsis: In a low-rent bar in an unnamed tropical country, an American bank cashier named Thompson, ashamed at the single act of dishonesty that has driven him from his home, tries to commit suicide. His
attempt almost succeeds, but the bartender, Dan McGinty, wrests the gun
away from him just in time. Not very sympathetic to Thompson's situation
or to his cowardly solution, McGinty launches into a story about his own
life and what he left behind in America—the governorship of a state.

The story flashes back to a city square on election night, where a soup
kitchen has been set up for the city's homeless people, courtesy of Mayor
Tillinghast. In return for the free food the men are encouraged to help the
mayor's bid for reelection: they will receive $2 for voting in the names of
registered voters who cannot make it to the polls. Seeing an opportunity
to help himself as well as to fulfill his debt, McGinty casts votes at thirty-seven different polling places, thereby earning an audience with The Boss,
the man who controls the city. Impressed with McGinty's boldness and
nerve, The Boss offers him a job collecting protection money from local

businesses, and on his first day McGinty brings in $1150 that The Boss had already written off.

Back in the bar McGinty fills in more details of his story for Thompson and the bar's female singer. He served as a collector for The Boss for a while, then was "elected" alderman, a position he could use to control bus franchises, garbage disposal, and other lucrative contracts. He did so well that The Boss was about to make him a superior court judge when outrage over corruption in the mayor's office put the heat on everyone.

As the story again moves back in time, the newspapers are full of reports about Mayor Tillinghast's graft-ridden administration and about the campaign by Dr. Jonas J. Jarvis of the Civic Purity League to clean up the city. In response to the trouble, The Boss hatches a plan to oust Mayor Tillinghast and replace him with an unknown man — McGinty. In preparation for his run, McGinty is told that he has to get married in order to secure the women's vote; a wedding is therefore arranged between the candidate and his secretary, Catherine. Although he does not view the union as anything more than a political necessity, McGinty soon takes a liking to Catherine's two children from her previous marriage. When the couple chooses a new apartment for the family to move into, McGinty has one room made into an elaborate playroom for the children. In addition, he and Catherine gradually grow fond of each other; after he is elected mayor and comes home drunk from the celebration, Catherine looks after him with the devotion of a real wife.

In his new role as mayor, McGinty is able to authorize enormous construction projects and take The Boss's payoff schemes to new heights. At home, however, he finds Catherine spending more and more evenings with her old suitor, George. When McGinty confronts her, the couple's true feelings for each other are revealed, and before long they turn their marriage of convenience into a traditional, family-centered life. Part of this transformation involves McGinty's new devotion to Catherine and her opinions, and she begins urging him to use his position as mayor to help the people of the city. McGinty explains that he cannot oppose The Boss, and that the people responsible for the sweatshops and tenements she decries are the very ones who put him in office. Still, Catherine makes him promise that some day, when he is in a position of unchallengeable power, he will turn his attention to the good of the people.

The scene shifts to the tropical bar again as McGinty provides more details: Catherine kept telling him it was just a matter of time until he could use his power for good, he went along with her ideas because he liked the way it made him look in her eyes, and finally he announced that the time was right.

As the action resumes, a series of parades and political speeches indicates that McGinty has entered the race for governor. With the backing of The Boss he wins easily, and during the inaugural parade Catherine tells him that now he must fulfill his promise to his constituents. Reluctantly, McGinty agrees, and the next day in the capitol he informs The Boss that he will not have any part of corrupt practices or unnecessary construction projects anymore. The two men argue and trade punches, finally almost shooting each other before The Boss is hauled off to jail and charged with attempted assassination. But even with The Boss behind bars, his political machine moves quickly into gear, and McGinty is soon arrested for fraud he committed while he was mayor. Although Catherine and George try every legal means to secure McGinty's release, it is The Boss's right-hand man who, posing as a guard, is able to get both men out of jail. The Boss and McGinty make their escape from the country, stopping only long enough for McGinty to call Catherine, apologize for what has happened, and tell her that it was impossible to make him into an honest man.

McGinty finishes telling his story to Thompson and the singer, but neither seems to believe him. He does not really care and simply sends them on their way, pocketing Thompson's bar tab when he thinks no one is looking. The owner of the club sees him, though, and in a moment McGinty and The Boss are once again at each other's throats, as the remaining members of the once-mighty political machine look on from the sidelines.

☉

From the first frames of *The Great McGinty*, Sturges's directorial debut, it is clear that any romantic or hopeful sentiments that may have been left over from his last script, *Remember the Night*, are not going to be put to use in this film. As the camera tracks in on the door of McGinty's tropical bar, the following words appear on the screen:

> This is the story of two men who met in a banana republic. One of them was honest all his life except one crazy minute. The other was dishonest all his life except one crazy minute. They both had to get out of the country.

With this statement Sturges gives us much of the philosophy that underlies this film: whether someone is immoral throughout his or her lifetime, or has only a momentary lapse of judgment, the end result is the same. Thus it makes sense simply to live your entire life without ethical constraints, especially since there is always the chance that dumb luck will turn up on your side (as it does for Trudy Kockenlocker in *The Miracle of Morgan's Creek*) or that the things you probably should be punished for will instead make you into a hero (as Woodrow Truesmith finds out in *Hail the Conquering Hero*).

But *The Great McGinty*, unlike *The Miracle of Morgan's Creek* or *Hail the Conquering Hero*, has no happy ending, and that is why the film is an especially potent example of Sturges's pessimism. He wants us to know from the beginning where this story will end up—in the seediest of bars, in what at that time would have been considered the seediest of countries. The title card and the flashback structure quickly lead us to this conclusion, even though as we view the film we see McGinty moving higher and higher up the ladder of success. The disparity between what McGinty had—all of it obtained illegally—and where we know he ended up increases throughout the film, allowing Sturges to build an almost scene-by-scene argument for his cynical point: it is not the immoral acts that did in McGinty, but the moral one.

Another important function of Sturges's opening words is to introduce us to McGinty and Thompson, the "two men who met in a banana republic." A casual viewing of *The Great McGinty* could easily leave the impression that Thompson's character serves little purpose other than to provide McGinty with a convenient excuse for telling his tale. By explicitly comparing the two men right at the start, though, Sturges stresses how crucial Thompson's presence is.

To reinforce the importance of Thompson, Sturges gives us a lengthy opening sequence that concentrates on the pathetic, drunken man. At first it appears that he is the main character in the story. Sturges tantalizes us with the vague mention of his "one crazy minute" (presumably theft from the bank he worked at) and with hints that Thompson is involved with the bar's female singer (who in the language of 1940s cinema would seem to be something more than just a vocalist). Since we know from the title card that this is the banana republic bar where the story ends, we assume that the attention being given to Thompson is the setup for telling his story.

Instead, Sturges shifts the focus from Thompson to the bartender, the other man referred to in the title card. While the opening words point out that both men wound up in the same place, Sturges is also carefully drawing a distinction between them—a distinction that will become clearer as we come to know Dan McGinty. Like him, Thompson has lost his home, his prosperity, and his U.S. citizenship, but he has also lost the one thing that McGinty has never been without: his self-reliance. Unable to live with his uncharacteristic misdeed, Thompson allows himself to fall into a drunken stupor and then tries to end his misery through suicide, an act that McGinty considers cowardly. McGinty, no matter what he experiences, never gives up his scrappiness, his willingness to accept whatever comes his way, and his determination to look out for himself.

When we first meet the two men there is not really much of a reason to like either character. In the real world we would be much more sympathetic to Thompson, a generally honest man who made one mistake, than to the perpetually corrupt McGinty. But for Sturges the cynic, society is such a depraved and dishonest place that it is not a person's morality that matters, but rather the way in which he or she deals with the inequities of everyday life. Throughout Sturges's films we see characters who are forced to react to base circumstances, and it is almost always those who respond most resourcefully—not those who act most morally—whom we admire. In McGinty, we see a man who is sure of himself, willing to take on The Boss both physically and politically, and unwavering in his belief that he has done his best, even after his "one crazy minute." The same cannot be said for Thompson.

While alerting us to this difference between Thompson and McGinty, the title card also leads us toward a major theme of *The Great McGinty*: you cannot, and should not try to, make people what they are not. Both McGinty and Thompson led a consistent type of life; for both, a single attempt to do something against their usual tendencies led to disaster. The fact that McGinty can deal with the consequences better may be a reason to admire him, but it does not change the fact that if he had kept to his corrupt ways he would have remained successful. The same would be true of Thompson had he continued his scrupulously honest lifestyle.

Sturges sets up his examination of McGinty's natural inclination by flashing back to a time when he was nothing but an unemployed vagrant. At the beginning of the film McGinty is a neutral character, a self-sufficient man who plays things his own way. As he rises within the political machine, he is forced to give up some of his independence, although he retains enough individuality to battle The Boss even though it endangers his position. When his marriage to Catherine turns from a political stratagem to a loving relationship, however, McGinty finds himself caught between the pull of two opposing forces.

The Politician and The Boss

In the characters of The Politician and The Boss, Sturges gives us not only an immoral magnet to pull on McGinty, but also an amusing and caustic portrait of American politics. From the top of the system to the very bottom, every person is corrupt and every decision is based on self-interest. The Boss represents the prototypical big-city power broker who runs absolutely everything within his reach, while The Politician exemplifies the cynicism and greed that feed the corruption and allow a person like The Boss to remain in power.

The first glimpse we get of political maneuverings is the soup kitchen scene in which food is being provided to homeless people, courtesy of the campaigning mayor. It would be an obviously contrived and hypocritical offering even if it were merely an attempt to land the recipients' legitimate votes; that it is really an act of bribery to get them to break the law makes it all the more cynical. Yet Sturges, primarily through the actions of The Politician, underplays the blatant corruption, treating it as though it were completely normal.

We first meet The Politician when he gives McGinty instructions for voting in the fraudulent election, after which the vagrant will receive his pay. Since the entire enterprise is based on deceit, it is logical that McGinty would wonder why he should take this man's word. When he asks how he can be sure that The Politician will be there to make the payoff, though, The Politician becomes indignant:

> How do you know I'll be here? How do you like that! Listen to this guy. You fill him full of soup and right away he don't trust nobody.... The nerve some guys got!

When McGinty asks about the payoff he would receive for repeating the voting trick, The Politician is annoyed that McGinty wants to upset the "honesty" of the system:

> Who said anything about repeatin'? Where do you think this is, Hicks Corners? Some people is too lazy to vote, that's all.... They don't like this kind of weather. Some of them is sick in bed and *can't* vote! Maybe a couple of 'em *croaked* recently! ... That ain't no reason why Mayor Tillinghast should get cheated outta their support. All we're doing is gettin' out the vote.

Later in the film, after McGinty has joined The Boss's organization as a city alderman, there is a scene in which The Politician and Catherine (then McGinty's secretary) discuss the crackdown on Mayor Tillinghast. Once again The Politician implies that corruption is a necessity in politics.

> *The Politician* [reading from a newspaper]: "In back of this agitation, said the Mayor, are so-called pious men who have accepted money from racketeers and gamblers in sanctiminious [*sic*] secrecy. The petition was filed by Dr. Jonas J. Jarvis, chairman of the Civic Purity League, Inc."
> Ah, they're always talking about graft, but they forget, if it wasn't for graft, you'd get a very low type of people in politics. Men without ambition. Jellyfish.
> *Catherine*: Especially since you can't rob the people anyway.
> *The Politician*: How is that?
> *Catherine*: What you rob you spend, and what you spend goes back to the people, so where's the robbing? I read that in one of my father's books.
> *The Politician*: That book should be in every home.*

In a piece of dialogue intended for the same scene but not used in the finished film, The Politician comments on the attempt to clean up the corruption: "They're always throwing guys out that's already got theirs to put in a bunch that needs everything from the socks up.... You'd think they'd learn." (Throughout this chapter, all examples of material not in the finished film derive from the screenplay as published in Brian Henderson, ed., Five Screenplays by Preston Sturges.)

For Sturges, this approach to politics is nothing new. It is not the mode of operation for this one group of politicians in this one city; it is the way the political game is always played. The remark of one shakedown victim—"Even in the days of Boss Herman we didn't have to pay *that* much for franchises! Even in the days of Bathhouse Jake!"—tells us that the city has always been corrupt. And by the time we reach the end of the film we have seen such pervasive fraud that there is no doubt that a new boss will immediately come forward, even though the current political machine has been driven out.

It is The Boss who most clearly demonstrates the way to use politics to achieve power and personal gain. As he explains to McGinty after his protégé's first round of collections, the possibilities in politics are virtually limitless:

> Yesterday you was a hobo on the bread line . . . today you got a thousand berries and a new suit. I wonder where you'll be tomorrow. This is a land of great opportunity. . . . You take me, for instance. Where I come from is very poor, see? All the richness is gone a long time ago, so everybody lives by chiseling everybody else. . . . It comes to me very natural. If I live five hundred years ago I guess I be a baron maybe, a robber baron. . . . I live on a rock and chisel the city below and everybody call me "baron." . . . Now, I live in a penthouse and everybody call me "Boss."

The Boss's speech suggests that the contemporary American political system has not really broken with a centuries-old tradition of exploitation, no matter how much we would like to think it has. Instead, it is a system in which a select few get rich and maintain control at the expense of the general public. For The Boss, much of the money is made by continually forcing businesses to pay for protection, although he convinces them that they have something to gain. It is "good protection, too," he tells McGinty. "If it wasn't for me, everybody'd pick on 'em. They'd be at the mercy." McGinty himself provides the best explanation of the protection arrangement when he goes to collect Madame LaJolla's unpaid bill:

> You've gotta pay protection. You want to be at the mercy of every slug that wears a uniform? You want the fire commissioner telling you that your joint is a trap? Or the health inspector telling you that your air is vicious? Or the plumbing inspector saying that your pipes stink? . . . You need somebody to cooperate all those guys, and protect you from human greed. You gotta pay somebody. . . . Buying from us is just like getting club rates.

As is apparent from McGinty's speech, The Boss has the entire city under his control. The protection money paid to him guarantees that the police, the fire department, and other city agencies will not harass the people whom he wishes to be left alone. Even the political parties themselves are under his authority.

> *The Boss*: Do you want to be Reform mayor? . . . The mayor of this city?
> *McGinty*: Whatta you got to do with the Reform Party?
> *The Boss*: I *am* the Reform Party. . . . In this town I'm *all* the parties. You think I'm going to starve every time they change administrations?

Finally, in the scene that takes place just after McGinty becomes governor, Sturges provides a picture of just how this unchecked power is used.

> *The Boss*: You should feel all right . . . with this [the governor's office] staring you in the face. What a wonderful opportunity. This state needs everything! They had honest governors so long the whole place is in wrack and ruin! . . . It's ridiculous. The roads, for instance. They're in terrible condition. In case of war we'd be at the mercy. We need a whole new highway system. . . . Then we'll need a new waterworks system, a state canal, and—you'll kiss me for this one—a new dam!
> *McGinty*: We do, huh?
> *The Boss*: I can see from your expression you don't know what a dam is. You think a dam is something you put a lot of water in. . . . A dam is something you put a lotta concrete in . . . and it doesn't matter how much you put in, there's always room for a lot more . . . and any time you're afraid it's finished you find a crack in it and you put some more concrete. It's wonderful.
> *McGinty*: What's the matter with the old dam?
> *The Boss*: It's got a crack in it.

As McGinty discovers just a few scenes later, it is hopeless to try to defeat such a corrupt political system. Even the people who are supposedly fighting the war against graft—in this case Dr. Jonas J. Jarvis and the Civic Purity League—are themselves part of the system. Before putting McGinty forward as a mayoral candidate, for example, The Boss checks with Jarvis, who is obviously working with the political machine. (In the script, the ties between Jarvis and The Boss are even stronger, and the civic reformer ends up in the banana republic bar with the rest of the political exiles.) The dishonesty is so pervasive that it is nearly impossible for McGinty not to be dragged down into it. The only force tugging him in the other direction is Catherine.

Catherine

As the sole counterweight to the overwhelming pull of private interest and corruption, Catherine is the only person who speaks up for the concerns and wishes of the electorate. She does not get very far with her efforts, though, not only because the political system is rotten through and through, but also because even she—the most moral of the film's characters— occasionally acts to further her own ends.

Catherine's first appearances in the film, initially as an obedient secretary and then as the inevitable love interest, do not give us much of a clue as to the important role she will play in the story. Her first line is only a brief comment made behind McGinty's back as he ushers another shakedown victim out of the office ("Aren't you ashamed of yourself?" she says to a photo of her boss). This glimpse of morality, however, is soon offset by her proposal that she and McGinty marry to further his political career. While there is an undercurrent of genuine affection on her part ("I'm so interested in your career, Mr. McGinty. You're sort of a favorite of mine"), there is also a clear sense of expediency. "I suppose it just seems so wonderful to me because it's so far beyond anything I could hope for," she tells McGinty, and then goes on to talk about being photographed on the steps of city hall, living in the mayor's house, and making speeches at the women's clubs. A marriage of convenience may be morally objectionable, but Catherine—who was abandoned by her husband and left to raise two children on her own—is resourceful enough to take advantage of the opportunity.

The issue of Catherine's ethics is particularly interesting in light of what Sturges left out of the film. In an extension of The Politician's graft speech that appears in a late version of the screenplay but not in the movie, the source of Catherine's practical experience becomes apparent.

> *The Politician*: How do you know so much about politics, anyway?
> *Catherine*: My father was a judge.
> *The Politician*: Oh, is that so? Well, don't the practical end of politics seem kinda ... I mean bein' a judge's daughter and all ... or was he a practical judge?
> *Catherine*: I'm afraid he wasn't, Skeeters. He didn't even leave any insurance money, the poor old sap.
> *The Politician*: Well, for heaven sake. And with all that opportunity! You'd think a man'd think of his wife and children, wouldn't you?

In the script, Catherine clearly has firsthand knowledge of the relative value of honesty, as well as an attitude that is not all that far from that of The Boss. Because her father was an honest, impractical judge who did not use his public position for private gain, his family had nothing to fall back on. Although Sturges tried to tone this aspect of Catherine's personality down a bit by removing the reference to her father, some of her opportunism remains in the film. Because her husband left her and their children without any means of support, for example, she is eager to enter the mock marriage with McGinty. As her thoroughly realistic defense of robbing from the people shows (in what is left in the film of her conversation with The Politician), she understands how the political system works. That is why she is willing to wait for McGinty to reach his position of power before he acts honestly. With Catherine, Sturges makes the caustically cynical point that even the people who seem to be the most moral and honest are really just *less* self-serving. The spectrum of human nature ranges not from unethical to ethical, but merely from very immoral to only mildly so.

But despite Catherine's jaded experience she is clearly the most honest person on display in *McGinty*, and as the film progresses she becomes a strong voice for moral action. The hint of warmth she displays in the marriage proposal sequence intensifies in later scenes, for example, when she chooses an apartment or cares for McGinty after his wild election party. Once she and McGinty settle down in a real marriage, her perspective begins to have a major effect on the mayor. Instead of drinking and running around with women, McGinty is now content to sit home at night and read bedtime stories to the children. As they spend more time together, Catherine also begins to push him to do something about the real problems in the city.

> *Catherine*: I think you're a fine man, Dan. . . . I think you're a fine, honest man with decent impulses and everything else. I couldn't have been as close to you as I have been and be mistaken. I don't think I could love you so much. I know I couldn't admire you so much. . . . You're just a tough guy, McGinty. You're not a wrong guy. If you were on the other side of the fence, you'd play just as hard the other way. . . . To have all that power you have and all the opportunities you have to do things for people and never to do anything but shake them down a little . . . it seems like a waste of something. It doesn't balance. . . .
> *McGinty*: What are you trying to do, reform me?
> *Catherine*: I guess I'm just being dull. I guess I went to one reform lunch too many this week. I've heard so much about child labor and sweatshops and the firetraps poor people live in. . . .

Catherine keeps after McGinty, telling him that one day he will be powerful enough to buck the system. When the day of his inauguration as governor arrives, Catherine is convinced the time has come: "You're strong enough for anything now. To do good for people. To justify the faith of your constituents." McGinty is still doubtful, though: "I'm the governor of the state. You're the governor's lady. Isn't that enough for you? Why don't we leave well enough alone? Everybody don't get to be governor."

Despite his love for Catherine, McGinty just cannot wholeheartedly support the idea of altruism, but to please her he does make the effort on

his first day in office. He tells The Boss that no more projects are going
to go through unless they are in the best interests of the people. "First, I'm
going to put through a child labor bill, then I'm going to stamp out the
sweatshops, then I'm going to banish the tenements," McGinty explains,
repeating the list of Catherine's ambitions. The Boss will have none of it,
however, and even after the scuffle that lands him in jail, he is still able to
set the wheels in motion to have McGinty arrested as well.

By the time Catherine visits her incarcerated husband, McGinty has
been jolted back to a sense of reality.

> *Catherine*: They can't do this to you, Dan. I'll go to the Supreme Court,
> I'll see the president, I'll get up a petition signed by every citizen of
> the state! They can't put a man in jail for doing something honest.
> *McGinty*: Maybe they can't, honey, but they're putting up a good bluff.
> *Catherine*: How long are they hoping to sentence you for?
> *McGinty*: They're hoping for ten years.
> *Catherine*: I'll stand by you, Dan. I'll fight for you night and day. We'll
> beat them if it takes twenty years.
> *McGinty*: Well, never mind about that part of it. You just get me out of
> here on bail and I'll take care of the rest of it.

Although Catherine may still have some faith in the political and legal
order, McGinty has come to his senses. He realizes that trusting his future
to the same system that he has manipulated and milked for years will only
result in a long jail term. His only hope is to leave the country and avoid
being the victim of the next Great McGinty.

McGinty

If McGinty in any way represents the average American—caught between self-interest and altruism—perhaps the most disturbing result of his
political rise and fall is not that he fails to do what is right, but rather that
he considers his mere attempt to do right a mistake. McGinty's movement
in the course of the film begins with him directly between The Boss and
Catherine, leads him first toward one side then toward the other, and finally deposits him back where he started. The only difference is that by the
end of his ordeal he has come to recognize the futility of being anything
other than himself.

In the first stages of McGinty's political career, he is clearly not motivated by the same type of greed exhibited by The Boss and his lackeys. The
initiative he takes in voting thirty-seven times may net him far more than
the $2 he has been promised, but his desire to live by his own code of honor
is more important than money. The most astute thing for someone in his
position to do would be to ingratiate himself with The Boss; McGinty,

however, cannot stop hurling insults and fighting with him. When The Boss offers McGinty all the money he has collected on his first day, which The Boss had already written off, McGinty is not at all grateful but instead is offended at the thought that he would be sent on a seemingly hopeless mission. Similarly, his first reaction to The Boss's plan to run him for mayor is not appreciation, but rather outrage that he should be expected to get married for the plan to work. And even though the marriage between McGinty and Catherine is one of convenience, McGinty never fails to take offense when The Boss speaks of Catherine as anything less than a lady.

Once McGinty comes under Catherine's influence, however, he begins to show a concern for others that goes beyond his usual values. He quickly develops a special feeling for Catherine's children, asking that the family's new apartment be equipped with a large playroom and feeling embarrassed and regretful when they see him in a drunken state. After the marriage turns into a real relationship, he takes a distinct pleasure in reading to the children, telling Catherine, "I don't feel no different toward them than if they were mine." Toward Catherine herself, of course, he feels such love that when she keeps urging him to do something to help people, he finally obliges by defying The Boss's plans for the state.

But the pull that Catherine exerts on McGinty is not nearly as strong as that exerted by The Boss. Even after McGinty has taken his stand and The Boss is in jail for attempted assassination, McGinty cannot help but side with his old ally.

> *Catherine*: It serves him right. I hope he gets twenty years for it.
> *McGinty*: I'm not going to press the charges. He ain't a bad guy, honey, according to his way of looking at things. You gotta remember he took me off a bread line...
> *Catherine*: But he tried to kill you!
> *McGinty*: Why shouldn't he? Don't you think *I'd* take a pop at a guy that slipped me the triple cross?

Only a few moments later, the authorities come to the door to arrest McGinty for the misdeeds of his mayoral administration. He soon finds himself in a jail cell next to The Boss, and true to form, he immediately begins fighting with the man he has just been defending. But like a married couple whose constant bickering actually serves to keep them together, McGinty and The Boss escape and set up new lives together, just as though nothing had ever come between them. Although McGinty may not realize just how much he and The Boss really need each other, he does understand that life with Catherine and the children (and with Catherine's moral values) does not suit his true nature. Before the escapees leave the country, McGinty takes the time to make one last phone call to Catherine.

McGinty (Brian Donlevy, *second from right*) and The Boss (Akim Tamiroff, *second from left*) are pulled apart from fighting after the newly elected governor has defied his mentor and the graft-ridden system.

Look, honey, you're not going to like what I've done, but I've only one life and I'm not going to live it in the icebox. . . . They got me dead to rights. Now listen: I know you'd come along with me but that ain't right, see. You gotta think about the little guy and the little lady. . . . It wouldn't do them no good to have their old man in stir or on the lam and the other kids razzing them about it. So this is what you do, see. It's kind of hard to say, honey, but you go see George to get you a divorce, see. . . .

Look, honey, there's just one more thing. You know the dresser in my room? You pull out the left top drawer, see, and there's a key fastened between the drawers with court plaster. It's got a number on it and the name of the safe deposit company. They won't ask you any questions. It's a little something I held out on you. It'll keep you going and put the kids through college without selling magazines.

So long, honey. I'm sorry it didn't work out, but you can't make a silk purse out of a pig's ear. Pat the little fellow for me.

In many ways, *The Great McGinty* is one of Preston Sturges's bleakest films. The only character in it who can be regarded in any way as moral completely fails in her efforts to impose her values on the other characters. Furthermore, by the movie's end the protagonist has been stripped of his wealth and position and driven out of the country; a couple who truly loved each other are permanently separated; two children who came to love their stepfather will never see him again; and the corrupt politicians, if they ultimately have not profited from their crimes, at least have not been punished for them. About the only positive outcome is that Dan McGinty, unlike Thompson the bank clerk, faces his failure and learns from it—even if all he learns is that he should never again try to do anything for the good of others.

Unlike the later *Hail the Conquering Hero*, in which Sturges comes to a slightly more heartening conclusion about the place of honesty in politics, here his message seems to be that it is impossible to reform the corrupt political system. What McGinty discovers by the end of the film is not that his crooked actions were wrong—he still tries to steal Thompson's bar tab behind The Boss's back—but rather that if he had not gone against his nature by trying to be honorable, he would be in the lap of luxury still. Now there is another lucky sap who has worked his way up and is reaping the rewards, doing the same things to the people that The Boss's machine did. And honesty has no place there.

SIX

Christmas in July

Produced by Paul Jones; Written and Directed by Preston Sturges; Photography: Victor Milner; Edited by Ellsworth Hoagland; Art Direction: Hans Dreier and Earl Hedrick; Sound: Harry Lindgren and Walter Oberst; Musical Direction: Sigmund Krumgold. Released by Paramount, 1940.

Cast: Dick Powell (Jimmy MacDonald); Ellen Drew (Betty Casey); Raymond Walburn (Dr. Maxford); Alexander Carr (Mr. Schindel); William Demarest (Mr. Bildocker); Ernest Truex (Mr. Baxter); Franklin Pangborn (Radio Announcer); Harry Hayden (Mr. Waterbury); Rod Cameron (Dick); Michael Morris (Tom); Harry Rosenthal (Harry); Georgia Caine (Mrs. MacDonald); Ferike Boros (Mrs. Schwartz); Torben Meyer (Mr. Schmidt); Julius Tannen (Mr. Zimmerman); Al Bridge (Mr. Hillbeiner); Lucille Ward (Mrs. Casey); Kay Stewart (Secretary); Vic Potel (Davenola Salesman).

Synopsis: Jimmy MacDonald, who enters every contest he learns about, and his girlfriend, Betty, are waiting to hear the results of the Maxford House Coffee slogan contest. The winner is supposed to be announced on the company's weekly radio program, but when the jury remains deadlocked at eleven to one, the program is forced to go off the air without a winner being chosen. Jimmy is still confident of his chances, and although Betty does not quite understand his slogan, she is rooting for him to win. It seems to be the only way he will marry her. Because he thinks that Betty and his mother deserve nice things, like cars and a house, he is waiting to "crash through" and win one of his contests before he will even think about marriage.

The next morning Jimmy goes to his job at the Baxter Coffee company, but before sitting down at his desk he places a call to Maxford House and finds out that a winning slogan has yet to be chosen. When three of his coworkers overhear the phone call, they decide to play a joke on Jimmy by sending him a phony telegram telling him he has won.

After being called into the boss's office and scolded for his recent work habits, Jimmy returns to his desk and finds the telegram. His excitement leads to such pandemonium in the office that the president of the company, Mr. Baxter, comes to see what has happened. When he learns the news he asks Jimmy into his office to discuss writing slogans for the Baxter company. Pleased with the suggestions Jimmy offers, Baxter promises Jimmy his own office and secretary before giving him and Betty the rest of the day off.

Jimmy and Betty go to the Maxford House Company to pick up the check from Dr. Maxford, who becomes upset at not having been informed by his jury that a winner was chosen. Nevertheless, he gives the couple the check, and they immediately head for a department store where they buy an engagement ring for Betty, the convertible davenport Jimmy's mother has always dreamed of, and gifts for everyone in their neighborhood. When they arrive home with their presents, Jimmy is treated to a hero's welcome.

In the meantime, Dr. Maxford has discovered that the jury is still deadlocked eleven to one and that no one at Maxford House sent Jimmy the telegram. He arrives at Jimmy's house to reclaim his check, followed by Mr. Schindel, the department store owner, whom Dr. Maxford alerted of the mistake. When Dr. Maxford admits that he wrote the check himself, Mr. Schindel urges everyone to keep the presents; he says he will sue Dr. Maxford to pay for them. Shortly afterward the three coworkers who sent the telegram arrive at Jimmy's house to apologize for the trouble they have caused.

That evening Jimmy and Betty go to the Baxter company to look at the office that has been prepared for him. There they run into Mr. Baxter, who reiterates his enthusiasm for Jimmy's new slogans until he hears that Jimmy did not in fact win the contest. At first he rescinds the job offer, but after a heartfelt speech from Betty, he relents and offers to give Jimmy a brief chance at the job, but with no increase in pay.

Back at the Maxford House Company, an exasperated Dr. Maxford is trying to put the day's events behind him when Bildocker, the one dissenting member of the jury, comes in and says that he has finally persuaded the eleven others to go along with his choice. And it turns out to be Jimmy's slogan.

❂

Perhaps it is because *The Great McGinty* and *Christmas in July* were originally conceived and written during the Depression that they both exhibit an especially pessimistic tone. Compared with *McGinty*, though, *Christmas in July* appears on the surface to be a much brighter movie, a boisterous tale that has its roots in the screwball comedies of the 1930s. The film is well stocked with sentiment, neighborly love, and a seemingly happy ending, as well as plenty of brilliant comic lines and memorable characters and performances.

But *Christmas in July* is much more than a humorous fable of a prank gone wrong; instead it explores rather scornfully the less rosy side of the American consumer's dream. Sturges presents a bleak view of the work ethic, showing us honest, hardworking people who not only have not succeeded, but who do not even seem to believe anymore that they can. These desperate characters are no longer motivated by self-respect and a concern for others, but by an overriding devotion to materialism. In America, Sturges demonstrates, money and possessions equal success, but even more, they equal life.

An Environment of Desperation

In *Christmas in July*, the one thought that seems to be on everybody's mind is money. Everyone constantly speaks of it, from Jimmy, who hopes to be able to buy success; to Mrs. MacDonald, who fondly remembers the day her conductor husband was overpaid by a subway passenger; to Dr. Maxford, who decries the ridiculous contest as a waste of his money. Even for Tom, Dick, and Harry, who send Jimmy the phony telegram, the realization that their joke has gone too far does not in their minds jeopardize their personal integrity or their reputation among their coworkers; instead, it will cost them one davenport.

The overwhelming emphasis on money reflects the film's roots in the Depression, when average Americans seriously questioned the work ethic and despaired of ever achieving (or regaining) success. In the movie's first scene, with Betty talking to Jimmy on their apartment roof, Sturges sets up the story's basic premise—that lack of money stands between the couple and happiness—and establishes the prevailing lack of hope that they and millions of other Americans feel. As the radio announcer runs down the list of contest prizes, we see a series of shots of people leaning over their radios, just as Jimmy and Betty are, poised and waiting for the results. The people are from all walks of life: nurses, a bartender, customers in a barbershop.* Since the degree of interest seems out of proportion for a simple radio contest, Sturges obviously intends the shots to be humorous. But the ensuing look at the judging of the contest adds another dimension to his message. The winning slogan will be selected by a group of twelve men, continually referred to as a jury. A problem arises when the men, who have been sequestered, are deadlocked eleven to one. The lone holdout,

---

Sturges can be glimpsed in the last of these shots, seated at a shoe-shine stand.

Bildocker, explains his opposition by saying that he is working for free, on behalf of all the contestants, and that he owes it to them to vote his conscience. Even the casual moviegoer has seen enough courtroom dramas to recognize this group as a jury struggling to reach a verdict, and the people gathered about their radios as the public waiting to hear the life-or-death sentence. By the end of *Christmas in July*, we realize that it is actually the people listening, the contest entrants, who are being sentenced. Sturges tells us that in this America, where hard work gets you nowhere, being the winner in such a contest is the only way to achieve the American Dream, the only way to be granted "life."

When the radio program ends with no decision in the contest, Sturges cuts back to the scene on the rooftop. Now Jimmy MacDonald talks for himself, describing his sincere yearning to win the contest. But Sturges has already undercut the reality of his hopes by showing us some of the three million other entrants, whose faces are just as eager as Jimmy's. The other entrants are presented in the same way, silent and unmoving, and when the litany of images ends with a shot of Jimmy and Betty listening on the roof in the same manner, the message is clear: This story is just one of the millions that could have been told. Everyone else who entered also wants to win—and needs to win—just as much as Jimmy.

The conversation between Betty and Jimmy reinforces the feeling of despair established by the wordless images. "Two can live as cheaply as one," Betty offers, to which Jimmy replies, "Who wants to live cheaply?" The answer of course is that no one does, but unfortunately for these characters, the hopes of being a success and of not living cheaply are virtually nonexistent. At no time does either Betty or Jimmy consider the possibility of the work ethic, of "working hard and getting ahead." Jimmy pins his hopes on winning one of the many contests he enters, most of which require no cleverness or skill, while Betty pretends that what little they already have is enough.

Perhaps the best example of this philosophy comes at the beginning of the rooftop scene, as Betty describes a one-room apartment with a revolving corner that sounds like something in a Disney cartoon. The corner turns to reveal the appointments of four different rooms: bathroom, bedroom, kitchenette, and nonworking fireplace. In this way, Betty explains to a skeptical Jimmy, a young couple just starting out can have four rooms for the price of one. The idea may sound ridiculous, but the underlying attitude represents a major theme of the movie and the edict by which the characters of this world live: if you cannot get what you really want, you can always fool yourself into believing that what you have is just as good.

The first part of *Christmas in July* also contains several speeches that highlight the mood of pessimism and defeat. On the rooftop, for example, Jimmy delivers a grim account of his family's troubles, which lingers throughout the film; even the comically happy ending does not completely wash away the memory. The speech begins when Betty tries to convince Jimmy that they are financially able to get married now. She points out that Jimmy's father was earning only $18 a week when he married Mrs. Mac-Donald, but Jimmy is not easily persuaded:

> Do you think that proves something? She's never been to the country for more than a day, never had any nice furniture. The dream of her life is a davenport that turns into a double bed at nighttime, with a crank. She's never had a nice dress except those she made herself. I wore the old man's stuff cut down until I got my first job, and he was worn out at forty-eight and croaked because he couldn't afford a decent doctor. Where do you get that eighteen bucks a week stuff?

Although Betty pushes, claiming that she makes $18 a week and he makes $22, Jimmy knows better: "Sure, and you got your Ma and I got mine. You get a kid and you have to stop work, and we're right back at the twenty-two again." He finishes by telling Betty that she should be looking out for herself, not wasting her time on a guy like him.

Sturges winds the rooftop scene down at this point, leaving the feeling of frustration hanging in the air. The film then moves to a brief scene in Jimmy's kitchen the next morning, where Mrs. MacDonald reminisces about her husband, a streetcar conductor, comparing him and his "crazy ideas" with Jimmy. She affectionately recounts to her son the story of what happened when her husband was once mistakenly given a five-dollar gold piece in change rather than a nickel. "We went to Coney that night," she remembers with a smile, offering up one of the film's many examples of how chance, not hard work, yields monetary success.* It is a lesson that Jimmy—who wants to be the one winner out of three million entrants—has learned well.

At the Baxter company headquarters, Sturges puts the final brush strokes on his portrait of desperation. The entire office, where the employees are referred to as numbers, don identical (and apparently unnecessary) smocks, and sit en masse in perfectly aligned rows, hardly suggests a rewarding employment experience; instead it conjures up a vision of a grade-school punishment session. It is not clear what all the employees are doing, but like Jimmy they seem to be simply adding up numbers. There presumably is some purpose to the work, but the numbers seem to be mere marks on a page, abstract and meaningless.

---

*The story of Mr. MacDonald's good fortune also touches on another favorite Sturges theme: the value of dishonesty. Like Diamond Jim Brady, who misleads Horsley to sell him under-trucks, or Dan McGinty, who makes money by impersonating dead voters, Mr. MacDonald seems to have one of his few successful moments when he decides not to return the extra money a nearsighted passenger gave him by mistake.

The routine is broken when Mr. Waterbury, the office manager, calls Jimmy into his office for a little talk. He points out that Jimmy's work has not been very good lately and wants to know why Jimmy is daydreaming on the job. When Jimmy explains that he has been distracted by thoughts of winning the $25,000 first prize in the Maxford House contest, Mr. Waterbury offers some advice:

> I used to think about $25,000, too, and what I'd do with it, that I'd be a failure if I didn't get a hold of it. And then one day I realized I was never going to have $25,000, Mr. MacDonald. And then another day, a little bit later, considerably later, I realized something else, something I'm imparting to you now, Mr. MacDonald. I'm not a failure—I'm a success. You see, ambition is all right if it works, but no system could be right where only half of one percent were successes and all the rest were failures. That wouldn't be right. I'm not a failure—I'm a success. And so are you, if you earn your own living, pay your bills, and look the world in the eye. I hope you win your $25,000, Mr. MacDonald, but if you shouldn't happen to, don't worry about it. Now get the heck back to your desk and try to improve your arithmetic.

With its repeated refrain, "I'm not a failure—I'm a success," Waterbury's speech implies that he is still trying to talk himself into accepting his lowly position in life. He has been denied the real object of his desire (money and status, the American version of success), but like Betty with her one-room apartment, he has fooled himself into believing that what he has gotten is just as good. And to further emphasize the irony in Waterbury's speech, Sturges shows us his actions just before he brings Jimmy into his office. Just as Sturges showed some of the other eager entrants before allowing Jimmy to speak of his contest hopes, here he uses the shots of Waterbury at work to undercut the boss's forthcoming assertion of his success. Wandering around the office, doing little except straightening the wooden paper holders on the desks, Waterbury hardly provides a model of achievement for anyone to emulate.

But while Sturges wants us to see that Waterbury's speech is not the answer to the prospect of living cheaply, he also inserts a sentence that essentially constitutes an indictment of ambition. If it works, Waterbury says, ambition is all right, but no system could be right that has so few successes. When combined with what we have already heard from Jimmy, the message is obvious: ambition, or at least the hard work encouraged by the American Dream, fails 99.5 percent of the time. The ones who are left behind either wait for a miracle, like Jimmy, or, like Waterbury, deceive themselves into thinking that they are not living cheaply.

With this background of desperation and futility firmly established, Sturges shifts gears to examine the effect it has on the people who have been forced to live with it. As soon as Jimmy leaves Mr. Waterbury's office, he finds the phony telegram informing him that he's won the Maxford House contest. The story then shifts to Jimmy's inevitable response to his newfound success: rampant consumerism.

Materialism and Lack of Respect

If the first section of *Christmas in July* shows how fraudulent the American work ethic is, then the second part demonstrates how unsatisfying are the values that are put in its place. Since people are so often denied any hope of success, it is only natural that they should come to value only material goods or whatever means they use to acquire material goods. This rampant materialism completely drives out any respect for oneself or for others and destroys any confidence in one's own abilities or convictions.

The lack of respect that people demonstrate toward one another is obvious throughout the entire film. The ongoing struggle between Dr. Maxford and the jury, for instance, contains countless examples. Bildocker refers to the contest entrants as "suckers" even though he claims to be working on their behalf, and he calls his fellow jurors "fatheaded, mealy-mouthed lamebrains." Dr. Maxford's opinion of the jury is not much better; after telling the group they have the combined brains of an amoeba, he asks: "What do you know about picking slogans anyway? You wouldn't know a slogan if you slipped on one." (One wonders why these men were assigned to make the decision in the first place.)

Other characters are just as guilty. The pranks that Tom, Dick, and Harry discuss in the locker room and their idea to send Jimmy the telegram all have a nasty streak more characteristic of the antics of ten-year-old boys than of the actions of grown men. Once Jimmy gets the telegram and starts a near riot in the office, Mr. Baxter fires him without listening to an explanation for his actions; this leads Waterbury to accuse Baxter of not caring about "these children [who] are part of your family." Mr. Schindel, the department store owner, calls Jimmy a lowlife, then reverses himself to hold up Jimmy's honesty and labels Maxford a burglar and a numbskull. And Mr. Zimmerman, a close friend of Jimmy's mother, describes the whole MacDonald family as "a little bit crazy" even as he is trying to defend them.

Jimmy's treatment of others also seems suspect at times. Despite apparent good intentions on his part, he really only shows concern for people by bestowing material goods on them. Although he claims to love Betty, he ridicules her idea of the apartment and says she is a sap who deserves better than him. But if Jimmy does not show much respect for her or her dedication to their relationship, Betty does not have complete confidence in Jimmy either. She vigorously points out that he has lost every contest he has entered, and try as she does to understand his slogan, she still thinks that it is bad and that he is being "pigheaded" in defending it. She even tries to make him feel better by saying, "And when you lose this one, just think how much better your chances will be on the next one."

But Sturges also points out how people turn this lack of respect inward so that they no longer have faith in their own abilities. In the rooftop scene, Jimmy hints at his lack of self-confidence when he tells Betty that she is a sap for sticking with him. After he goes to Dr. Maxford's office to pick up his check, Jimmy delivers a speech that more fully expresses his view of himself:

> I don't know whether you've ever had anything like this happen to you, Dr. Maxford, but to be poor and unknown one minute and be sitting on top of the world the next minute—that's a feeling nobody can ever take away from me. To know I won this contest because I thought of a better slogan than anyone else means more to me than anything else on earth. And I'll tell you why. You see, I used to think maybe I had good ideas, and was going to get somewhere in the world, but now I know it. And that's what I want to thank you for, Dr. Maxford, even more than the money.

The money is important, however, because it gives Jimmy status not only in his eyes, but also in the eyes of the rest of the world. When Jimmy and Betty are shopping for engagement rings, Mr. Hillbeiner treats them somewhat casually until he shows them the $12,000 ring. "I wouldn't care to spend that much," Jimmy says. "But I could if I felt like it!" With his new wealth Jimmy is aware that he now commands the kind of esteem he has never had before, and Hillbeiner's reaction—"Well, that puts everything on an entirely different basis"—bestows that respect.

Even Mr. Baxter, the head of a large coffee company, does not believe in himself. Although he quickly latches onto Jimmy's slogan for his coffee ("It's Bred in the Bean") and proclaims him a genius, Baxter's true feelings about his own business judgment are revealed later, when Jimmy asks if it would make a difference if he had not won the contest:

> Of course it would make a difference. Certainly it would. I'm no genius. I didn't hang on to my father's money by backing my own judgment, you know. I make mistakes every day, sometimes several times a day. I've got a whole warehouse full of mistakes. I should say it would make a difference. You see, I think your ideas are good because they sound good to me, but I know your ideas are good because you won this contest over millions of aspirants. It's what you might call commercial insurance, as, when a horse wins the Derby, you back him for the Preakness.

Both Jimmy, a failure, and Mr. Baxter, a success, think they have good ideas, but both need to rely on someone else's opinions for a confirmation

A startled Dr. Maxford (Raymond Walburn, *right*) presents a check for $50,000 to the "winner" of the Maxford House contest, Jimmy MacDonald (Dick Powell), and his girlfriend, Betty (Ellen Drew).

of self-worth. As soon as he discovers that Jimmy did not actually win the contest, Mr. Baxter goes from wildly praising him ("I mean it sincerely," he says) to rescinding the new job offer. The ideas that a few moments before had "pungency, brevity, crispness" are now back in that nether-world of unconfirmed maybes. And while one would expect Jimmy to offer a spirited and heartfelt rebuttal, to fight for his chance to prove himself, he only stands by silently as Betty delivers the speech that helps change Baxter's mind. "I'm like Mr. Baxter," he later explains to her. "That's why I understood him and didn't say anything."

There is, in fact, only one character in the entire movie who does not need the approval of others to believe in himself, and that is Bildocker. Stubborn as an ox, Bildocker refuses to give in to the eleven jurors who agree on the slogan or to the company president who would like to have the contest end on time. He takes his role on the jury seriously and claims that he works not for Maxford, but for the contest entrants, and that he is going to vote the way he thinks is right even if it takes ten years to settle the issue. He simply will not buckle under and vote for a slogan that he thinks is "putrid."

Chaos takes over the neighborhood as Jimmy (Dick Powell) and Betty (Ellen Drew) distribute all the gifts they bought for their friends.

In the character of Bildocker, Sturges once again gives us a dose of irony. The positive impressions we have of him—his tenacity and integrity, his guts in standing up to the president, his willingness to defend his choice with his fists—are undermined at the end of the film when we learn that the slogan he has been holding out for is Jimmy's. The slogan chosen by the other jurors, "Maxford—Magnificent and Mellow," may not be brilliant, but it is respectable. But Jimmy's creation, "If You Don't Sleep at Night, It Isn't the Coffee, It's the Bunk," is downright bad. Any admiration developed for Bildocker for sticking to his principles is totally destroyed when we learn that he has been fighting for this foolish entry. It is also important to note that Bildocker—the one person who seems to have any self-esteem—was the cause of all the trouble in the first place. If he had not felt the need to be so honorable, the winner would have been announced on time and the fake telegram would not have been sent.

While this kind of disrespect for others is clearly in keeping with the tradition of film comedy, the overwhelming lack of self-confidence exhibited by characters in *Christmas in July* is not so common. By the end of most comic films, any self-doubting protagonists have at least come to the realization that they are capable people, even if they still have no respect for others. But Preston Sturges isn't interested in providing such an unrealistic resolution; for him, self-esteem is not so easily gained.

An Illusion of Happiness

With the last scenes of *Christmas in July*, Sturges accomplishes the amazing feat of giving us an ending that has all the earmarks of being happy and satisfying when in fact it resolves almost nothing. The ending does more to uphold the impression that Sturges has provided of a desperate environment than it does to refute it. The key to understanding Sturges's message lies in the speech delivered by Betty, after Mr. Baxter informs Jimmy that he does not deserve the new job and that it is not practical to give him a chance.

> It *is* practical, Mr. Baxter—it's the most practical idea you ever had. He belongs in here because he thinks he has ideas, he belongs in here until he proves himself or fails, and then somebody else belongs in here until he proves himself or fails, and somebody else after that, and somebody else after him, and so on and so on for always. Oh, I don't know how to put it in the words like Jimmy could, but all he wants, all any of them want, is a chance to show, to find out what they've got, while they're still young and burning, like a shortcut or a stepping-stone. Oh, I know they're not going to succeed. At least most of them aren't. They'll all be like Mr. Waterbury soon enough, most of them anyway. But they won't mind it, they'll find something else, and they'll be happy because they had their chance. Because it's one thing to muff a chance when you get it, but it's another thing never to have had a chance.

Betty's speech seems to make an appeal for opportunity, for giving the Jimmy MacDonalds of America the chance to see whether they can succeed. So when Mr. Baxter relents and agrees to give Jimmy that chance for "a very short time," it appears that the comic bad guy—the person holding the protagonist down—has been won over.

If this were a truly happy ending, however, Mr. Baxter would realize that Jimmy's ideas were good even though he did not win the contest. Baxter would see that the "minor employees" whom he had ignored for years actually had much to offer, and he would vow to deal with them in a much more enlightened manner from now on.

Sturges is going after something more realistic, though. He knows that genuine conversions do not normally take place and that the protagonist in real life is rarely left to triumph. So Mr. Baxter is not won over at the end of the film; in fact, he gives Jimmy the job primarily because his name is already painted on the door. Even as Baxter leaves the office, he is having second thoughts about his decision: When Betty assures him, "You'll never be sorry," he replies, "Well, I'm a little bit sorry already."

At the end of the film, then, Jimmy has almost nothing more than he had when he started. The money he thought he had won is largely gone: all the things he bought with it (which Mr. Schindel intends to make Mr.

Maxford pay for) belong to the neighbors, with the exception of Betty's ring and his mother's davenport. The self-confidence he briefly had has also disappeared, and he is back to not knowing whether his ideas are good. All he has is a shot at a slogan-writing job that will last only a very short time, with no increase in pay. His chances for success seem dim if the foolish and incomprehensible slogan he devised for the Maxford House contest is any indication.

Still, Jimmy's situation is not entirely miserable (especially after we learn that the jury *has* chosen his slogan), at least not compared with the prospects for all the other Jimmy MacDonalds of the world. At the beginning of the film, Sturges makes it obvious that the problems of achieving success are not confined to Jimmy alone, and Betty's speech to Mr. Baxter returns to that broader view. Betty starts by pleading for Jimmy to keep his new job—"He belongs in here until he proves himself or fails"—but quickly shifts to include everyone—"All any of them want is a chance to show . . . what they've got." That chance, however, is all but destined to fail, and sooner or later they will end up like Mr. Waterbury, who thinks he is a success though it is apparent to us and to Betty that he is not. When these ambitious young men do not make it, though, they will not mind. "They'll find something else"—probably, like Waterbury, the ability to fool themselves into accepting their defeat as success. In many ways, Mr. Waterbury is an older version of Jimmy, a man who once dreamed the same dreams but who did not have the luck Jimmy had. He speaks from a lifetime of disappointment and resignation when he says, "Ambition is all right if it works, but no system could be right where only half of one percent were successes and all the rest were failures."

Waterbury means to say that since no system like this could be right and since we know that ours *is* right, then there must be many more successes than one-half of one percent. By the end of the film, however, we realize that Sturges has turned that statement on its head. Because no one in the film has cashed in on the promises of the work ethic, we are forced to reinterpret Waterbury's words: since only one-half of one percent actually do succeed and since any system like that could not be right, there must be something wrong with our system. In this way, *Christmas in July* portrays the futility of the ambition and hard work that the American Dream encourages and the desperation these broken promises can generate. Sturges's dark view of America and its economic system tells us that the country needs the Mr. Waterburys, not to triumph, but only to do the drudge work while convincing themselves that they are successes for doing it.

SEVEN

The Lady Eve

Produced by Paul Jones; Written and Directed by Preston Sturges; Based on a story by Monckton Hoffe; Photography: Victor Milner; Edited by Stuart Gilmore; Art Direction: Hans Dreier and Ernst Fegte; Sound: Harry Lindgren and Don Johnson; Musical Direction: Sigmund Krumgold. Released by Paramount, 1941.

Cast: Barbara Stanwyck (Jean Harrington/The Lady Eve); Henry Fonda (Charles "Hopsie" Pike); Charles Coburn (Colonel Harrington); William Demarest (Muggsy Murgatroyd); Eugene Pallette (Mr. Pike); Eric Blore (Sir Alfred McGlennan-Keith); Melville Cooper (Gerald); Robert Greig (Burrows); Torben Meyer (Ship's Purser).

Synopsis: On its way back from South America, the cruise ship *Southern Queen* stops to pick up an important passenger—Charles Pike, the heir to a family fortune amassed through the sale of Pike's Ale ("The Ale That Won for Yale"). A nerdy bookworm with the nickname Hopsie, Charles has been up the Amazon for a year studying and capturing snakes. His presence on the ship causes an immediate sensation, as every eligible young (and not so young) woman attempts to grab his attention, and ultimately his fortune. Charles shows no interest in any of them, though, at least until he literally runs into Jean Harrington. A con artist traveling with her father, "Colonel" Harrington, and their valet, Gerald, Jean cleverly manages to play on Charles's shyness and sense of propriety as she makes him think he has affronted her by tripping over her and ruining her shoes. Back in her cabin to get a new pair of shoes, she deliberately flirts with Charles to send the young man's head spinning—then promptly takes him to the ship's game room where she and her father can begin the process of bilking him of thousands of dollars. They use the first night as the setup and let Charles win $600 before Jean lures him back to her cabin and again flirts with him mercilessly, leaving the young heir dizzy with love.

The next morning, Charles's bodyguard and lifelong protector, Muggsy, warns him that the Harringtons may not be what they seem. Charles brushes off the warning, however; he spends the entire day with Jean and becomes completely infatuated with her. Unexpectedly Jean has begun to fall in love with Charles as well. That evening, when the Colonel tries to take him for a fortune at cards, Jean intervenes to prevent Charles from losing much more than he had won the previous night. When she excuses herself for a few minutes, the Colonel tries to con Charles once again and succeeds in getting him to write a $32,000 check for money he lost just cutting cards. Returning just in time to see the end of the transaction, Jean makes her father tear up Charles's check. She and Charles then move to the deck, and their talk turns to romance and finally to the subject of marriage.

Still too skeptical to believe Charles's claim that Jean loves him, the ever-watchful Muggsy approaches the ship's purser the next day with his suspicions. The purser provides Muggsy and Charles with a police photograph that identifies the Harringtons as con artists, and Charles is forced to confront Jean with the photo. She claims that she really loves Charles and that she was going to confess to him about her past, but the devastated Charles does not believe a word of it. The couple part, furious with one another for not having faith in their love. As Jean and her father wait to disembark at the end of the voyage, the Colonel shows her Charles's $32,000 check, which he did not actually destroy. Claiming that Charles's money is not enough, Jean vows to somehow get revenge on the man whom she feels jilted her.

Back in the United States, Jean and the Colonel run into a con artist friend who is currently passing himself off as Sir Alfred McGlennan-Keith. Making the rounds of rich families in Connecticut, Sir Alfred gets invited to parties, wins money at bridge, and ingratiates himself in any profitable way. When Jean hears that the Pikes are one of the families he knows, she insists on using Sir Alfred in a scheme to get back at Charles. Sometime later, at a party given at the Pike home, Sir Alfred shows up with his "niece," the Lady Eve, accompanying him. Claiming to be just off the boat from England, she is the hit of the party. At first Charles cannot believe that Eve is not the same woman as Jean, and Muggsy agrees with him. But Charles gradually comes to accept Eve's story, especially when Sir Alfred pulls him aside and tells him the dark family secret: there is an illegitimate daughter who looks just like the proper Lady Eve but who is thoroughly immoral.

After Eve's constant flirting with him, Hopsie is once again hooked. In short order he proposes to this new woman, and Eve accepts. Following a huge wedding at the Pike home, the newlyweds embark by train on their honeymoon and Jean sets her plan in motion. She tells Charles that it seems like a good time to let him know about her previous marriage—an elopement at age sixteen that, much to Charles's chagrin, resulted in her spending a number of nights with another man. Although greatly upset, Charles finally agrees to consider it a youthful mistake and put it behind them, but Jean has no intention of stopping. She details relationships with at least five more men, so infuriating Charles that he asks to be put off the train in the middle of nowhere, still clad in his pajamas.

The Pike family lawyers jump into action, ready to arrange the details of Charles's divorce. Feeling sorry for what she has done, however, and realizing that she is still in love with Charles, Jean announces that she does not intend to seek any financial settlement. All she wants is to see Charles one more time; but he adamantly refuses to see or speak to Eve. In order to forget the entire ordeal, he boards a cruise ship headed for South America to go back to studying his snakes. Much to his surprise, he encounters Jean Harrington and the Colonel on the ship, and he immediately recognizes the mistake he made in ever letting her go. The two embrace and kiss, with Charles still unaware of the truth behind the Lady Eve.

◉

Although considered by many critics to be one of Sturges's best movies, *The Lady Eve* is the one major film that seems least distinguishable as a Preston Sturges creation. His best works all have Sturgean plots and characters that no other director could ever duplicate. For all its undeniable quality, however, *The Lady Eve* just does not have those ingredients. There are no characters like the Wienie King or the members of The Ale and Quail Club in *The Palm Beach Story,* and no plot elements similar to the creation of the Diddlebock cocktail in *The Sin of Harold Diddlebock* or the Marine and his mother complex in *Hail the Conquering Hero.* Instead, *The Lady Eve* offers a good but not especially unusual plot, finely written characters, a particularly satisfying performance by Barbara Stanwyck, and a lot of witty dialogue. It is by no means a poor film; it is simply the one major Sturges work that could most easily be mistaken for someone else's.

Perhaps Sturges was inclined to pattern *The Lady Eve* along lines drawn by others because he was working with a central topic—romance—different from that of most of his films. Although romance certainly played a part in many of the films he directed, he often wove his stories around such issues as success, small-town life, politics, and the American class structure. With love and courtship as its themes, *The Lady Eve* harkens back to the earlier *Remember the Night,* as both films tell the story of a petty criminal who is eventually awakened and reformed by love. In *The Lady Eve,* the machinations that lead up to that conversion are the real focus of the movie, and it therefore falls more easily than any other Sturges-directed film into the genre of romantic or screwball comedy. Within that model,

The Harringtons (Charles Coburn, *left*, and Barbara Stanwyck) total up their losses on the first night of card playing with Charles Pike (Henry Fonda, *seated*), while a suspicious Muggsy (William Demarest) keeps watch.

however, he still found room to explore a favorite subject: deceit and its rewards.

The Pervasiveness of Fraud

For Sturges to populate a film with con artists and wealthy heirs and not imbue it with some of his biting views on America would be almost impossible. Throughout the movie there are subplots and undercurrents that form the background to the Jean Harrington–Charles Pike romance, but are in perfect keeping with the worlds of Dan McGinty, Tom Jeffers (*The Palm Beach Story*), Jimmy MacDonald, or Norval Jones (*The Miracle of Morgan's Creek*). The most notable of these is the corruption that exists in every corner. No matter where one looks illegal deeds are taking place, and just as in Dan McGinty's political domain, everyone seems to accept them as a given.

The most obvious example is provided by the Harringtons and their ability to thrive at their chosen work. They are able to travel on an exclusive cruise ship, and Colonel Harrington can "lose" $600 to Charles Pike, only because the Harringtons have built up a sizable fortune conning people. What is more, Colonel Harrington and Gerald seem to feel that *everyone* is fair game for a con, including relatives. When Jean chastises them for planning to "take" Charles even though she has announced her intention to marry him, the Colonel asks her, "If you can't rob your own son-in-law, then who can you rob?" Later she tells her father, "You're such an old scoundrel you'd skin *me* if you got the chance."

The Harringtons are not alone in their business, however, and they receive indirect support from some unlikely accomplices. In the ship's game room, where Charles and the Colonel play cards, a sign on the wall warns passengers to beware of professional gamblers, adding that the cruise ship company takes no responsibility for losses incurred by its passengers. Although the disclaimer seems routine and innocuous, the company's true position on gambling becomes evident the next morning when a suspicious Muggsy confronts the ship's purser to ask if he can provide evidence concerning possible con artists on board.

> *Purser:* A passenger is a passenger, my friend. If he pays for his ticket and doesn't steal the ship's towels, who are we to go slandering him? Furthermore, what do you mean by card shark? One man's card shark is another man's bridge expert.
>
> *Muggsy:* I mean a guy who cheats.
>
> *Purser:* What do you mean by "cheating"? It's a very hard thing to prove. The companies have been trying for years.
>
> *Muggsy:* You don't happen to be a mouthpiece, do you? You talk like a law school.
>
> *Purser:* I was admitted to the bar, if that's what you're talking about.

The double-talk that's intended to protect the company rather than the passengers comes to a quick stop, however, once the purser finds out who employs Muggsy.

> If I should discover that Mr. Pike was in any danger of being swindled, not that I admit there is any such possibility, you understand, I would consider it my duty to warn him. . . . In the event that I should consider it necessary, I *might* have some photographs, confidential, of course, of some of the better known *alleged* professional card players . . . NOT THAT I ADMIT THERE ARE ANY ON THIS SHIP, YOU UNDERSTAND.

The purser's speech reveals that passengers aboard the cruise ship are treated according to a double standard. Passengers of average means are not likely to receive much protection from the ship's authorities should they encounter a card shark; passengers as wealthy as Charles Pike, however, will get as much help as they need. The reason for the double standard seems very practical: because the cruise ship relies on income from the tickets purchased by people like the Harringtons, it is in the company's interest to keep the card sharks in business—unless the fraud starts to threaten the rich passengers. As in *Sullivan's Travels*, Sturges makes it clear that the level of justice that is doled out is based entirely on how much money and influence a person has.

Sturges portrays the widespread corruption in the world of *The Lady Eve* in other ways as well. Muggsy, for instance, a man who has been around the block a few times, has learned to be suspicious of everyone and everything he sees. Others who are less astute will always find people ready to play them for fools. Sir Alfred can pass himself off as a wealthy nobleman and take the rich families of Connecticut over a period of months without being discovered and cast out. Even Mr. Pike, who falls for Sir Alfred's scam, has some understanding of the dirty reality of life: when Eve says she wants no money from her divorce settlement with Charles, he replies, "I think you're a sucker." The corruption exists everywhere, but as in so many Sturges films, only those who make use of that fact really find success.

The Profits of Dishonesty

Throughout *The Lady Eve*, Sturges sets up a dichotomy between those people who are honest and those who are dishonest. As is so often the case for Sturges, the canny ones who act with little regard for propriety are the people who ultimately succeed. Because they think the worst of everyone and look out for themselves, they are one step (or more) ahead of those fools who think life is based on honesty, hard work, and clean living.

The obvious examples of crafty operators are Colonel Harrington and Jean, who make their living preying on gullible souls like Charles Pike. The ironic thing about Charles Pike is that he is wildly successful (because he is wealthy), but he has done nothing himself to achieve that success. He is the epitome of the bumbling fool who lucked out by being born into a rich family. Perhaps because he did not use any cleverness in making money he is incapable of holding on to what he has. The only thing that keeps him from a lifetime of being suckered and conned is his streetwise companion, Muggsy. Early in the film, Charles explains his relationship with Muggsy:

> My father took him off a truck to watch over me when I was a kid. You know, kidnappers and stuff like that, and he's been sort of bodyguard, governess, and a very bad valet ever since. He saved my life one time in a brawl, so the family's crazy about him.

However, it is apparent from the way Muggsy is treated at the dinner party that the Pike family is not really fond of him at all. More likely the parents understand that their son *needs* a Muggsy so that he will not be taken in by every con artist who comes along.

Even with Muggsy to protect him, Charles comes very close to being done in by his naïveté. He has no idea that Jean is after him for his money, despite Muggsy's efforts to alert him. When Jean teasingly tells Charles that some of his romantic words sound like a marriage proposal and that he could be taken advantage of in such a situation, Charles replies, "Not by girls like you." And after she warns him that it is dangerous to trust people you barely know, he says in all sincerity, "But I know you very well."*

It is not just in his dealings with women that Charles is blind to the ways of the world. He is oblivious to being set up by Colonel Harrington during their first night of card playing, and on the second night he does not notice that the Colonel and Jean are planting cards and vying to turn him into a winner or loser. Charles even accepts the Colonel's contention that he wants to cut cards to even things between them, and naïvely writes out a check for the $32,000 that he thinks he has lost fair and square.

The most outrageous example of Charles's gullibility is seen at the party his family gives for the Lady Eve. Although his own instincts tell him that Eve is really Jean, Charles lets himself be persuaded that she is not, thanks to the wild story that Sir Alfred tells about a lusty coachman and an illegitimate daughter. Muggsy is not fooled, however, and continues to try to convince Charles of his error. But even at the end of the movie, when Charles finds Jean again and realizes that he loves her, he still does not see that the two women are one and the same. "Oh, you still don't understand," Jean sighs. To which Charles replies, "I don't want to understand. I don't want to know."

As gullible as he is, Charles is not alone in his capacity to be taken for a ride. Sir Alfred has set up a lucrative practice of conning the millionaires in Bridgefield, Connecticut, and as he tells the Harringtons, it is very easy to keep the con going.

> *Sir Alfred:* I have my horses, I have my dogs, I have my little house, I have my antiques. We play a little game here and a little game there, and then we play somewhere else. Sometimes my luck is good and sometimes my luck is better, and what with one thing and another, my dear boy... What a dream!
>
> *Colonel Harrington:* How did you meet them?
>
> *Sir Alfred:* The chumps? My dear boy, when your name is Sir Alfred McGlennan-Keith, R.F.D., you don't *have* to meet them—you fight them off with sticks. And just think ... there's no hurry. You have them by the year, like a lease.

*"You don't know very much about girls," Jean tells him. "The best ones aren't as good as you probably think they are, and the bad ones aren't as bad ... not nearly as bad." Even such a direct statement does not get through to Charles, but its implication—that things are not as polarized as Charles thinks, because everyone is "bad" to some degree—certainly fits with the film's undercurrent of corruption.

Muggsy (William Demarest) leans in for a close-up look at the Lady Eve (Barbara Stanwyck), convinced that she is really Jean Harrington.

Sir Alfred and the Harringtons are able to succeed because they know how to take advantage of a situation. At best, honesty is a neutral factor that may not hinder you in achieving success and wealth. Mr. Pike, for instance, seems to have earned his fortune honestly by selling a good brand of beer (at least we are never told otherwise), and his upright son, Charles, was lucky enough to be born with a rich father. The con artists, on the other hand, prove by their actions that dishonesty is a sure road to success. They are perfectly capable of swindling Charles out of thousands of dollars and of swindling the millionaires of Connecticut on an ongoing basis. Wealthy but credulous people such as the Pikes are no match for the Harringtons and Sir Alfreds of this world. The only thing that saves Charles from losing a fortune is dumb luck—the fact that Jean falls in love with him.

Sturges presents the con artists not only as more successful, though, but also as more appealing. Early in the film, Jean comments to the Colonel that she would like to see him "giving some old harpy the three-in-one." The Colonel is not pleased with the remark. "Don't be vulgar, Jean," he chides. "Let us be crooked but never common." It is a small moment that plays against the stereotype of low-class crooks, but later in the movie it becomes clear that the Colonel's comment indicates a certain tasteful

standard not shared by everyone. The Colonel's refinement is in complete
contrast to the manners displayed by Mr. Pike when he turns to the Lady
Eve at the dinner party and says, "Come on, let's put on the feed bag."

But even if the Pikes were as well mannered as the Harringtons, they
would still be less attractive. The relationships between Mr. Pike, his wife,
and Charles are all characterized by self-centeredness and a complete lack
of respect for one another, and the lives they lead do not seem very exciting. From playing bridge with the other rich families of Bridgefield to
making sure that the ale ferments correctly, the Pikes' life appears so dull
that it is easy to understand why Charles spends so much time with snakes.

Probably the best illustration of how boring the lives of the Pikes and
their ilk can be is provided by Colonel Harrington when he and Jean are
discussing her possible marriage to Charles.

> *Jean*: You can come and live with us, part of the time, anyway. We prob-
> ably have a very beautiful place. And think how peaceful you can
> be. . . .
> *Colonel Harrington*: You mean playing cribbage with the gardener. I can
> just see myself wandering around your estate with a weed sticker and
> fifty cents a week . . . and some new slippers for Christmas. The
> trouble with people who reform is they always want to rain on
> everybody else's parade too. You tend to your knitting, and I'll play
> cards.

There is not much question that cruises in high-class style win out over
Colonel Harrington's picture of life with the Pikes any day. Being dishonest is not only more profitable, it is also a lot more fun.

By the end of *The Lady Eve* Sturges has provided his audience with
an unsparing look at life among the honest and dishonest: the con artists
have essentially come out on top. Jean will marry into one of the richest
families in the country thanks to the life of deceit that allowed her to travel
among them; Sir Alfred will continue to live and operate among Connecticut's upper crust; and the Colonel will continue to defraud people for
years to come. They are never caught and punished for their behavior: for
them, crime *does* pay. The most that can be said for the Pikes is that they
lucked out and did not get taken for a real ride, either in the Harringtons'
card games or in Eve's divorce settlement. But their family now includes
two con artists as in-laws, and Sir Alfred is still among their circle of
friends. As in McGinty's political world, the honest folks are always at the
mercy of the corrupt—the ones who know how life *really* works.

EIGHT

Sullivan's Travels

Written and Directed by Preston Sturges; Associate Producer: Paul Jones; Photography: John Seitz; Process Photography: Farciot Edouart; Edited by Stuart Gilmore; Art Direction: Hans Dreier and Zack Hedrick; Sound: Harry Mills and Walter Oberst; Musical Direction: Sigmund Krumgold; Musical Score: Leo Shuken and Charles Bradshaw. Released by Paramount, 1941.

Cast: Joel McCrea (John L. Sullivan); Veronica Lake (The Girl); Robert Warwick (Mr. LeBrand); William Demarest (Mr. Jones); Franklin Pangborn (Mr. Casalsis); Porter Hall (Mr. Hadrian); Byron Foulger (Mr. Valdelle); Margaret Hayes (Secretary); Robert Greig (Sullivan's Butler); Eric Blore (Sullivan's Valet); Torben Meyer (Doctor); Vic Potel (Cameraman); Richard Webb (Radioman); Charles Moore (Chef); Almira Sessions (Ursula); Esther Howard (Miz Zeffie); Frank Moran (Tough Chauffeur); George Renavent (Old Tramp); Harry Rosenthal (The Trombenick); Al Bridge (The Mister); Jimmy Conlin (Trusty); Jan Buckingham (Mrs. Sullivan); Chick Collins (Capital); Jimmie Dundee (Labor).

Synopsis: At night, with a mountain in the background and a river in the foreground, a freight train hurtles toward us. On top of the train two men are fighting a vicious battle, chasing each other from car to car, rolling precariously toward the edge, and struggling for their lives. The dramatic conflict lasts only a few minutes, until both men fall into the swirling river beneath the train. As they sink below the surface and to their deaths, the words "The End" appear on the screen.

The scene is from the latest movie by John L. Sullivan, a successful Hollywood director whose passion for the serious drama is obviously not shared by the studio heads for whom he works. Although "Sully" tries to convince his bosses that the two men on the train represent Capital and Labor, and that the movie makes a profound statement about the times in which they live, the executives want him to go back to making comedies. They are reluctant to give him the support he wants for his next project, an adaptation of the socially conscious novel *O Brother, Where Art Thou?* The studio heads argue that Sully has led a pampered life and does not know the first thing about being down-and-out. Taking that as a challenge, Sully resolves to find out what it is like—he will dress like a tramp (courtesy of the studio's wardrobe department) and travel the roads until he has experienced real trouble.

At his mansion, Sully elicits the help of his butler and valet in choosing the most suitable set of hobo clothes. The butler does not find the plan terribly amusing and warns Sully that poverty is not something to play around with, but the director has his mind set on going through with his plan. Before he leaves, though, the studio executives arrive and insist that the entire trip be used as a public relations vehicle: a "land yacht" (an elaborate motor home) equipped with a bar and carrying a doctor, a photographer, a writer, a cook, and a secretary will follow Sully on his journey and make it an event known throughout the world. People everywhere will hear about Sully's expedition, and *O Brother, Where Art Thou?* will play to immense crowds.

Forced to accept the studio's plan, Sully begins his trek, but quickly finds the close-tailing land yacht a major hindrance. He hitches a ride with a teenage speed demon to try to shake his entourage, but after a wild chase they all end up in a haystack. Sully then convinces the crew to give him a couple of weeks alone, after which he will meet them in Las Vegas. Finally left to his own devices, Sully finds work as a handyman with the widow Miz Zeffie, though it soon becomes apparent that she is less interested in Sully's work than in the handsome young man himself. After an awkward evening together at the picture show, Sully makes his escape from the house and falls into a bucket of freezing water along the way. A sympathetic truck driver allows Sully to crowd in alongside his freight, but when the driver arrives at his destination the next morning and wakes Sully up, the director finds that he is right back where he started—in Hollywood.

Sully wanders into a roadside diner and orders a cup of coffee with the only dime he has, but a friendly young woman offers to buy him a full breakfast. While he eats, the woman tells him that she came out to Hollywood to be an actress, but that now, with no job and little money, she is about to begin hitching her way back to her home in the East. Without letting on who he really is, Sully offers her the use of a "friend's" house and some letters of introduction to directors and studio executives whom he claims to have known in his more prosperous days. While she waits at the diner Sully fetches one of his expensive cars—borrowed from a friend, he explains—to drive her where she needs to go. Before they can get very far, though, the police arrest Sully and The Girl for stealing the car, and Sully's butler and valet have to come to the prison to identify their boss and secure his release.

After resting at his house, Sully sets out once again on his trip, this time taking The Girl along with him. They spend the night on a freight train with scores of other tramps, but by morning the two are hungry and Sully has a severe cold. They make their way to a lunch stand, only to find that they have no money to buy food—a fact that the owner magnanimously overlooks. The town they have landed in turns out to be Las Vegas, and just down the road from the lunch stand they find the land yacht. Sully and The Girl gladly turn to the studio crew for food and hot showers, but the studio doctor refuses to let Sully out of the vehicle until his cold is gone.

Once recovered, Sully strikes out again with The Girl. A montage sequence shows us what they see: temporary shacks and tent colonies full of poor, struggling people; soup lines; bug-infested flophouses; communal showers; missions; homeless shelters (in one of which Sully's boots are stolen right off his feet); and people scrounging for food in garbage cans.

Sully and The Girl eventually make it to Kansas City, where they find the studio entourage and rest at a plush hotel. Sully's adventure is almost over, but before he returns to Hollywood he has one last thing in mind: he will hit the streets as a tramp once again, but this time he will distribute five-dollar bills to needy people. While he is handing out the money a tramp follows Sully to a train yard, hits him over the head, steals the cash, and dumps him in an empty freight car. As he escapes with his prize, though, the tramp is hit by an oncoming train. The mangled corpse is found the next morning, and the only identifying mark on him is the card of John L. Sullivan sewn in the soles of his boots.

When Sully finally staggers out of the freight car he is unable to remember his name. He starts a fight with a railroad yardman, strikes the man with a stone, and is arrested and tried for trespassing and assault. Still unsure of who he is or what is happening, Sully is sentenced to six years of hard labor in a camp run by a sadistic warden. There Sully finally recalls his name, but he cannot make contact with the outside world; because of his belligerent attitude all his privileges have been taken away—with the exception of one. On a weekend night, the incarcerated men, including Sully, are led in shackles to a local church where they join the congregation in watching a selection of movies. When the first film—a Disney cartoon—lights up the screen, Sully experiences firsthand just how important comedy can be to people who have nothing else in their lives.

Having read in a fellow inmate's newspaper that Hollywood director John L. Sullivan was killed in a train yard, Sully comes up with a plan to ensure his release: he confesses to the murder of the director. With his picture splashed across front pages all over the country, the prisoner comes to the attention of the studio heads, who recognize his true identity. In no

time at all Sully is released from the labor camp and is on his way back
to Hollywood. Much to the dismay of the studio executives, who would
like to capitalize on this great publicity, Sully announces that he is no
longer interested in making *O Brother, Where Art Thou?* Instead he wants
to continue making comedies, because now he realizes that they are all
some people have in their lives.

•

By 1941, Preston Sturges was a major success in Hollywood. As the
writer of numerous well-received films, the director of three recent hits,
and the recipient of an Academy Award, he had a growing reputation for
creating witty, raucous, unique comedies. Despite a sometimes stormy
relationship with the Paramount executives, he probably could have pushed
through any film that he really wanted to make. He was, in many ways,
not all that much different from John L. Sullivan.

When any filmmaker decides to make a movie about someone who
makes movies, there is a natural tendency to psychoanalyze the director,
portray the lead character as an alter ego, and recast the real director's
career in light of the words and actions of the fictional creation. On a very
basic level, *Sullivan's Travels* can certainly be seen as Sturges's statement
on his own career: Sully discovers that the public needs good comedies
more than anything else, and Sturges's response, in 1941 and throughout
his career, was to make comedies. But the film's references to the movie
business do not so much comment on Sturges's own position as they allow
him to play with the medium and, more importantly, convey his message
about the need for laughter.

In many of his films, Sturges played loosely with the strict conventions
of cinema, particularly if it meant he could throw in another joke. In *Sullivan's Travels* he continually toys with the viewer's suspension of disbelief.
The film opens with the final sequence from Sully's film, which the audience thinks is the first part of Sturges's film until the words "The End"
appear on the screen after only a few minutes. From that point on Sturges
will not let us forget that even Sullivan's story itself is just a movie we are
watching. In the police station where Sully has been taken for stealing his
own car, the sergeant asks the director how The Girl fits into the picture.
"There's always a girl in the picture," Sully replies sharply. "Haven't you
ever been to the movies?"

Near the end of the movie, Sully makes a similar remark as he is trying
to figure a way out of the labor camp. Just before he comes up with the
idea of confessing to his own murder, he tells the guard, "If ever a plot
needed a twist, this one does." A few moments later that is exactly what
Sturges the writer provides for Sullivan the director. And Sturges's movie

gags do not stop there: he puts himself in a brief shot as a movie director who is working with The Girl when she reads that Sullivan is still alive; he names the man (William Demarest) who is in charge of the studio's land yacht Mr. Jones, in all likelihood a reference to Sturges's producer, Paul Jones; and he pokes fun at movie titles with the triple feature that Sully and Miz Zeffie go to see (*Beyond These Tears, The Valley of the Shadow,* and *The Buzzard of Berlin*).

But Sturges offers a more serious take on motion pictures in present-ing the movie's primary message—that people need to be entertained more than they need to be preached to. He expresses this view most strongly at the end of the film, when Sully realizes how the value of a movie can vary greatly depending on the circumstances of the people watching it. To give the moment of Sully's discovery its maximum impact, Sturges shows us in the preceding scenes how little the director knows about what type of movies people prefer. The following conversation takes place while The Girl and Sully are driving in Sully's car, before she learns who he really is:

> *Sully*: Did you see *Hey, Hey in the Hayloft* [one of Sullivan's directorial efforts]?
> *The Girl*: Oh, I was crazy about that.
> *Sully*: I thought that would just about fit.
> *The Girl*: Do you remember that scene where the two are up in the hayloft?
> *Sully*: Perfectly.
> *The Girl*: And she made him close his eyes and count three before kissing her . . . and the pig came out and he kissed the pig instead!
> *Sully*: That was on a very high plane.
> *The Girl*: And then he fell through the hole and sneezed at the horse?
> *Sully*: And the horse sneezed back at him.
> *The Girl*: Oh, that was a wonderful scene. Of course it was stupid, but it was wonderful.
> *Sully*: Don't you think with the world in its present condition, with death snarling at you from every street corner, people are a little allergic to comedies?
> *The Girl*: No.

A few minutes later, Sully admits that he used to be a movie director.

> *The Girl*: What kind of pictures did you make?
> *Sully*: More along educational lines.
> *The Girl*: No wonder. There's nothing like a deep-dish movie to drive you out in the open.
> *Sully*: What are you talking about? Film is the greatest educational medium the world has ever known. You take *Hold Back Tomor-row . . .*
> *The Girl*: *You* hold it.

If Sully were not so blinded by his abstract ideas, he would probably be able to see that The Girl's views closely represent those of the average moviegoer. In fact, by not giving her character a name but simply referring to her in the script as The Girl, Sturges makes her a symbol, a spokesperson for the viewing public.* That she would express a preference for "stupid" comedies and a dislike for "deep-dish" movies should tell Sully all he needs to know about the reception *O Brother, Where Art Thou?* would find. But it is only after he sees the Disney cartoon—whose slapstick antics are not all that different from *Hey, Hey in the Hayloft*—that Sully will really understand what his own comedy films can mean to people.

Sully's deep connection to the movies goes well beyond the fact that he is a director; no matter where he goes he cannot escape motion pictures. Miz Zeffie takes him to see a triple feature; he meets up with The Girl, a down-and-out soul who failed in her dream to make it in the movies; and his only privilege in labor camp is to go to the picture show. Yet only after he ventures far away from Hollywood does Sully begin to understand the role films play in the lives of the public, or the role he ought to play in making them. Until then Sully thinks that movies should teach people about trouble, and he therefore wants to learn about it firsthand, although people around him try to dissuade him. Ultimately he comes to realize that they are right and that in some cases it is best not to know what life can be like in America.

Washing the Elephant

In at least one of the early drafts for *Sullivan's Travels*, Preston Sturges placed the film's opening dedication within the movie itself, spoken by John L. Sullivan. In this draft, Sully declares at the very end of the movie that he wants to make a comedy and that he already knows what the prologue will be, then recites a slightly different version of the words that now appear at the beginning of the film:

> To the memory of those who made us laugh: the motley mountebanks, the clowns, the buffoons, in all times and in all nations, whose efforts have lightened our burden a little, this picture is affectionately dedicated.

That Sturges could so easily apply the dedication from Sully's film to his own must have meant that he agreed strongly with the lesson Sully learns. In addition to paying tribute to the laugh makers of the world, the words clue the audience in to where Sullivan's travels are going to lead

---

Throughout this chapter, all references to the script and to material not in the finished film come from the screenplay as published in Brian Henderson, ed., Five Screenplays by Preston Sturges.

John L. Sullivan (Joel McCrea) is forced to reveal his true identity to The Girl (Veronica Lake) after they're released from prison for auto theft.

him. But in order to move Sully's spoken dedication to the beginning of *Sullivan's Travels*, Sturges had to delete his original epigraph for the film:

> This is the story
> of a man who wanted
> to wash an elephant.
> The elephant darn
> near ruined him.

While the elephant adage suggests a slightly different aspect of Sullivan's journey, its implications are pertinent even though the saying does not appear in the final film. Like the man washing the elephant, Sully is taking on a much more daunting task than he initially imagined when he set out on a quest to "find trouble." In addition, Sturges insinuates that like the man with the odd ambition to wash an elephant, Sully should have known better than to attempt such foolishness in the first place.

Certainly everyone in the film thinks that this is the case, for right from the start Sully's journey meets with unanimous disapproval. All the people he knows try to tell him that he does not have a clue about what he's getting himself into, beginning with Mr. Hadrian, one of the studio executives:

What do *you* know about troubles? . . . You want to make a picture about garbage cans. What do you know about garbage cans? When did you eat your last meal out of one? . . . You want to make an epic about misery. You want to show hungry people sleeping in doorways. . . . You want to grind ten thousand feet of hard luck and all I'm asking you is what do you know about hard luck?

When they fail to stop Sully from going on his journey, the studio executives try instead to protect him while he is on the streets. They send the land yacht and its crew to follow their star filmmaker and see that he does not get into *too much* trouble. The Girl also insists on accompanying Sully in his travels, contending, "You don't know anything about anything. You don't know how to get a meal, you don't know how to keep a secret. . . . I know fifty times as much about trouble as you ever will." (And Sully does stay out of real trouble as long as he's with her; his crisis occurs only when he goes out by himself.) Even his valet thinks that Sully needs some looking after, so he has identification cards sewn into the director's boots.

Despite the efforts of all these people to tell him what he ought to know, Sully still keeps trying to wash the elephant. The gifted creator of successful musicals and comedies still wants to make a socially conscious documentary, as he says when he explains to the studio executives the motivation behind *O Brother, Where Art Thou?*

> *Sully*: I want this picture to be a commentary on modern conditions . . . stark realism . . . the problems that confront the average man. . . . I want this picture to be a document. I want to hold a mirror up to life. I want this to be a picture of dignity, a true canvas of the suffering of humanity. . . .
> *Hadrian*: How about a nice musical?
> *Sully*: How can you talk about musicals at a time like this? With the world committing suicide . . . corpses piling up in the streets, grim death gargling at you around every corner . . . people slaughtered like sheep.
> *Hadrian*: Maybe they'd like to forget that.

But Sully carries his illusions with him into the real world and utterly fails to grasp what truly deprived people have to deal with. He often makes foolish statements about poor people, as when he tells The Girl, "I don't starve and suffer because I like it, you know." ("Neither does anybody else," she replies wisely.) Similarly, when they are later riding the rails, Sully asks The Girl what other bums do to get food.

> *The Girl*: They steal chickens and roast them over campfires with baked potatoes and green corn on the cob roasted in the ashes with melted butter and. . .
> *Sully*: Where do they get the butter?

> *The Girl*: They steal it.
> *Sully*: Well, they don't. It isn't as easy as all that. There is a lot of suffering
> in this world that ordinary people don't know anything about.

Sully's failure to comprehend what real trouble may be like also colors the way in which he hopes to find out about it. Time and again he tries to engage the people he meets in conversation about how hard things are, but they always rebuff his attempts. In the roadside diner, when The Girl complains that she has been locked out of her room, Sully tells *her* how hard things are: "Things are tough every place. The war in Europe, the strikes over here.... There's no work, there's no food...." Her reply to his lecture is, "Drink your coffee while it's hot." Later, when Sully and The Girl jump the freight train and find some tramps in the car with them, Sully greets them with a proper "How do you do?" and then inquires, "How do you feel about the labor situation?" Without a word, the tramps promptly get up and leave for another freight car.

By the time Sully reaches his Kansas City hotel room, he has had the chance to live among the troubled people and experience their lives, but the irony is that he still does not understand their suffering. He thinks he can solve their problems by going out, in the words of Mr. Jones, "for a quick tour ... to hand [five-dollar bills] out to these bums, in gratitude for what they did for him." Sully calls it "the payoff." (In a line that appears in the script but not in the film, Sully admits at this point in the story that he does not know anything more about curing what is wrong with the world than he did when he started.)

Sully's friends and colleagues insist that his journey will be futile and that he should stay in Hollywood where he belongs. Even fate tries to put him back in his place: When he escapes from Miz Zeffie's house and thumbs a ride with a trucker, he winds up back in Hollywood the next morning; when he takes his car to drive The Girl where she wants to go, the police arrest him and drag him back home; and when he and The Girl end up at a lunch stand without any money, the land yacht happens to be parked just a few yards away. Even the thick-headed Sully momentarily glimpses the truth after this last incident:

> It's a funny thing the way everything keeps shoving me back to Hollywood or Beverly Hills or this monstrosity we're riding in, almost like, like gravity. As if some force was saying, "Get back where you belong. Don't try sticking your nose out here. You don't belong to real life, you phony." ... Maybe there's a universal law that says, "Stay put! As you are, so shall you remain." Maybe that's why tramps are always in trouble. They don't vote, they don't pay taxes, they violate the law of nature...

The universal law of nature may be trying to save Sully, but he is too dumb to realize it. The most compelling argument Sturges provides for Sully to stay in his place is voiced by his butler, Burrows.

> *Sully*: I'm going out on the road to find out about what it's *like* to be poor and needy, and then I'm going to make a picture about it.
> *Burrows*: If you'll permit me to say so, sir, the subject is not an interesting one. The poor know all about poverty and only the morbid rich would find the topic glamorous.
> *Sully*: But I'm doing it *for* the poor, don't you understand?
> *Burrows*: I doubt that they would appreciate it, sir. They rather resent the invasion of their privacy, I believe quite properly, sir. Also, such excursions can be extremely dangerous, sir. I worked for a gentleman once who likewise, with two friends, accoutred himself as you have, sir, and then went out for a lark. They have not been heard from since.
> *Sully*: That was some time ago?
> *Burrows*: 1912, sir. You see, sir, rich people and theorists, who are usually rich people, think of poverty in the negative, as the lack of riches, as disease might be called the lack of health. But it isn't, sir. Poverty is not the lack of anything, but a positive plague, virulent in itself, contagious as cholera, with filth, criminality, vice, and despair as only a few of its symptoms. It is to be stayed away from, even for purposes of study. It is to be shunned.
> *Sully*: Well, you seem to have made quite a study of it.
> *Burrows*: Quite unwillingly, sir.

This scene is one of the most important in the movie, for in it Burrows states directly and succinctly all the reasons that Sully should not embark on his excursion. And Sturges does not simply rely on the words to make his point; he photographs the crux of the scene (beginning with "You see, sir, rich people and theorists...") in virtually the only extreme close-up in the entire film. With a heavy scowl, actor Robert Greig sternly warns Sully against this folly, his acid tone underscored by narrowed eyes and an intent expression. For the first time in the film, the tone shifts drastically from the broadly comic to the deadly serious.

Burrows's speech also perfectly predicts what eventually does happen to Sully when he ventures out on his own. He sees filth in the bug-infested flophouses; he is the victim of criminality, both when his boots are stolen and when he's beaten and robbed; he experiences despair firsthand when he is sentenced to the labor camp; and he also is not heard from and presumed dead. Like the man who tried to wash the elephant, Sully's adventure darn near ruins him.

When he first hears them, of course, Sully does not believe Burrows's words. He thinks that poor people can be helped if he can just gather enough information to make a film about them. When he finally does collect the facts, though, Sully discovers that Burrows is right. The only thing he can do for the oppressed is make them forget their misery for a couple of hours. But while that realization may justify Hollywood's role in making lightweight comedies even in troubled times, it also implies that there is little hope for changing the living conditions of society's poor.

Justice for All?

In *The Great McGinty*, Sturges explored the idea that certain people are intended for certain types of lifestyles and should not try to go against their natural inclinations. McGinty had no more business trying to help the state's citizens than Thompson had trying to steal money from his employer. In *Sullivan's Travels*, Sturges seems to be implying the same thing, both in the way in which everyone tries to keep Sully from "finding trouble" and with Sully's mention of a "universal law" that keeps people in their places. The context in which Sturges places these notions here is much more serious than that in *McGinty*. If the most Sully can offer is a few hours of laughs, the implication is that nothing can be done to help society's disadvantaged. Sturges paints a very bleak picture of the life that America's poor people were leading in 1941, and his prescription of laughter provides no real hope for improving their plight.

Through the first two-thirds or so of the film, Sturges for the most part plays Sully's attempts to find trouble for laughs. But once Sully and The Girl finally start living among the poor the tone turns decidedly serious. The lengthy montage sequence shows us the brutal reality that Sully observes: people living in shacks put together with plywood and cardboard (one even has a For Sale sign on it); flophouse denizens sleeping virtually on top of one another; and men and women looking old and haggard well beyond their years, and with a hard edge to their faces that could only have developed after a lifetime of outright suffering.*

Sturges elicits a feeling of nightmarish horror in the audience through the photography and editing of these scenes. They were shot without any dialogue, relying simply on the strong images and the musical score to convey the point. Most of the scenes are also set at night, with strong shadows cast on the nameless people, in contrast to the clean, brightly lit shots that Hollywood studios (and Sturges) generally preferred for comedies. And finally, there are the crowds. Nearly every shot in the sequence is teeming with people, lined up for food, crowded into a dining hall, jockeying for a spot to sleep, or filling the benches in a midnight mission. And every face

---

*Only in very serious Hollywood films of the day, such as The Grapes of Wrath (1940), was anything approaching such a miserable image of the poor presented. Thus it is ironic that at the end of Sullivan's Travels Sturges shows us a glimpse of the novel O Brother, Where Art Thou? and we see that it was written by Sinclair Beckstein, a parody of Sinclair Lewis and John Steinbeck.

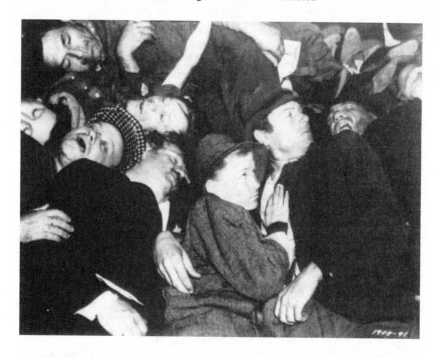

Sully (Joel McCrea) and The Girl (Veronica Lake) experience life among the downtrodden at a mission shelter for homeless men.

we see is sullen, withdrawn, defeated, disengaged, or just asleep. The scene in the mission is particularly powerful, as the camera tracks down the length of the hall passing row after row of overcrowded pews, not one of which bears an alert face or an engaged mind.*

Later, out on his own, Sully encounters an even more barren world. His attempt to hand out five-dollar bills ends with one of the recipients knocking him out and stealing the money; his fight with the railroad yard-man (echoing the scene from Sully's movie that opens the film) results in Sully's trial, conviction, and unfairly harsh sentence; and his demands for justice run afoul of the labor camp's sadistic Mister, who is all the more frightening because we are told that he is one of the nicest wardens at any of the prison camps. Just as Burrows warned him, poverty and trouble are things Sully knows nothing about, and he would have been much better off leaving them alone.

---

*The entire treatment of homeless people is much different from that in The Great McGinty, where McGinty, the representative tramp, is self-assured and resourceful rather than beaten down. The harsh vision of human suffering in Sullivan's Travels is almost reminiscent in tone of the scene in Remember the Night in which Lee goes home to see her mother, only to be greeted with hatred and spite.

Sturges has one final point to make with the trial and labor camp sequence, and it goes well beyond his principal message concerning the importance of laughter. By linking the inhumane treatment that Sully receives in the camp with the larger trouble he sets off to find, Sturges suggests that such injustice is part of the everyday life of poor people. Sully is shocked at this injustice; it goes against everything he has ever learned about America and everything he wants to believe *O Brother, Where Art Thou?* can do for people. He has discovered that justice is not blind and privilege is not equal, but dependent on position.

We can see Sturges's point clearly if we compare the film's two arrest scenes. Early in the film, after Sully "steals" his own car to drive The Girl home, he is arrested and taken to jail. Burrows and the valet arrive and inform the sergeant that Sully is indeed the owner of the car, but the perplexed officer presses Sully on his lack of a driver's license.

> *Sergeant*: Driving without a license, huh?
> *Sully*: Yes, isn't it terrible? That must call for a dollar fine and ten minutes in jail.
> *Sergeant* [to Burrows]: You sure this is Sullivan?
> *Burrows*: Oh quite, sir.
> *Sergeant*: Then what are you doing in those clothes?
> *Sully*: I just paid my income tax.
> *Sergeant*: All right, case dismissed. But you don't drive that car without a license.

Even though technically he has broken the law, Sullivan's tone throughout the scene is belligerent. His responses imply that the officer is bothering him with a frivolous matter and that he has done nothing that warrants investigation. The case is quickly dismissed, undoubtedly because it is relatively unimportant but also in part because the police in Hollywood are used to giving in to wealthy, powerful people such as Sully.

Contrasted with this scene is the trial in which Sully tries to answer the assault charges against him.

> *Judge*: Guilty or not guilty to trespass and atrocious assault with a rock upon the person of the employee of the railroad?
> *Sully*: I guess I hit him all right, the way my hand feels. I'm sorry. I'll make it up to you, pay any damages you want.

Here Sully is much more contrite and deferential to the law, but because he is a nobody he is treated far differently. The fact that he's dazed and wounded (he was hit in the head and is seeing double) means nothing to the judge, who takes Sully's inability to remember his name as a deliberate offense rather than as a result of his injury. Later, in the labor camp, when his memory does return, Sully is not allowed to make a phone call or write a letter until he shows respect for the Mister and has his privileges reinstated.

In one of the last scenes in the film, Sturges has Sully discuss his imprisonment with the camp trusty.

> *Sully*: Don't you understand? They think I'm dead but I'm not dead.
> *Trusty*: Well, that's fine. Just think what a nice surprise they'll have when you get out.
> *Sully*: I haven't got the time to spend six years here.
> *Trusty*: But you were sentenced.
> *Sully*: I know that, but I still haven't time.
> *Trusty*: Well, you'll have to *find* the time.
> *Sully*: Look, they don't sentence people like me to places like this for a little disagreement with a yard bull.
> *Trusty*: Don't they?
> *Sully*: No.

Sully, of course, is absolutely right. As soon as the executives at the studio hear that he's still alive, they move into action and get him out of the camp, although the specifics of what they do are never explained. You should not *have* to ask how Sully got released, or why he could get out when he actually did assault a man and trespass on railroad property, or how a legitimate court sentence was subverted. Sully is important, so he merits special treatment. The trusty, who doesn't even know that such treatment exists for some people, is left at the camp along with the dozens of other men who are paying an unfair price for their crimes, simply because they do not have the wealth, power, and position that Sully has. What these people really need is some justice, but as Sturges tells us, there's no use in even trying to get it for them. About all Sully can do is make funny movies to entertain and distract them for a few hours, while he stays far away to avoid being sucked into their misery again.

It is ironic that in *Sullivan's Travels*, Preston Sturges uses the most compelling visuals and sophisticated techniques of his directorial career to make a point about the need for simple comic films. Sequence after sequence—from the montage chronicling Sully's life as a bum to the powerful images of prisoners in chains marching to the church against a background of gospel singing—proves that Sturges was fully capable of more conspicuous directorial touches than his films normally exhibit. Unlike John L. Sullivan, though, who wants to hit his audience over the head with his moral, Sturges understands the power of subtlety. His prevailing message—the need for more laughter—is there for everyone to see, but just below the surface lies a darker, much grimmer comment on a society that can offer only amusement to its downtrodden members.

NINE

The Palm Beach Story

Written and Directed by Preston Sturges; Associate Producer: Paul Jones; Photography: Victor Milner; Edited by Stuart Gilmore; Art Direction: Hans Dreier and Ernst Fegte; Sound: Harry Lindgren and Walter Oberst; Musical Score: Victor Young. Released by Paramount, 1942.

Cast: Claudette Colbert (Geraldine Jeffers); Joel McCrea (Tom Jeffers); Mary Astor (The Princess Centimillia [Maude]); Rudy Vallee (John D. Hackensacker III [Snoodles]); Sig Arno (Toto); Robert Warwick (Mr. Hinch); Arthur Stuart Hull (Mr. Ormond); Torben Meyer (Dr. Kluck); Jimmy Conlin (Mr. Asweld); Vic Potel (Mr. McKeewie); William Demarest, Jack Norton, Robert Greig, Rosco Ates, Dewey Robinson, Chester Conklin, Sheldon Jett (Ale and Quail Club Members); Robert Dudley (The Wienie King); Franklin Pangborn (Apartment Manager); Arthur Hoyt, Al Bridge (Train Conductors); Esther Howard (Wife of the Wienie King).

Synopsis: During the opening credits, a cryptic story plays out as a man and a woman race to get ready for a wedding. The man quickly gets dressed and into the car that is waiting for him, but the woman has other things to worry about. Locked in a closet in her room is a second woman, bound and gagged but struggling to kick her way out. The bride ignores the captive woman and just manages to finish dressing and leave for the ceremony before the prisoner escapes from the closet. At the church the man and the woman meet and the wedding proceeds; a series of dates flashing on the screen then leads us to the film's real beginning—five years into the couple's marriage.

In her Park Avenue duplex, Gerry Jeffers is still clad in her morning robe when the building manager comes in with an elderly couple who are interested in renting the suite. While poking around upstairs the man finds Gerry, who explains that she and her husband are being evicted for not paying their rent. The man introduces himself as the Wienie King, a wealthy sausage mogul; taken with Gerry's beauty, he gives her $700 to pay the rent and buy herself some nice clothes.

When Gerry's husband, Tom, a struggling inventor, returns home, he is not so happy about the old man's generosity. He is convinced that Gerry must have done *something* to get the money from the man and that sex must have been involved. Gerry contends that she did not have to do anything because men are naturally inclined to help beautiful young women. Furthermore, she claims that if Tom would only let her, she could easily obtain the financing he needs to realize his latest project: an airport suspended over a city. Since Tom insists—despite her urging—on getting money through his own hard work, Gerry argues that he would really be better off if they divorced so that he would not have to use his meager earnings to support her in style. Throughout the rest of the evening, Gerry persists with this argument, telling Tom that after the divorce she would be a help, not a hindrance, to him. Posing as his sister, she could persuade the rich men courting her to include him in their business deals. To convince Tom to go along with her plan she declares that she does not really care about him anymore, but despite her protestations the two spend the evening in each other's arms.

The next morning Tom awakes to find the other side of the bed empty and Gerry packing to leave for her divorce. He chases after her and even wrests the suitcase away from her, warning that she will never get anywhere without any money. But she proves him wrong by securing a free cab ride to Penn Station and a complimentary ticket to Palm Beach, courtesy of a group of traveling millionaires, The Ale and Quail Club. Tom's attempts to stop her are futile, but back at his apartment he runs into the Wienie King, who gives him the money to fly down to Palm Beach and intercept Gerry.

On the train, in the meantime, the Ale and Quail Club members fortify themselves with liquor and become rowdier and rowdier, eventually holding skeet-shooting competitions in the club car. Wearing nothing more than a pair of borrowed pajamas, Gerry is able to escape the mayhem and find an empty Pullman berth just before the club car is disconnected from the train and the millionaires are left to fend for themselves. The next morning, without clothes or money, Gerry is rescued by the man in the berth below her. He is so impressed with her looks that he treats her to breakfast and gets off the train with her to buy her some clothes. After spending thousands of dollars on her, he takes her on his yacht to Palm Beach. Along the way Gerry discovers that the man is John D. Hackensacker III, one of the richest men in the world. Thinking quickly, she hatches a plan to marry Hackensacker after her divorce, which she tells him she can obtain only after he pays Tom $99,000.

When the yacht arrives in Palm Beach, Gerry and Hackensacker meet up with the millionaire's sister, Maude (whose current title is the Princess Centimillia), and her latest kept man, Toto. But onshore Gerry also finds Tom waiting for her; before he can say anything she introduces him as her brother, Captain McGlue, and steers him toward the arms of the husband-collecting princess.

At Hackensacker's Palm Beach home, Maude urges her brother (whom she calls by his nickname, Snoodles) to marry Gerry, but the cautious millionaire proposes a mock marriage to test the waters—an idea that's greeted with ridicule by everyone. That evening at a nightclub Gerry tries to convince Hackensacker to give her "brother" the money he needs to build an airport. When Snoodles quickly agrees, Tom announces that his partner in the deal is Gerry's husband—a scoundrel whom Hackensacker surely would not want to assist. Although the millionaire insists on funding the project anyway, Gerry is furious with Tom for trying to thwart her efforts to get him his money. As mad as she is, though, she cannot deny that she is still in love, and the couple end the evening in a passionate embrace, even as Snoodles and a full orchestra serenade Gerry through her bedroom window.

By the following morning, Hackensacker has already purchased the engagement ring he will give to Gerry and Maude has her sights set on capturing Captain McGlue as yet another husband. When they go to Tom and Gerry's suite, however, they are confronted with the sight of their guests packing, and the truth about the relationship finally comes out. At first Snoodles is devastated, although he still plans on funding Tom's airport idea because he sees merit in it. What makes for a truly happy ending, though, is the discovery by Snoodles and Maude that Tom and Gerry both have twin siblings—allowing the film to conclude with a wedding ceremony for Tom and Gerry, Snoodles and Gerry's identical twin, and Maude and Tom's identical twin.

•

Although it may be a stretch to call Preston Sturges a feminist film-maker, at a time when many Hollywood films cast women in traditional roles Sturges was looking at them in a different light. Not all his movies display strong female characters (*The Great McGinty* and *Christmas in July*, for example, contain fairly conventional leading-lady roles), but in several of his films the women drive the action. *The Lady Eve, The Miracle of Morgan's Creek*, and *The Beautiful Blonde from Bashful Bend* feature plots that center on female characters who are more resourceful and intelligent than their male counterparts. Unlike film noirs, in which the strong women are usually evil, or Bette Davis–style soap operas, in which the women often suffer in spite of (or because of) their independence, many of Sturges's films present strong women who face few repercussions or at least wind up on top at the end.

In *The Palm Beach Story*, Sturges gives us one of his strongest female characters in Gerry Jeffers. Although we don't know it at the time, he sets us up for the role that she is to play right from the opening sequence. The manipulations that lead to Tom and Gerry's wedding are completely handled (at least as far as we see them) by Gerry. Tom is racing to get dressed and to the church on time, like any bridegroom, but Gerry has bound and gagged her twin sister to keep her from reaching the altar. The exact details are never revealed ("That's another plot entirely," Tom tells Snoodles and Maude at the end of the film), but whatever happened, it is clear that Gerry took control of the situation to see that she got what she wanted: Tom's hand in marriage.

From that brief opening Sturges moves ahead in time five years, introducing the couple's financial problems and the short-term solution in the form of the Wienie King's money. But while the Wienie King may think he is being chivalrous in giving Gerry the $700, it is obvious that Gerry is not totally unaware of the effect her youth and good looks are having on him. "It's a privilege to do a favor for such a beautiful lady," he tells her as he is leaving. "It makes me feel young again." For her part, Gerry does nothing to dissuade his generosity and even subtly encourages it through her expressions and mannerisms. With the Wienie King incident serving as the basis, Sturges launches into a lengthy sequence that functions as both the setup for the film's action and an outline of male and female roles in society.

Sturges first gives us a brief glimpse of Tom at his office, trying to sell his airport idea to a skeptical client. When Tom arrives home to find that the rent and bills have all been paid, we get a more complete picture of him. His simplistic view of how Gerry might have obtained the money begins a verbal skirmish between the two as Gerry tries to explain how things work for women in this world.

> *Tom*: He just [gave you] $700 . . . just like that? . . . Sex didn't even enter into it?
>
> *Gerry*: Oh, but of course it did, darling. I don't think he would have given it to me if I'd had hair like excelsior and little short legs like an alligator. Sex always has something to do with it, dear.
>
> *Tom*: I see.
>
> *Gerry*: From the time you're about so big and wondering why your girlfriends' fathers are getting so arch all of a sudden. Nothing wrong, just an overture to the opera that's coming.
>
> *Tom*: I see.
>
> *Gerry*: You don't, really. But from then on you get it from cops, taxi drivers, bellboys, delicatessen dealers . . .

Tom: Get what?
Gerry: The look! You know, "How's about this evening, babe?"

Tom does not know, though, and that is what continues to make him so mad. Despite his wife's protestations that nothing happened between her and the Wienie King, Tom refuses to believe it or to accept the idea that Gerry could possibly use "the look" to bring him success. Partially it is a matter of ignorance and partially it is a matter of false nobility, as Sturges illustrates later in their conversation.

> *Gerry*: I'm so very tired of being broke, darling, and feel so helpless about having my hands tied. I could have helped you so many times, but every time I tried to, you tried to punch the man in the nose.
> *Tom*: Don't talk rot.
> *Gerry*: How about that president of the smelting company?
> *Tom*: That wolf!
> *Gerry*: He's still the president of a smelting company. We might have been in the smelting business now and paying our rent. . . . He liked you very much, he said!
> *Tom*: The less I hear about that hyena the better I'll like it.
> *Gerry*: That's what's so irritating! To know that I could get you some-place, without doing any harm, either. You have no idea what a long-legged gal can do without doing anything.

To Gerry, Tom just seems dense and foolishly virtuous, unable or unwilling to see the practicality of the situation:

> I'm a rotten wife. I can't sew, I can't cook . . . . But just because I'm a useless wife doesn't mean I couldn't be very valuable to you as a sister . . . very valuable. . . . And all the boys who wanted to go out with me would naturally have to be in your good graces. . . . Or I wouldn't go out with them. . . . They'd probably offer you partnerships. . . . They'd work you in on deals, and let you in on all the good things that were happening on the market, and that kind of business. Well, very few pretty girls' brothers have failed, you know, if they knew enough to come in out of the hail-storm.

So despite a brief lapse back into Tom's arms that evening, Gerry is determined to show that Tom's way of living—working hard, being noble, and waiting for success to arrive—is a way to get nowhere fast. Her own scheme of taking advantage of her youth, beauty, and feminine charms will get them both much further, much faster. And as Sturges has Gerry set out to prove her point, he also gives us a lesson in the differences between men and women in America.

Women and Practicality

Throughout *The Palm Beach Story*, Sturges shows us women, such as
Gerry in the opening sequence, who are practical and keenly aware of the
way in which the world functions. Firmly in control of nearly all things—
including the success of their husbands—they generally defer to men in
much the same way in which one might humor a child.

Gerry, of course, provides the primary example of female practicality.
In addition to thoroughly understanding the potential of female beauty,
she also recognizes the drain that she exerts on Tom:

> I'm no good for you, darling. I don't mean I'm not good for somebody,
> but . . . I can't cook or sew or whip up a little dress out of last year's win-
> dow curtains. . . . You see, by yourself you could live so simply. I mean
> just a little room anywhere, or maybe move in with your brother, or even
> use the couch in your office. And you wouldn't keep slipping back all the
> time. You could balance what you earn, look the world in the eye, and
> maybe even get ahead a little.

It is significant that Gerry doesn't suggest cutting back on her living
expenses (the couple's Park Avenue apartment is quite plush for a struggling entrepreneur). She accepts as a given that she deserves such a lifestyle
and that Tom, on his own, will never be able to provide it. "Men don't get
smarter as they get older," she tells her husband, "they just lose their hair."*
To Gerry, the solution to not having enough money to pay the bills
is to find someone who can provide more money—a task she *knows* she is
up to. Although Tom has no idea how she can be so sure about her fortunes, as soon as she is away from him she begins proving that she is right.
She secures a free taxi ride to the train station and a complimentary ticket
to Palm Beach; borrows a set of pajamas and armfuls of clothes when she
finds herself without a wardrobe; and receives not only a free breakfast but
also thousands of dollars' worth of clothes and jewelry, a private yacht trip,
and luxury accommodations from one of the richest men in the world. All
these favors are bestowed on her not because she has done anything to
deserve them, but rather because she is young and beautiful—a fact that
Gerry completely understands. As the Wienie King tells Tom, "A pretty
girl like that can get anybody. Why hang around with a man that can't pay
the rent?"

*The movie is filled with examples of the extraordinary amount of material goods that people
need to live comfortably. There is the luxurious duplex and its furnishings; the thousands of
dollars' worth of clothes that Snoodles buys for Gerry when she really only needs a few dresses
and some underwear; the yacht that Snoodles has been on only once before; and the jewelry that
Maude and Snoodles buy for Tom and Gerry after knowing them for only a few days. Even
Tom's airport is nothing more to Gerry than a way to make more money, which they can then
spend. As in so many Sturges films, success is equated with money and possessions.

Maude, the other female character in the film, also has no illusions about how things work in this society. She is, as her brother puts it, "a woman of iron determination, and once her mind's made up you might as well yield." Because, unlike Gerry, Maude has no financial worries, she is able to play even more aggressively at romance. Her six marriages attest to her dedication to enjoying her youth and good looks, which she uses in just the same way that Gerry does. ("Oh, thank goodness," Maude exclaims when she discovers that Tom did not respond to her advances because he is not really Gerry's brother. "I thought I was losing my grip!") She shares none of her brother's foolish notions of romantic love, as she demonstrates when she questions his plans concerning Gerry.

> *Maude*: Why don't you marry her? She's lovely.
> *Snoodles*: In the first place, she isn't free yet; in the second place, you don't marry somebody you just met the day before. At least I don't.
> *Maude*: But that's the only way, dear. If you get to know too much about them you'd never marry them. I'd marry Captain McGlue tomorrow, even with that name.
> *Snoodles*: And divorce him next month.
> *Maude*: Nothing is permanent in this world except Roosevelt, dear.

With three divorces and two annulments behind her, Maude shows no signs of stopping. She is still married to the prince, spends her time with Toto, and begins pursuing Tom all within the twenty-four-hour period in which we see her. To her, life—and love—are obviously meant for pleasure, and concepts such as propriety and commitment are useless constraints.

Men and Their Foolish Notions

While the women in *The Palm Beach Story* take a no-nonsense view of life, the men in the film are concerned with nothing but impractical ideas, such as chivalry and honor. Unrealistically noble and gladly willing to give up their money or even their lives for their ideal of a woman, they are often involved in silly or futile enterprises. (Only Toto, the lone non–American man, is different; like the women in the film, he seems much more attuned to the practical, namely, getting the princess to put him up and pay his way, just as Gerry wants Snoodles to do for her.)

To Tom, becoming successful means achieving his goals on his own, without his wife's convincing someone to help out. He balks at the thought of Gerry getting money from the Wienie King, and even after he finds out that no real sex was involved he still wants to give the money back. Also, although he goes along with the ruse that he is Gerry's brother, he nonetheless tries to sabotage Gerry's attempts to get the $99,000 from Snoodles. "Don't you ever get tired of being noble?" Gerry finally asks him. "Everything I build up for you, you knock down."

But as bad as Tom is, Snoodles is worse. He is simply full of ideas of what should and what should not be, nearly all of which contradict Gerry's and Maude's proven views. When Maude first meets up with him in Palm Beach, the differences between the siblings are immediately apparent.

> *Maude* [to Gerry]: My, you do get prettier as one gets nearer. How did you manage it? He's stiffer than a blanket. It must have done him a power of good.
> *Snoodles*: This is my sister, Maude ... Mrs. ... ah...
> *Maude*: Don't tell me he doesn't even know your name! Why that's perfectly marvelous! Now tell me he picked you up on the train and you'll make me a happy woman.... Wait till I tell the papers. Did he pick you up on the train?
> *Gerry*: Well, I was in awful trouble until he nobly came to my rescue.
> *Maude*: Oh, now you've ruined everything. I hoped for once that he hadn't done anything noble, that he was really cooking with gas.

For Maude, marriage is something you enter into as casually as you would a dinner date, but for Snoodles it is so sacred that he wants to set up a mock marriage (perhaps even "rent" some children) to see whether Gerry is appropriate for him.

In every other respect, Snoodles is similarly tied to ceremony and to how men and women *should* act. "The homely virtues are so hard to find these days," he tells Gerry, "a woman who can sew and cook and bake, even if she doesn't have to." During his breakfast with Gerry on the train he brings up the topic of her lack of money.

> *Snoodles*: Now you say you have no ticket?
> *Gerry*: That's right.
> *Snoodles*: Naturally I can't buy you a ticket—I mean, a perfectly strange young woman.
> *Gerry*: Naturally.
> *Snoodles*: In the first place you wouldn't accept it and in the second place...
> *Gerry*: There's the expense.
> *Snoodles*: I wasn't actually thinking of that.... Now I get off in Jacksonville...
> *Gerry*: I guess I do too, unless they throw me off sooner.
> *Snoodles*: Suppose we go to a little store in Jacksonville and buy you the few little things you need, and then you come the rest of the way with me by boat. You wouldn't have had to accept a ticket from someone you don't know, but you'll still get to where you're going.

Snoodles fails to understand not only that Gerry is actively seeking a ticket, but also that by providing her with clothes and transportation he is playing right into her hand. She has no sense of nobility that would lead her to refuse his offer; such a sense exists only in the minds of the men in

When Gerry (Claudette Colbert, *right*) learns that Snoodles (Rudy Vallee, *right*) wants a mock marriage with her, she and Maude (Mary Astor) share a knowing laugh while he and Tom (Joel McCrea) are left on the sidelines.

the film. Still, Gerry is always ready to play along with their notions. When the Ale and Quail Club members invite her to travel for free to Palm Beach in their reserved car, she at first politely turns them down, not because she believes it is not proper, but because she knows that the men think so. And when the Wienie King wants to give her $700 she respectfully declines, thus giving him the opportunity to insist that she take it.

With Gerry's behavior, Sturges demonstrates that men just do not understand how they are manipulated by women. Nearly all the male characters make sacrifices for Gerry: Tom compromises on his work to continue to support her lavishly; the Wienie King pays her rent and bills; the cab driver gives her a free ride to the train station; the Ale and Quail Club millionaires pay for her ticket to Palm Beach; and Snoodles buys her breakfast, clothes, and jewelry. These men all think that they are being noble and chivalrous as they implore Gerry to allow them to help her, when in fact she is banking on such notions to get exactly what she wants.

That none of the men perceive what the women are up to is obvious from a number of incidents. "It isn't how you look," a police officer tells Gerry, "it's how you behave in this world"—a statement contradicted by every scene in the film. Similarly, when Gerry tells Snoodles that her husband wants $99,000 to divorce her, the millionaire is outraged. "The days of serfdom, I mean bondage—I mean the days you bought a wife for a cow are over. I never heard of such a thing," he declares, even though we later learn that his sister has paid off many of her ex-husbands to get rid of them.

Gerry believes that such foolish thinking has kept her husband from succeeding as he should have. "I've always done what you wanted, and it's always turned out a disaster," she reminds him. To put him on the road to success she urges him to follow her methods of pretense and cunning. "Can't you ever learn to be practical?" she entreats him. "Don't you know that the greatest men in the world have told lies and let things be misunderstood if it's been useful to them? Didn't you ever hear of a campaign promise?" But Tom still does not see: "The way you are is the way you have to be, honey. It's the way I am. If I'm supposed to be a flop..."

If not for Gerry's interference, Tom would continue pursuing the same strategy that for five years has kept him just a half-step ahead of his creditors. With no clue as to how to achieve success himself, Tom is little different from Snoodles. The millionaire has a book of expenditures he never adds up and an office that he does nothing in; if not for the money he inherited, he would probably be just as bad off as Tom.

That Tom and Snoodles are able to come together and agree to build the airport makes for a seemingly happy conclusion to *The Palm Beach Story*. Yet with all that has gone before, it is hard to be too encouraged by the outcome. The whole idea of an airport suspended over the city is dubious at best (it sounds a little too much like Jimmy MacDonald's half-baked contest entries in *Christmas in July*), and there is not much reason to believe that Tom and Snoodles have the business skills to carry out the plan. If it does work, it will most likely be through sheer luck rather than good judgment. The only person in the film who actively works to get ahead is Gerry, who not only gets to keep Tom but also secures the money for his airport, provides her sister with a millionaire husband, and steers Tom's brother into the arms of a wealthy woman who will make him rich at the time of their divorce. The irony of Tom's success is twofold, however. On the one hand, he cannot take any credit for his achievement, as Sturges clearly shows the men to be fools. On the other hand, the success does not come about through any great talent or hard work on Gerry's part, either, other than her skill in using the one thing that she is least responsible for: her youthful, feminine beauty. Our society may talk about the "homely virtues," but when it comes right down to it, Sturges tells us, it is not how you behave in this world—it is how you look.

TEN

The Great Moment

Written and Directed by Preston Sturges; Based on the book *Triumph Over Pain* by Rene Fulop-Miller; Photography: Victor Milner; Edited by Stuart Gilmore; Art Direction: Hans Dreier and Ernst Fegte; Set Decoration: Stephen Seymour; Sound: Harry Lindgren and Walter Oberst; Musical Score: Victor Young. Released by Paramount, 1944.

Cast: Joel McCrea (W. T. G. Morton); Betty Field (Lizzie Morton); Harry Carey (Professor Warren); William Demarest (Eben Frost); Louis Jean Heydt (Horace Wells); Julius Tannen (Dr. Jackson); Edwin Maxwell (Vice President of the Medical Society); Porter Hall (President Franklin Pierce); Franklin Pangborn (Dr. Heywood); Grady Sutton (Homer Quimby); Donivee Lee (Betty Morton); Harry Hayden (Judge Shipman); Torben Meyer (Dr. Dahlmeyer); Vic Potel (Senator Borland); Robert Greig (Morton's Butler); Esther Howard (Dental Patient); Jimmy Conlin (Mr. Burnett).

Synopsis: Under the opening credits, a massive parade is marching from the dental offices of Dr. William T. G. Morton, through streets lined with people, to the beautiful home where the dentist's family waits for him. Morton and the man we will later come to know as Eben Frost are at the center of this parade, riding in an open carriage and waving to the onlookers, who hold signs proclaiming the end of pain, the miracle of Letheon, and the greatness of Morton.

The film opens with a shot of a large honorary medal in the window of a pawn shop. A much older Eben Frost sees the medal and purchases it for the widow of the man to whom it was originally given—William T. G. Morton. As Frost visits with Mrs. Morton, we learn that William has recently died and that she alone was there at the end. After the great contribution he made to humankind, Morton has been disgraced and forgotten, and his discovery of painless surgery has been disputed as fraudulent and stolen from the work of others.

A flashback sequence then presents the details of Morton's last attempt to gain recognition. As a farmer laboring in his fields, Morton is interrupted by his children, who hand him a telegram from Washington, D.C. The telegram informs Morton that Professor Warren of Massachusetts General Hospital wrote to Congress and the president on his behalf and the government is about to appropriate $100,000 to him for his discovery of ether. Morton goes to Washington and meets with President Franklin Pierce, who is willing to sign the bill that Congress has passed. The only catch is that the president first wants Morton to bring a patent infringement suit against a military hospital that is currently using ether, to obtain once and for all a court ruling establishing Morton as the legal owner of his discovery. When the case reaches court, however, the judge rules that such a discovery cannot be patented, and Morton is left without money or recourse. The public turns completely against him, calling him a cheat and a profiteer, and after assaulting a store owner who sells ether devices, Morton ends up a sick, broken man, his dental practice destroyed. As the scene flashes forward to Eben's visit with Lizzie Morton, we are told that William died shortly afterward.

Next the film moves to Morton's college days, when he was a boarder with Lizzie's family. Morton realizes that he cannot afford to continue his medical studies, and he decides to become a dentist instead. Before going to dental school he asks Lizzie to marry him. We next see them a few years later in the dental offices that Morton has rented and is showing off to his bride. At first, things look promising for the young couple. They soon have a child, and Morton builds a profitable practice. Still, unable to overlook the pain and fear his patients feel when they come to him, Morton struggles to find a way to make dentistry a painless science.

Morton's quest takes him to Dr. Jackson, a former teacher from his medical school days. The old man, whom Morton finds half-drunk in a bar, suggests that the dentist might try chloric ether, though Jackson doubts that anything can alleviate the pain of dentistry. Undaunted, Morton goes to a pharmacy and, unable to remember the type of ether Jackson told him to get, buys a bottle of chloric ether and another of sulfuric ether. At home that night, the cork loosens on one of the bottles, and as Morton studies nearby, he is quickly overcome by the liquid's fumes. When Lizzie finds him passed out she scolds him for coming home drunk, but Morton insists that he had no more than a drink or two. To discover what caused him to lose consciousness Morton returns the next day to the pharmacist, who tells him that the noxious fumes of the sulfuric ether knocked him out.

Shortly afterward Morton is visited at his office by Horace Wells, a friend from dental school who is also searching for a technique for painless dentistry to use in his practice in Hartford. Claiming that he is experimented successfully with nitrous oxide (laughing gas), Wells asks Morton to accompany him to Harvard Medical School where he is scheduled to demonstrate his method. Although doubtful that laughing gas is the answer, Morton agrees to act as Wells's assistant, on the condition that they seek Dr. Jackson's opinion first. This time Dr. Jackson is not only skeptical but also wholly opposed to the types of experiments that Morton and Wells are conducting. Their meeting with Jackson merely strengthens their resolve, though, and the dentists proceed to Harvard, only to have the test fail miserably when the patient becomes violent instead of losing consciousness.

Back at Morton's office, Wells still insists that laughing gas will work, but Morton convinces him that the dosage needs to be perfected before they can administer it to patients. While Morton is procuring an animal on which to experiment, a woman arrives at the office seeking help for an aching tooth. Wells takes the opportunity to anesthetize her with laughing gas, and although he is able to pull the tooth without any pain, the anesthetic very nearly kills the woman. A shaken Wells vows not to carry on with his experiments, while the incident gives Morton further proof that laughing gas is not a step in the right direction. When Morton discovers that ether has the same sleep-inducing properties as nitrous oxide, he is anxious to continue his own research. First he tries to give ether to the family dog, then successfully renders his goldfish unconscious, and finally inhales the fumes himself. When Lizzie finds him in his study, he is lying unconscious with a letter spike driven through his hand—and with no memory of feeling any pain from the puncture.

Certain that his search is finally over, Morton decides to patent his discovery as Letheon and begins advertising painless dentistry or "double your money back." But when he tries ether on Eben Frost, the first patient, Frost becomes agitated and violent. After another consultation with Dr. Jackson, Morton learns that he should have been using highly refined ether rather than a less pure mixture. In return for Dr. Jackson's help, Morton offers him 10 percent of the Letheon patent, which the doctor accepts even though he does not think it will ever work. When an angry Frost returns to Morton's office to get a refund, the dentist lures him back into the chair, successfully anesthetizes him, and pulls his tooth with no pain at all.

With an exclusive on pain-free dentistry, Morton's practice thrives, so much so that he has to bring in a number of assistants to handle all the patients. His success prompts Dr. Jackson to demand a greater percentage of the Letheon patent and to threaten a lawsuit if he does not get it. In the meantime Morton continues experimenting with ether, usually on Eben Frost, trying to increase the dosage and the amount of time Frost stays under. If patients could remain unconscious a little longer, Morton believes, Letheon could become a valid option in general surgery. Approaching Professor Warren of Massachusetts General Hospital after the doctor has performed an especially painful amputation, Morton convinces him to try Letheon in an upcoming operation. Morton and Frost nearly miss their historic chance, however, when Horace Wells shows up at Morton's office just as they are about to leave. Wells claims that the Boston dentist stole the painless dentistry idea from him, but Morton brushes Wells's threats aside. Morton and Frost race to the hospital and arrive just as Warren is about to proceed without the Letheon. They administer the anesthetic, and the operation is a complete success.

Before a second surgical experiment, scheduled for later in the week, can take place, members of the Massachusetts Medical Society confront Professor Warren. Appalled at the idea of a dentist being involved in their profession, they claim that Morton is just looking to get rich from his discovery. Reminding Warren of medical ethics, they persuade him that he should not in good conscience administer Letheon if he does not know exactly what it is. On the day of the operation Morton meets with Warren and the society members to attempt to answer their charges. Morton is willing to give Letheon, free of charge, to all doctors and hospitals in the world, he says, but he cannot reveal its exact nature for fear of losing his edge in his dental practice. Coerced by his fellow physicians, Professor Warren refuses to use Letheon and prepares to perform the surgery without the anesthetic. A frustrated Morton turns to leave the hospital, but on the way out he encounters the young servant girl who is about to undergo the operation. When he tells her that she is very brave, she says she is not worried because someone has discovered a way to make surgery painless, and Morton assures her that she is right. As the doors to the operating room open, Morton steps ahead of the girl's stretcher and hands the ether to Professor Warren.

•

Of all of Preston Sturges's films, *The Great Moment* is perhaps the most difficult to assess fairly. Since its release in 1944, the movie has been dismissed as unsatisfying almost wholly because of the nearly two years of re-editing it received at the hands of Paramount, against the wishes and judgment of Sturges. Its odd mixture of seriousness and humor, of melodrama and slapstick, has often been attributed to the studio's lack of vision; if they had just let Sturges alone, the theory goes, he would have made another brilliant film.

Such an argument is especially plausible because *The Great Moment* was the sixth of eight films that Sturges directed at Paramount, all of which (with the exception of *The Great Moment*) are fully realized artistic achievements. It is entirely reasonable to think that in the middle of such an extraordinary streak Sturges would have been unlikely to lose his touch; left

Elizabeth Morton (Betty Field) watches as her husband William (Joel McCrea) continues his ether experiments on the family's goldfish.

to his own devices he surely would have turned in something just as special as the five films that came before and the two films that followed. Further bolstering this view is the example of *Hail the Conquering Hero*: Sturges also differed with Paramount over the editing of this film, but in the end he won out and created what is undoubtedly one of his strongest works.

But much as we might like to believe that *The Great Moment*'s weaknesses are wholly attributable to studio meddling, the facts do not seem to bear out this theory. According to all Sturges's biographers, Paramount's version was not all that different from the one the director had prepared. Much of the support for a great discrepancy between the two versions has come from Sturges's own comments in the wake of the film's release, when he accused Paramount of having ruined his film by cutting it solely for comedy. But as Diane Jacobs points out, on at least one occasion after the film's release Sturges phoned a reporter and "claimed full responsibility for the movie."* She also argues very persuasively that the comedy in the film was always intended to be there and that Paramount merely removed one flashback sequence and much of the dramatic balance and subtlety. While these changes are by no means minor, they also do not uphold the common perception that the movie's structure or story was substantially

*Diane Jacobs, Christmas in July, p. 319.

altered by the studio. Many issues were in dispute between Sturges and Paramount in the mid–1940s, only some of which were related to *The Great Moment*; for Sturges, however, this film became a lightning rod for the contention and ultimately one of his primary excuses for leaving the studio.

From various sources, a reasonable outline of the beginning of Sturges's version of the story can be derived.

1. The film opens with a spoken prologue, substantially different from the written prologue that precedes the released version.
2. Eben Frost finds the medal in the pawn shop, buys it, and brings it to Lizzie at the farmhouse.
3. After some reminiscences between Eben and Lizzie, the scene flashes back to the day when Professor Warren is able to amputate a patient's leg painlessly. A parade through the streets of Boston hails Morton as the discoverer of Letheon, but after a party that night Lizzie expresses worry about what will happen if people find out what Letheon is. Morton then admits that in order for the operation to take place that day, he had to sacrifice the secret of his discovery by telling the doctors that Letheon was only ether. The reason he told them, he vaguely explains to Lizzie, was for a servant girl.
4. Although Morton is acclaimed worldwide, the assistants in his dental office, who now know the secret of painless surgery, all leave him to open their own practices, taking patients with them.
5. A glassmaker copies the design of Morton's ether inhaler and begins making and selling the inhalers himself. Morton confronts the man but cannot convince him to stop.
6. Horace Wells and Dr. Jackson both publicly claim that they discovered the anesthetic first, while Morton, watching his practice and his life fall apart, becomes ill trying to fight for what is rightfully his. A doctor orders him to the country to rest.
7. After another brief scene at the farmhouse with Eben and Lizzie, the film flashes back to an older Morton working on his farm. When word arrives that Congress has voted him money in recognition of his discovery, he goes to Washington to meet with the president. The president suggests that Morton file a suit to establish his legal right to a patent, but the court rules against him.

From this point the film moves back in time to Morton's days in medical school, and with the exception of an extra scene during Morton and Lizzie's courtship (which takes place at a party where all the guests inhale ether for amusement), Sturges's version appears to be essentially the same as the Paramount release.*

This outline illustrates clearly what Paramount did to the beginning of Sturges's film. The studio removed the initial flashback sequence that detailed Morton's acclaim in the aftermath of the surgery, the squabbling over Letheon's discovery, and the demise of Morton's practice; it moved the scene with the glassmaker ahead in time to follow the failed court case; it put the parade scene under the opening credits (where it makes no sense); and it did away with Morton's comments about relinquishing his hopes of great wealth for a servant girl. As Diane Jacobs observes, this last change completely eliminated a rather enticing carrot that was dangling in front of the audience's nose. Sturges planned to have Morton tell his wife that he had in effect thrown away his patent because of "some servant girl," then to fade out and offer no further explanation until the movie's last scene. Because of its provocative nature, the comment would not only have kept up the audience's interest, but it would also have left viewers far more affected by Morton's eventual sacrifice, since they would have expected a baser motive.

Thus Sturges's opening sequences were much more coherent and dramatically powerful than those in the released film, which kept many of the scenes but rearranged them in a confusing order. Perhaps the greatest change that Paramount made, however, was redoing the prologue to the movie, because it was in the prologue that Sturges had placed the message he wished *The Great Moment* to convey. Once that original opening is known, it is much easier to fit the remaining parts of the film into an intelligible picture.

A Doomed Prophet

As he did in *The Great McGinty* and *Sullivan's Travels*, Sturges often liked to set a story in a specific context by opening the film with an explanatory maxim or paragraph. He did the same with *The Great Moment*, but since the executives at Paramount were determined to impose their will on the film, his original prologue was radically rewritten. The studio's version, printed on a plain background in two succeeding frames, reads as follows:

> It does not seem to be generally understood that before ether there was nothing. The patient was strapped down ... *that is all*. This is the story

The account of Sturges's version comes primarily from Jacobs, pp. 281–83, 318. Details of Sturges's plan for the film can also be found in James Curtis, Between Flops, *pp. 168–74; Donald Spoto,* Madcap: The Life of Preston Sturges, *pp. 183–85; and* Preston Sturges by Preston Sturges, *pp. 296–98, 302–3.*

of W. T. G. Morton of Boston, Mass., before whom *in all time surgery was agony*, since whom science has control of pain.

Of all things in nature great men alone reverse the laws of perspective and grow smaller as one approaches them. Dwarfed by the magnitude of his revelation, reviled, hated by his fellow men, forgotten before he was remembered, Morton seems very small indeed until the incandescent moment he ruined himself for a servant girl and gained immortality.

What Sturges had in mind was much less confusing and much more trenchant. According to his plan, the film would have opened with a shot of "a vast plain, dotted with the wreckage of war—half a cannon, half a triumphal arch, half an equestrian statue (the rear half)." There would be no sign of life in the shot, "the only movement coming from the swirls of poison gas." Over this scene, in a cheerful tone, a voice would read the following words:

> One of the most charming characteristics of *Homo sapiens*, the wise guy on your right, is the consistency with which he has stoned, crucified, hanged, flayed, boiled in oil and otherwise rid himself of those who consecrated their lives to his further comfort and well-being, so that all his strength and cunning might be preserved for the erection of ever larger monuments, memorial shafts, triumphal arches, pyramids, and obelisks to the eternal glow of generals on horseback, tyrants, usurpers, dictators, politicians, and other heroes who led him, from the rear, to dismemberment and death.
>
> This is the story of the Boston dentist who gave you ether—before whom in all time surgery was agony, since whom science has control of pain. It should be almost unnecessary then to tell you that this man, whose contribution to human mercy is unparalleled in the history of the world, was ridiculed, reviled, burned in effigy and eventually driven to despair and death by the beneficiaries of his revelation.
>
> Paramount Pictures, Incorporated, has the honor of bringing you, at long last, the true story of an American of supreme achievement—W. T. G. Morton of Boston, Massachusetts, in a motion picture called *Triumph Over Pain.**

To Paramount, the revised opening probably appeared to convey essentially the same information conveyed by Sturges's words, but with a better presentation. The studio included the reference to the servant girl that had been cut from the film itself, and noted that Morton had been at

---

*Preston Sturges by Preston Sturges, *pp. 302–3.* Triumph Over Pain, *which came from the Rene Fulop-Miller book on which the movie was based, was the title Sturges preferred for the film. But Paramount executives thought that this title would turn audiences off and insisted on a different one. According to Donald Spoto (p. 184), Sturges submitted several alternatives, including* Great Without Glory, The Great Day, Out of the Darkness, *and* The Magic Moment, *before Paramount overruled him and gave the film its current title. As with the final cut of the movie itself, Sturges hated the studio's choice.*

best forgotten and at worst reviled for his actions when he should have been praised as a benefactor of humankind. But it probably would have been difficult to emasculate Sturges's prologue any more than Paramount did. Though much shorter, the revised opening is far more cryptic. Its second paragraph is so overwritten and vague that it makes almost no sense, and the allusion to the servant girl has none of the dramatic power that Sturges gave it by placing it within the film: by the time Morton finally ruins himself, the audience has completely forgotten this brief mention of her.

But the worst transgression of Sturges's original meaning is the removal of any *responsibility* for Morton's rejection. The studio's version makes it sound as though such a great man was berated and ignored simply because of a fluke of nature; Sturges is not so generous, however. He makes it clear that Morton's renunciation was completely predictable, just one more example of humankind's foolish inability to distinguish between those people who want to help us and those who want to take advantage of us. "It should be almost unnecessary . . . to tell you," Sturges states, just how poorly this man was treated: anyone who has observed human beings for any time at all should know. And not only does Sturges hold his fellow humans responsible for not recognizing greatness, but he also chastises them for being stupid enough to honor those individuals who time and again lead us to dismemberment and death.*

Greed and Self-interest

With Sturges's opening in mind, it is easy to conclude that Sturges saw *The Great Moment* as the story of a man whose attempt to help people was undermined by their innate selfishness. To further emphasize his point he designed the film's nonchronological structure as a way of coloring the audience's view of the characters before their story was told. We find out in the opening minutes that Morton received a medal inscribed "To the benefactor of mankind, with the gratitude of humanity," but that he died a broken man because others tried to claim the credit for his discovery. Before we ever meet Dr. Jackson or Horace Wells, we hear Lizzie's perspective on the events that took place just after her husband's death:

---

*Written in the midst of World War II, Sturges's prologue was scathing indeed, and the scornful reference to military leaders was the primary reason Paramount decided to change Sturges's opening (Preston Sturges by Preston Sturges, p. 303). At a time when patriotism and devotion to the war effort were almost universal in this country, criticizing war and militarism was undoubtedly a dangerous proposition.

Sturges was able to keep one cynical antimilitary jab in the film, in the scene in which President Pierce suggests that Morton file a lawsuit to legally establish his patent. "I'd hate to have it look as though I was trying to make the government pay to relieve wounded soldiers from pain," Morton asserts, to which Pierce replies, "The government pays for the guns, don't it?"

> The papers spoke of him as the man who *claimed* to have discovered the use of ether. They dug up the whole nasty business—that Dr. Jackson had told him how to do it; that he, Jackson, had known about it for years.... Can you imagine anyone keeping a secret like that? And then they brought in poor Horace Wells's claim that he did it first, and Dr. Crawford Long's claim that he had done it four years before. Well, maybe they all did do it first, maybe they all did discover the use of ether. I guess they did all right—why should they lie about it? But it seems so cruel to have let people go on suffering for so long after they knew how to stop it. All I know is that three months after my husband discovered anesthesia, the whole world was using it.

Sturges later claimed that by changing the order in which he presented the events in Morton's life he was simply moving the man's triumph from the middle of his life, where it fell chronologically, to the end of the movie, where it would be more dramatically satisfying.* In the process, though, Sturges was also making it clear right from the start of the film how Morton's colleagues were to be regarded. We may observe Horace Wells's apparent dedication to finding a workable anesthetic, but in the back of our minds is the fact that he will also be low enough to try to claim Morton's eventual discovery as his own. Similarly, we would view Dr. Jackson's opposition to Morton's research in a different light if we did not know that after ether's acceptance, he, too, wanted to wrest the credit away from Morton.

As the story of Morton's research develops, the scenes involving Wells and Jackson are not, on their own, terribly incriminating. The worst that can be said of Wells, who seems just as concerned as Morton with perfecting painless dentistry, is that he is a bit premature in trying his method at Harvard. (Morton can be criticized for similar foolishness, particularly when he administers cleaning fluid instead of ether to Eben Frost.) And Dr. Jackson might seem to be nothing worse than an older, overcautious scientist who has been doing the same thing for so long that he is unable to see the potential in a new procedure. If not for Sturges's nonchronological structure, the audience would probably leave the film surprised at the accusations Wells and Jackson eventually make against Morton, but not with an overwhelmingly negative attitude toward them.

By presenting the story as he does, however, Sturges not only turns the audience against Wells and Jackson from the start, but also highlights one of his favorite themes: the tendency for people to look out for themselves. In reality, Morton is not much different from either Horace Wells or Dr. Jackson; he continues his search for anesthesia primarily because he wants an edge on competing dentists. Although he is deeply bothered by

---

Curtis, p. 172.

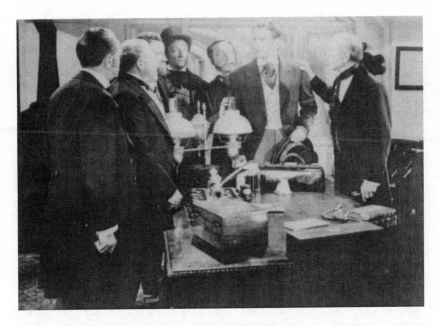

Morton (Joel McCrea, *second from right*) tries in vain to convince the board members of the Massachusetts Medical Society to use Letheon.

the pain that any patients feel (especially after he witnesses his first operation), he is also concerned because all the screaming in his office is scaring away his own waiting patients. Where Morton differs from Wells and Jackson is in being determined enough (and, Sturges makes clear, unwise enough) to keep experimenting. Horace Wells gives up his research after he nearly kills the woman in Morton's office, while Jackson, who knows a good deal about ether's properties, never even begins an investigation.

The contrast between the men is drawn even more sharply when the money from Letheon starts to roll in. Just as Wells and Jackson, neither of whom wanted anything to do with Morton's ether before, rush forward to claim a portion of the windfall, Morton becomes dedicated to seeing that Letheon is used for the good of humankind. Although he looks out for himself by trying to keep his discovery safe from other dentists, he also offers the anesthetic to all hospitals and charitable institutions throughout the world in perpetuity. When that is not enough to satisfy the medical profession, Morton is forced to decide either to limit the ether to his own dental practice or to reveal its composition and therefore relieve all surgery patients of the burden of pain. He gives up his secret but continues to seek a patent for Letheon. Like Dan McGinty and other Sturges characters, though, Morton is essentially doomed. As long as he pursued his own self-interest he was successful; as soon as he made a moral choice he set himself up for destruction. He loses his dental business, watches a fickle public go from honoring him to vilifying him overnight, and finally descends into poverty and an early death.

Sturges makes it clear who is responsible for coercing Morton into a decision with such disastrous consequences. Both Horace Wells and Dr. Jackson have at least *some* basis for making a claim on Letheon, but in sheer selfishness they are outdone by the Massachusetts Medical Society. Threatened by the usurpation of their power by a mere dentist, the representatives of this group are perfectly willing to allow a young woman to go through a needlessly painful amputation just to exert their control. To protect the superiority of their profession, these people would have denied their colleagues the means for providing painless surgery. The members of the Medical Society, with their lofty status and the influence they undoubtedly wielded, would surely have been included in Sturges's list of the tyrants, politicians, and heroes who lead humankind to (a very painful) dismemberment and death.

Despite all the changes made to *The Great Moment* without Sturges's approval, the movie as it exists remains an interesting example of its creator's vision. Whether the movie would have been more coherent if Sturges had been allowed to edit it seems clear: it would have been. But whether it would have been as artistically successful a film as the seven others he directed at Paramount seems much less certain. Presented as Sturges had planned, the film still would have been confusing, with an uneasy combination of drama and slapstick, and it still would not have fulfilled the potential Sturges thought it had.

There are several possible reasons to account for the great attraction that Rene Fulop-Miller's book and the life of William T. G. Morton held for Sturges. An inventor himself, Sturges may have been sympathetic to the plight of a fellow experimenter who was not appreciated as he should have been. Sturges may also have been drawn to the deep irony of the situation, as Morton relieved the world from pain only to have his own life turned into an agonizing nightmare. The appearance of several of Sturges's recurrent themes in the film—from the material advantages to be gained from selfishness, to the fickleness of the public, to the utter futility of believing that hard work equals success—reveals the closeness he felt to the material.

The Great Moment, as much as any other Sturges film, has a near-overwhelming sense of cynicism, especially in Sturges's version with its caustic prologue. Characters are not simply looking out for themselves; they are overtly inhumane in their willingness to deny people anesthesia. No one's motives are anything close to pure and noble—even Morton's great sacrifice is followed by years of trying to gain financial reward. And

Sturges's original preamble makes it clear that such incidents are by no means unique and that all of us in the audience may be just as guilty of such greed. It is particularly ironic that *The Great Moment*—a movie that celebrates the discovery of anesthesia—would be the one film to be cut against Sturges's wishes and cause him such personal and professional pain.

ELEVEN

The Miracle of Morgan's Creek

Written and Directed by Preston Sturges; Photography: John F. Seitz; Edited by Stuart Gilmore; Art Direction: Hans Dreier and Ernst Fegte; Set Decoration: Stephen Seymour; Sound: Hugo Grenzbach and Walter Oberst; Musical Score: Leo Shuken and Charles Bradshaw; Musical Direction: Sigmund Krumgold. Released by Paramount, 1944.

Cast: Eddie Bracken (Norval Jones); Betty Hutton (Trudy Kockenlocker); William Demarest (Officer Kockenlocker); Diana Lynn (Emmy Kockenlocker); Al Bridge (Mr. Johnson); Julius Tannen (Mr. Rafferty); Porter Hall (Justice of the Peace); Emory Parnell (Mr. Tuerck); Vic Potel (Newspaper Editor); Georgia Caine (Mrs. Johnson); Brian Donlevy (McGinty); Akim Tamiroff (The Boss); Jimmy Conlin (The Mayor); Frank Moran (Military Policeman); Torben Meyer (Doctor); J. Farrell MacDonald (The Sheriff).

Synopsis: In the town of Morgan's Creek something extraordinary has happened. The editor of the local paper, the *Bugle*, is frantically trying to reach Governor Dan McGinty* to tell him about the news. While the governor shares the editor's excitement, we never hear exactly what it is that is causing all the commotion. With The Boss by his side, McGinty tries to get some simple answers out of the editor, but the man insists on relating the story his way—from the beginning. As he launches into his tale, the film flashes back a number of months to the day on which it all started.

The typical small town of Morgan's Creek is a bit more lively than usual, with the streets full of soldiers trying to get in a last bit of fun before shipping out from the local base the next day. Officer Kockenlocker, the

---

The characters from The Great McGinty *are heralded in the opening credits here not as Brian Donlevy and Akim Tamiroff, but as McGinty and The Boss. As clever as their inclusion is, however, McGinty actually was not governor long enough to do any of the things he does in* Morgan's Creek.

gruff town constable, attempts to rein the boys in, but it is his daughter Trudy who is really attracting their attention. In Rafferty's Music Shop, where she works as a clerk, she promises a group of soldiers that she will attend that evening's going-away dance, much to the dismay of Norval Jones. Denied entrance into the army because of his extreme nervousness (he gets so worked up he sees spots in front of his eyes), Norval has held an unrequited love for Trudy ever since they were children. Although he hoped to take her to the movies that night, he loses out once again to men in uniform.

When Officer Kockenlocker finds out about the soldiers' dance, though, he forbids Trudy to attend. A disappointed Trudy phones Norval to come to her rescue, letting him think that he is finally getting his date with her. But Trudy simply wants to use him as a cover so that she can go to the dance without telling her father the truth. Although it is against his better judgment, Norval is finally persuaded by Trudy's tears to let her drive his car to the dance while he sits in the movie theater by himself. Throughout the night Trudy moves from one party to the next, dancing with all the soldiers, drinking lemonade and champagne, and, during one particularly vigorous dance, hitting her head and nearly knocking herself out. When she finally arrives at the movie theater to pick Norval up, it is eight o'clock in the morning, Norval's car is a wreck, and Trudy seems suspiciously drunk. To top it all off Norval is nearly beaten up by Officer Kockenlocker when he brings the constable's daughter home at that hour.

With her sister Emmy's help, Trudy begins to revive herself and to remember what happened during the evening. A group of soldiers and girls thought it would be a great joke to get married, so, giving false names and using curtain rings as wedding bands, all of them—including Trudy—exchanged marriage vows. Now Trudy has no memory of the name she used or that of the man she married (other than Ratzkiwatzki). Trudy and Emmy figure that no one will ever know about the incident—until Trudy finds out that she's pregnant. Turning to the local lawyer, Mr. Johnson, for advice, Trudy learns that even though she gave a false name she's still married. To get Trudy out of this jam Emmy begins lobbying her to marry Norval, who, she says, was born to play the sucker.

That evening, after Norval has dinner with the Kockenlocker family, Trudy plays up to him in order to coax a marriage proposal, and she succeeds. But Trudy's acceptance makes Norval so deliriously happy that she feels guilty not telling him the truth. When Norval finds out, he realizes that he is the one who is going to bear the brunt of Officer Kockenlocker's wrath. Later Trudy and Emmy weigh another option—that Trudy not get married—but quickly determine that in a small town like Morgan's Creek that will not work. About the only thing they are sure of is that they should not have told Norval the truth.

Word of Norval's late night date with Trudy soon gets around town, and rumors begin to circulate that the announcement of the couple's engagement is imminent. Norval pleads with Trudy to marry him because it is her only way out, but she remains reluctant. Meanwhile, Officer Kockenlocker has heard the gossip in town and he pulls Norval aside for a private talk. With gun in hand the constable tells Norval that the pair *will* be getting married. Though Trudy learns what her father has said, she is still concerned about committing bigamy; Norval promises to come up with a plan within a day.

Norval sets his scheme in motion when he picks Trudy up the following night on the pretense of going to the movies. Equipped with a secondhand wedding ring and a World War I army uniform, he will pose as Ignatz Ratzkiwatzki. He and Trudy will be married at the office of a justice of the peace twenty-five miles away and get the certificate they need in order for Trudy to obtain a legal divorce. The plan looks as if it is going to work until a very nervous Norval mistakenly signs the register with his real name. The justice of the peace suspects foul play and has Norval arrested and hauled back to Morgan's Creek. With everyone from the FBI to the military police wanting to take possession of the prisoner, Officer Kockenlocker decides to lock Norval up in the town jail until everything can be straightened out. Despite the confusion, the justice of the peace manages to get a moment alone with Kockenlocker, and he offers to destroy the evidence—the marriage certificate—in order to help out a fellow officer of the law. Kockenlocker agrees, thinking that he is saving Trudy a lot of grief. Only when he tells his daughters that he has taken care of everything does he get the full story.

With a clear understanding of the predicament, Kockenlocker agrees with Trudy and Emmy that their only hope is to find the real Ratzkiwatzki. After sneaking Norval out of his prison cell, they break into the bank where Norval works so that he can "borrow" the money he has in his account there. They then return to the jail, where Trudy and Emmy tie Officer Kockenlocker up and knock him out to simulate Norval's prison break. In the meantime Norval sets off in the Kockenlockers' car to find Trudy's real husband.

The scene then flashes forward to the phone conversation between Governor McGinty and the newspaper editor. The governor insists that Trudy *must* be married, but the editor replies that the townspeople still are not sure and that in any case Norval is back in jail. Next the scene flashes back to the day preceding the governor's phone call, as Norval arrives in Morgan's Creek just before Christmas. From Mr. Johnson, the lawyer, he learns that the Kockenlockers left town six months earlier, after Officer Kockenlocker was discharged for his role in Norval's escape. When Norval says that he wants to find Trudy and give himself up, Johnson advises him to leave town, change his name, and forget that any of it ever happened. Refusing to abandon his search for Trudy, Norval makes a visit to her former boss, Mr. Rafferty, who says he has been secretly providing Trudy with help. Rafferty is about to bring Norval to see her when they are spotted by the bank president and Norval is once again arrested.

Rafferty races to the small country farmhouse where the Kockenlockers are staying to give them the news. When Trudy hears that Norval has come back, she insists on going to Morgan's Creek with her father to tell the whole story and save Norval from jail. In the next scene, Officer Kockenlocker interrupts a meeting of the town leaders to say that his daughter has arrived to give them the truth about Norval; while waiting in the car, though, Trudy goes into labor and is rushed to the hospital. With the town leaders outside plotting their revenge, a tense Emily, Rafferty, and Officer Kockenlocker watch in amazement as Trudy delivers one baby boy, then another, then another—until there are six in all.

With the miracle making headlines around the world, the governor tells the newspaper editor to get Norval out of jail immediately. McGinty informs him that the uniform was actually from the state guard and that Trudy has always been married to Norval—the nervous groom just stuttered and was misunderstood to say "Ratzkiwatzki." On the basis of McGinty's word that everything is in order, Norval is released from prison, but he is still in the dark as to what is going on. Dressed in full state guard uniform, he is escorted to the hospital to see his wife and given a hero's reception at the door. Neither he nor Trudy knows anything other than that her labor is over. Thus when Emmy takes Norval to the nursery he nearly faints at the sight of six babies. He—and we in the audience—see the spots in front of his eyes, as Sturges ends with the written quote, "Some are *born* great, some *achieve* greatness, and some have greatness *thrust upon them.*"

•

In *Remember the Night,* Preston Sturges painted a warm and glowing portrait of small-town life in America, complete with church socials and sing-alongs around the piano. John Sargent's small Indiana hometown, with its time-tested values of honesty and generosity, nurtured him and provided him with a lifetime of insulation from the city's callousness. It is difficult to believe that just a few years after upholding the virtues of small towns in *Remember the Night,* Sturges would harshly ridicule their drawbacks as he does in *The Miracle of Morgan's Creek.* Rather than the simple, quiet beauty of the scenes with John Sargent and his mother, Sturges fills *Morgan's Creek* with scenes of the verbal and physical abuse that Emmy Kockenlocker and her father inflict on each other. Whether Sturges changed his opinion of rural America between 1939 and 1944, or whether he simply had a unique ability to see both sides of the coin with great clarity, he certainly delivered quite a blow to small-town life both in *Morgan's Creek* and in its follow-up, *Hail the Conquering Hero*.

Sturges claimed that he had a different target in mind with *Morgan's Creek*, though. He intended the film to "show what happens to young girls who disregard their parents' advice and who confuse patriotism with promiscuity."* Included in the original screenplay is a scene in which the local preacher sermonizes against such imprudence, but Sturges maintained that Paramount made him remove the scene and with it his explicit moral for the film. But a close reading of the version that appears in the script shows that the scene is meant to be far more comic than serious, with Trudy and Emmy sitting in church and making snide comments about the preacher's remarks.† The sermon contains such lines as "When the abominations we have committed seem at last to have filled the cup till it overfloweth, when the world is being destroyed, when God seems to have abandoned us to our own miserable devices and the race of men is rapidly vanishing from this earth ... it may be particularly appropriate to talk about creation, and particularly creation in wartime when it is so needful ... for future wars." Sturges could not really have meant for this sermon to be taken seriously as the main point of his film. It is also hard to reconcile his supposed moral — that children ought to listen to their parents — with the picture he gives us of Officer Kockenlocker, a bumbling dolt who seems incapable of ever giving Trudy any valuable advice.

Despite Sturges's claims, *Morgan's Creek* seems more a satire of small-town values than a warning against teenage rebellion. The film stands in sharp contrast to MGM's immensely popular paean to idealized small-town life, the Andy Hardy films. Begun in earnest in 1938, the series focused on the family of James Hardy, a highly respected judge in the town of Carvel who always decided cases fairly and justly while reaffirming traditional American values. His only real problem came in getting his teenage son Andy out of various jams. With the aid of a man-to-man talk, though, and some quotations from Thomas Jefferson or Abraham Lincoln, the judge would invariably convince his son of the error of his ways, leaving Andy a wiser and more obedient young man.

With their respect for the wisdom of parents, the Andy Hardy films promoted the moral that Sturges claimed to be dispensing: listen to your parents, obey their rules, do not question the status quo, and you will be better off. Sturges would hardly have wanted to offer up the same trite

---

*Preston Sturges by Preston Sturges, *p. 300*.

†*Throughout this chapter all references to material in the script or not in the finished film come from the screenplay as published in John Gassner and Dudley Nichols, eds.*, Best Film Plays of 1943–1944.

message as that of Mickey Rooney's endearing Andy. The town of Morgan's Creek in fact provides a perfect snapshot of dysfunctional families. Far from venerating family life, Sturges pulls the rug out from under the institution, offering us one example after another of unhappy family members and disdainful observers. And nowhere does he make his point more clearly than right in the middle of the Kockenlocker household.

Family Life in Morgan's Creek

While Andy Hardy may always have had a loving, respectful family to fall back on—no matter what kind of trouble he got himself into—the children in the Kockenlocker family have no such stability. In the first place there is no nuclear family unit; Mrs. Kockenlocker has apparently died, leaving her husband to raise fourteen-year-old Emmy and her older sister, Trudy. Instead of respecting their father, Emmy and Trudy view Officer Kockenlocker as most teenagers probably see their parents: out of touch with the contemporary world, unsympathetic to the problems of their children, and hypocritical because they believe that adults have a different standard of acceptable behavior than minors do.

Although Trudy constantly belittles and deceives her father, the relationship between Emmy and Officer Kockenlocker takes Sturges's mocking of small-town family life to its extreme. Not only do father and daughter not get along, they actually have contempt for one another. Emmy continually taunts her father, and Officer Kockenlocker is always suspicious of what his younger child might be doing or even thinking. After reading an editorial in the *Bugle* about the dangers of wartime weddings, for instance, Officer Kockenlocker immediately confronts Emmy, who is quietly playing a wedding march on the piano.

> *Kockenlocker*: You wasn't thinking of getting married, was you?
> *Emmy*: At fourteen? I was thinking of going down to the corner and having a soda.
> *Kockenlocker*: I didn't mean what you was thinking about right now. I mean generally.
> *Emmy*: Generally, yes.
> *Kockenlocker*: Generally, yes what?
> *Emmy*: Generally, yes, I think about marriage. What else do you think I think about?
> *Kockenlocker*: Oh, you do, do you?
> *Emmy*: Anybody can think about it, can't they? It doesn't cost anything to think about it. It's only when you do it that it costs two dollars.
> *Kockenlocker*: *What* costs two dollars? You seem to know a great deal about a subject far beyond your years....

The absurdity of the entire encounter—with Kockenlocker assuming first that Emmy might actually be thinking about getting married, and then completely contradicting himself by being outraged that she would even know what getting married entails—sets the tone for all the confrontations between the father and his daughters. Because he can't even tell the difference between what his children should and should not know, or even what they might or might not do, he can never give them firm guidance and sensible advice. Later in the same scene, after Trudy announces her plans to attend the soldiers' going-away dance, Kockenlocker forbids it on the grounds that he was in the army once and he knows what goes on at such parties. In this one case, of course, Kockenlocker proves to be right. But rather than rationally explaining the facts to Trudy, Kockenlocker simply blusters and bellows, giving his daughters all the more reason not to respect him. Upset at the implications of her father's words, Emmy shoots back, "If you don't mind my mentioning it, Father, I think you have a mind like a swamp." In response, Kockenlocker aims a forceful kick at Emmy's rear end, only to wind up on the floor when the girl moves out of the way in time.

This sparring between Emmy and Kockenlocker continues throughout the movie. When Norval arrives to pick up Trudy for their date, Emmy cannot resist getting in a few jabs at her father. "There's a new little boogie-woogie joint...," she starts to tell Trudy after their father's admonition to be home early.

> *Kockenlocker* [sternly]: Now what do you know about this little boogie-woogie joint?
> *Emmy* [with feigned innocence]: Nothing. I just heard you were there . . . digging quite a trench.

Later the verbal bickering between Emmy and her father turns physical once again, this time after Trudy has coaxed a marriage proposal out of Norval but then has second thoughts about using him. Hearing Trudy's sobs and thinking that his daughter has been treated poorly, Kockenlocker grabs Norval and, with Trudy and Emmy on the other side, begins a tug-of-war with the bewildered young man. After the girls are finally able to rescue Norval, Emmy yells at her father, "Papa! Can't you learn to be a little more refined?" Her remark earns her another attempted boot in the rear from her father, but once again she is faster than he is and Kockenlocker ends up flat on his back.

There are a number of other tussles between Kockenlocker and his daughters in which Norval is caught in the middle. When Trudy arrives home at eight o'clock in the morning after her date, Kockenlocker is ready to kill Norval on the spot; he even throws Emmy to the ground as she tries to stop him. Only when Trudy pulls Kockenlocker's arm and Emmy leaps on her father's back and then painfully twists his leg is Norval finally able

The violence that Officer Kockenlocker (William Demarest, *left*) directs toward Norval Jones (Eddie Bracken) is exceeded only by that which Emmy and Trudy (Diana Lynn, *left*, and Betty Hutton) inflict on their father.

to escape. Such episodes are the norm within the Kockenlocker family. Even when Emmy *wants* to act in a loving way she is not allowed to, as in the scene in which she waits for Trudy and Norval to return home from the mock marriage. Worried that something might have gone wrong because they are late, she sits down in her father's lap only to have him respond, "Get off my lap!! What's the matter with you?" It seems as if Kockenlocker cannot be near Emmy without trying to insult her, hit her, or push her aside. He may never land any of his attempted kicks, but there's a tremendous amount of force—and anger—behind each one.

The hostility in the Kockenlocker family reaches a peak when the two sisters and their father are trying to devise a plan to help Norval escape from the Morgan's Creek jail. "Couldn't you think of some bright way of doing it?" Emmy asks her father. Then, unable to resist the opportunity, she adds, "You're always having bright ideas!" Fed up with his daughter's insolence, Kockenlocker fires back, "Listen zipper-puss! Some day they're just gonna find your hair ribbon and an axe some place—nothing else! The Mystery of Morgan's Creek!" Such an extreme example of intimidation perfectly sums up the relationship between Kockenlocker and Emmy:

since he has no respect for her and does not make any attempt to understand her, his only means of control is violence, real or threatened.

But the Kockenlockers are not the only dysfunctional or incomplete family in Morgan's Creek. Norval is an orphan, and Mr. and Mrs. Johnson appear to have no children (although they are very close to Norval, who rents a room from them). Sturges also implies that a biological family cannot necessarily provide the comfort and nurturing that people need. The biological offspring in the film (Trudy and Emmy) have a far less loving relationship with their father than do the "adopted" children with their parent figures (Norval and the Johnsons, Trudy and Mr. Rafferty). At the end of the movie, Sturges mocks the entire idea of a natural family unit consisting of mother, father, and children, as the Jones family is created by the edict of corrupt politicians.

In Morgan's Creek, though, it is not surprising to find people whose family ties are either troubled or nonexistent, since all relationships between men and women—especially marriage—are viewed with distrust. The *Bugle*'s editorial about the danger of military marriages, like the minister's sermon that was cut from the final film, claims that there are "by necessity of the laws of average, some scoundrels and some fools."* Young women are urged to be aware of such men and not to confuse promiscuity with patriotism—a warning implying, of course, that these men will use any argument at all to get women in bed with them. These soldiers are hardly decent young men idealistically defending their country, as Officer Kockenlocker knows all too well. When Trudy informs him that she is going to the soldiers' party and that the boys will bring her right home afterward, he replies, "Yeah, by way of Cincinnati, with a side trip to Detroit. I was a soldier too, you know, in the last war." For one of the only times in the film, Kockenlocker is right.

The people of Morgan's Creek don't hold women in much higher regard. By contending that they might mistake promiscuity for patriotism, the *Bugle*'s editor insinuates that women are impetuous and misguided at best, and wanton at worst. Even when the subject turns from loose men and women to young people in general, the attitude remains negative. Kockenlocker's speech to Norval offers a representative picture of the viewpoint in Morgan's Creek.

> *Kockenlocker*: [Daughters are] a mess no matter how you look at them . . .
> a headache till they get married. *If* they get married, and after that
> they get worse. Either they leave their husbands and come back with
> four children and move into your guest room, or their husband loses
> his job and the whole caboodle comes back. . . . Or else they're so

---

*In the film, the editorial does not appear on the screen long enough to be read in its entirety, but the complete text does appear in the script.

homely you can't get rid of them at all and they hang around the
house like Spanish moss and shame you into an early grave.
Emmy: How about sons? They're no bargain either.
Kockenlocker: That's right, but there's one thing don't happen to them.
They never turn into old maids.

Other people in Morgan's Creek agree with Kockenlocker that women
are a continual burden on men, first on their fathers and then on their
husbands. During the mock marriage Norval trembles and stammers,
barely able to speak or stand up. "Oh, that certainly made me nervous,"
he says as the service ends. "If you knew what it was like," the justice of
the peace counters, "it would make you still nervouser."

But the most hostile opinion of marriage comes from Mr. Johnson,
the lawyer, when Trudy and Emmy consult him about the possibilities of
divorce for the "friend" who's gotten herself into this jam.

> *Johnson*: Well, since you are here on behalf of a friend who does not wish
> to appear, all I can say is that your friend ought to be ashamed of
> herself.
> *Emmy*: She's a *very* nice girl. It just happened, that's all.
> *Johnson*: I mean because of her carelessness. The responsibility of record-
> ing a marriage has always been up to the woman; if it weren't for
> them marriage would have disappeared long since. No man is going
> to jeopardize his present or poison his future with a lot of little brats
> hollering around the house unless he's forced to. It is up to the
> woman to knock him down and hog-tie him and drag him in front
> of two witnesses immediately, if not sooner. Any time after that is
> too late.

Such an attitude toward marriage hardly reflects the love, generosity,
and concern for others that are supposed to flourish in small towns. But
the disrespect is in no way limited to relationships between men and
women, or between spouses, or among family members. The Kockenlocker family is emblematic of the utter disdain that nearly everyone in
Morgan's Creek has for everyone else. The residents lie, cheat, steal, and
treat each other miserably; all of these offenses, though, are committed under the pretense of upholding the propriety and good name of their town.

Deception, Hypocrisy, and Small-Town Values

From the most mundane actions—such as Norval's claim that he has
come to the music store to buy phonograph needles when he really wants
to ask Trudy out—to the most sacred personal commitments, the entire
population of Morgan's Creek seems to be involved in one game of deception after another. When Trudy decides to attend the soldiers' dance, for

example, she starts weaving an entire web of lies. After she deceives her father into thinking that she will only be going to the movies with Norval, she then fools Norval into thinking that she is actually calling him for a date. Once Norval finds out that he is being used he balks at going along with Trudy's plan, but then he agrees to the ruse as Trudy convinces him that she is doing this for the soldiers, not for herself.

When the evening of dancing is over, of course, one deception is piled on top of another. Trudy and Ratzkiwatzki marry under false names; Norval is persuaded to keep the truth from Officer Kockenlocker; Emmy and Trudy do not tell their father about Trudy's pregnancy; the sisters set up a plan to get Norval to propose to Trudy before he knows what has really happened; and Norval arranges a fake wedding, an act that is also illegal. The deceptions reach outside the family as well. Mr. Rafferty, for example, is forced—by the hypocrisy of the townspeople—to risk his own status by secretly looking after Trudy during her pregnancy, bringing the Kockenlockers food, and arranging for a doctor.*

It seems that everyone in Morgan's Creek is ready to turn to deceit if it will keep some image of propriety intact, and a number of people will go so far as to break the laws they have sworn to uphold. After Norval is arrested and jailed, the justice of the peace—the person who captured the subject and is pressing the charges—offers to help Officer Kockenlocker out of his predicament by tearing up the Ratzkiwatzki–Kockenlocker marriage certificate. Even though as an officer of the law he knows he cannot condone the destruction of evidence, Kockenlocker goes along with the plan in order to save his daughter's reputation. For the same reason he aids Norval not only in escaping from jail but also in "borrowing" money from the bank.† The most egregious oath breaking takes place in the state capital, however, at the highest level of government. Governor McGinty declares that the facts will be disregarded, new documentation will be created, and state lines will be redrawn if necessary (to make sure that Morgan's Creek is securely within his state's boundaries), all so that no one can question any aspect of the town's miracle.

Ironically, the people of Morgan's Creek have become so concerned with keeping up a proper image that they have lost all semblance of basic

---

*One of the funniest and most cynical examples of deceit appears in the script but did not make it into the film, thanks to the cuts that removed the minister's sermon and the reading of the complete editorial on military marriages. The sermon, which Trudy and Emmy listen to from the pews, was lifted nearly word-for-word from the Bugle's editorial. It seems that in Morgan's Creek even clergymen cannot be trusted to be honest.

†Mr. Johnson, the lawyer, also breaks his oath, or at least the ethics of his profession. When Norval returns to town on Christmas Eve, Johnson more or less tells him to evade the law, especially since everyone has just about forgotten the jail break and bank robbery. Earlier in the film Johnson summed up his position by saying, "Look, I practice law. I am not only willing but anxious to sue anybody, for anything, any time. . . . "

Norval (Eddie Bracken, *sitting*) clings to the hopeful bride Trudy (Betty Hutton) as the justice of the peace (Porter Hall) holds a gun on him.

human kindness. Throughout the film Sturges presents numerous examples of people's looking for the worst in others. When Norval arrives home tattered after his late-night date, his neighbors sneer at his appearance and at what they imagine he has done. When Trudy returns to Morgan's Creek and Officer Kockenlocker tells the town leaders that she isn't feeling well, the bank president snidely replies, "Well, is that so?" And even Norval falls prey to the mistrust: when Trudy asks him for help on the day after their date, he responds, "Where's the party tonight?"

A further irony, of course, is that although the town tries to champion its strong family values by banishing the wrongdoer (Trudy) from its midst, everyone in Morgan's Creek realizes how hypocritical everyone else is. At one point when the sisters are struggling with possible solutions to their problem, Trudy protests to Emmy that, just like a widow, she once had a husband.

> You don't have to convince me, Trudy. I love you. I know you wouldn't do anything wrong, except you take after Papa's side of the family a little.

> It would hurt me just as much as it would you to have you hurt and miserable and ashamed and everything. That's the only reason I want you to get married. You can't tell how a town's going to take things—a town that can produce schnooks like Papa—all suspicious and suspecting the worst in everything.

Such statements are uttered throughout the movie by a variety of characters. Early on, the ever-perceptive Emmy tells Trudy, "Nobody's going to believe [that you're already married]. Nobody believes good unless they have to, if they've got a chance to believe something bad." And when Rafferty tells Trudy about Norval's return to town and his imprisonment, she volunteers to explain to the town leaders the truth about all that has happened.

> What are you talking? How about your reputation? We spend six months planning, fixing everything, building up a secret.... Now you got to build it down overnight? . . . How about your father? Ain't he got enough trouble? How about your sister? How about me? How about. . . Anyway, they wouldn't believe you.

In the end, despite all the supposed concern about morals and upright behavior, about whether young women are sleeping with soldiers out of misguided patriotism, and about whether Norval has corrupted a minor or impersonated an army officer or robbed a bank, all anyone in Morgan's Creek really cares about is the image of the town. As Norval is being led to prison by Officer Kockenlocker, a woman from the neighborhood chides, "That'll teach you to besmirch the name of our fair city." These are almost the same words that Governor McGinty uses later as he fixes the problem: "Well, she's got to be married—that's all there is to it! We can't have a thing like that hanging over our fair state—besmirching our fair name!"

With the birth of Trudy's six babies, it suddenly becomes much more important for the people of Morgan's Creek to accept her and Norval, to go along with the altering of evidence, and to make believe that nothing wrong ever happened, than it is for them to stand by their small-town values. Morgan's Creek gladly welcomes the sextuplets because their presence makes the town *look* like a bastion of familial love, togetherness, and harmony, even if this particular family unit is based on deceit and dubious sexual morals. And even though Trudy and Emmy decry the hypocrisy and narrow-mindedness of the townspeople, in the end they tacitly accept the status quo by going along with the one huge deception in which everyone in Morgan's Creek is happy to participate. Even Norval is willing to go along with it; it seems doubtful that he will ever, for the remainder of his life, do anything to suggest that he is *not* the father of Trudy's children.

But Norval's situation also touches on another favorite Sturges topic: the power of the unstable masses. At the film's end Norval is as baffled by the greatness that has been thrust upon him as he was by the ignominy that plagued him earlier. He has almost nothing to do with the happy ending, nor does Trudy, except by the sheer accident of her motherhood. It is the forces around them both, and specifically the malleable moral compass of the townspeople, that ultimately determine their fate. Sturges had explored this theme before and would delve more deeply into it in the context of small-town life with *Hail the Conquering Hero*.

TWELVE

Hail the Conquering Hero

Written and Directed by Preston Sturges; Photography: John F.
Seitz; Edited by Stuart Gilmore; Art Direction: Hans Dreier and
Haldane Douglas; Set Decoration: Stephen Seymour; Sound:
Wallace Nogle and Walter Oberst; Musical Score: Werner Hey-
mann; Musical Direction: Sigmund Krumgold. Released by Para-
mount, 1944.

Cast: Eddie Bracken (Woodrow Truesmith); Ella Raines (Libby);
William Demarest (Sergeant Julius Heffelfinger); Raymond
Walburn (Everett Noble); Franklin Pangborn (Chairman of the
Welcoming Committee); Elizabeth Patterson (Libby's Aunt);
Georgia Caine (Mrs. Truesmith); Al Bridge (Noble's Campaign
Boss); Freddie Steele (Bugsy); Bill Edwards (Forrest Noble);
Harry Hayden (Doc Bissell); Jimmy Conlin (Judge Dennis); Jimmy
Dundee (Marine Corporal).

Synopsis: In a waterfront bar a group of six Marines—with five days'
leave and only fifteen cents among them—meet up with Woodrow Truesmith when he buys them all beer and whiskey. The son of a great World
War I hero, Woodrow was expected to live up to his late father's accomplishments and had been sent off to war with great fanfare a year earlier. He
was almost immediately discharged from the Marines, however, because
of chronic hay fever. Ashamed and dejected because his enlistment lasted
only a few weeks, Woodrow has not returned home or notified anyone of
his discharge. The Marines feel sorry for him, especially when Sergeant
Heffelfinger finds out that the young man's father was the hero who gave his
own life to save Heffelfinger's unit in World War I. While the Marines try to
hatch a plan to help Woodrow, Bugsy, an orphaned member of the outfit
with an obsessive mother complex, takes it upon himself to phone Woodrow's mother and tell her that her son is coming home the next day, a hero.

The following morning, against Woodrow's better judgment, the
Marines hustle him—dressed in his Marine uniform and wearing some of

their medals—on a train to his hometown of Oakridge. They plan to disembark quietly, take the back roads to the Truesmith home, and deliver
him into the arms of his waiting mother. What they do not count on, however, is the enormous crowd that turns out at the station. Woodrow is
greeted with a hero's welcome, complete with bands, parades, and a
wreath-placing ceremony at the town's monument to General Zabriski. In
all the excitement Mayor Noble's reelection placards get lost in the shuffle,
and Woodrow's girlfriend, Libby, does not have a chance to tell the returning hero that she is now engaged to Forrest Noble, the mayor's son. When
he finally does get home, Woodrow quickly takes off his uniform just before the entire entourage heads off to church. Already out of his head with
worry over the fraud he is perpetrating, Woodrow is further alarmed when
the minister burns the mortgage on Mrs. Truesmith's house, announcing
that the townspeople have paid it off to show their appreciation for her
son's heroism. To make matters worse, Woodrow learns on leaving church
that Oakridge intends to erect a joint statue to him and his father—the two
local heroes. Fearful of what might happen when the truth comes out,
Woodrow seeks the advice of Sergeant Heffelfinger, who simply says that
in a few days everyone will forget all about it.

But events swirl around Woodrow faster than he can deal with them.
He is barely home from the church service when Judge Dennis, Doc
Bissell, and other town leaders come calling and ask him to run for mayor
against Everett Noble. Although Woodrow tries to refuse, the men have
obviously made up their minds; outside the Truesmith house a huge crowd
already waits to hail their new candidate. Forced to speak to the people,
Woodrow once again tries to turn down the honor, but the crowd will not
have it. They are quickly whipped into a frenzy, especially when Sergeant
Heffelfinger tells them detailed—but fictitious—stories of Woodrow's
wartime exploits.

Meanwhile, at his campaign headquarters the mayor is working with
Forrest on his acceptance speech for the upcoming election. Libby arrives
at the office, followed by Mrs. Noble and the mayor's campaign boss, all
bringing the news that Woodrow will be running for mayor. A fight ensues
over Libby's loyalty to the Nobles, and Libby leaves saying that she will
never work as Everett's secretary again. When Forrest chases after her to
smooth things over, he not only finds out that she has not told Woodrow
about her engagement yet, but he also begins to suspect that she may still
be in love with her old boyfriend.

That evening, the rally outside Woodrow's house is bigger and louder
than before. Led by Sergeant Heffelfinger, the Marines regale the crowd
with increasingly fantastic tales of Woodrow's bravery, to which the people
respond by cheering and singing the newly written "We Want Woodrow"
theme song. As Woodrow sits in the kitchen, drinking cooking wine and

contemplating his inevitable downfall, Libby arrives and finally breaks the news about her impending marriage. Though he is still in love with her, Woodrow is thrilled that she will be spared the horrible fate that awaits him when the townspeople learn the truth. To get some privacy, the pair escape the house and take a long walk while Woodrow tries to explain to Libby that he is not really a hero. Libby is skeptical and asks Woodrow if he is feeling well, and when Heffelfinger and the other Marines arrive to take Woodrow home they reassure her that he is just overcome by the excitement of the day. But not everyone is so easily convinced of Woodrow's glory: at Noble headquarters, the campaign boss, wondering what the real story with Woodrow is, decides to contact the Marine base at San Diego for the facts of Woodrow's military record.

Woodrow grows more and more panicky and tries to run away from the house that night, but the Marines standing guard outside his bedroom do not let him. When he comes down to breakfast the next morning with a newfound zeal for his status as a hero, Sergeant Heffelfinger and the other Marines are therefore suspicious, especially when Woodrow gets a phone call from the Marine base in San Diego telling him to report for service again immediately. By the time the Marines finally figure out that one of their unit had slipped away to make the fake call, Woodrow has told Judge Dennis and Doc Bissell that he will be leaving that day. He agrees to participate in the parade and the rally for his candidacy, though, as a last gesture to the town. As the parade moves through the streets of Oakridge, Noble and his campaign boss get the telegram they have been waiting for with the information on Woodrow's medical discharge. Heading to the town hall—the site of the Woodrow rally—they take seats in the front of the auditorium to wait for the right moment to drop their bombshell.

But Woodrow has a surprise of his own. As the audience listens in shock, he admits that he intended to announce his reenlistment with the Marines but that he cannot do that to the fine people he has known all his life. He then confesses the whole story: how he was discharged from the Marines for hay fever, how he returned under the false pretense of being a hero, how he did it all because he thought he was saving his mother from disgrace, and how he is not fit to be his father's son. The only element he leaves out is the Marines' involvement in the plot; he says that he tricked Sergeant Heffelfinger and the other men into believing the hero story as well. After Woodrow, his mother, and five of the Marines leave the town hall, Sergeant Heffelfinger insists that everyone else stay and hear the *whole* truth.

As Woodrow packs to leave town, Libby arrives and says that she's broken off her engagement to Forrest and will follow Woodrow wherever he goes. Escorted by the five marines, they hurry off to the station to catch the next train out of town. But before they can make their getaway, all the townspeople come marching down the street and into the train station, with Sergeant Heffelfinger in the lead. Telling Woodrow that they now know the complete story, Judge Dennis, Doc Bissell, and the others declare that any man who would jeopardize his own reputation and future to save his mother humiliation is the kind of man they want for mayor. With the crowd cheering in approval, the six Marines get on the departing train, salute Oakridge's conquering hero, and ride off into the distance to the accompaniment of the Marines Hymn.

•

In discussions of Preston Sturges's films, *Hail the Conquering Hero* is often spoken of as a companion piece to *The Miracle of Morgan's Creek*. The movies, shot one right after the other, were both released in 1944 and star Eddie Bracken in similar nebbish-type roles. But the connections between the two films also go much deeper, into the basic setting that Sturges chose and the themes that he explores. Both films deal with life in a small town and the values of the townspeople, particularly in regard to families, and both treat soldiers less as idealized heroes than as characters who disrupt the fine balance of the town's strict morality. In addition, in both movies the people respond to a flagrant violation of their moral standards by doing a complete about-face and making a paragon of the offender. The strict rules and moral codes that these characters claim to abide by are absolutely sacred—at least until it is in everyone's best interest for them to be pliable.

The thematic link between the two films is so strong that it is possible to see *Hail the Conquering Hero* as something of a continuation of *The Miracle of Morgan's Creek*. In the first half (*Morgan's Creek*), the Norval/Woodrow character tries to live up to external standards (the heroic ideal of the soldier), fails miserably, and finally, through no effort of his own, has greatness "thrust upon him." In the second half (*Conquering Hero*), the setup condenses the action of *Morgan's Creek*—having lost his attempt to achieve military glory Norval/Woodrow has greatness bestowed on him by Sergeant Heffelfinger and the other Marines—before the movie takes off in its own direction. Woodrow's return to his hometown extends the story of the false hero: how he struggles with the praise and honor that have been heaped on him for no genuine reason and how he finally admits his deception, only to garner even greater acclaim.

But as similar as the themes are, there are subtle differences in the way in which Sturges approaches them. In *Hail the Conquering Hero* he focuses not on dysfunctional family relationships but rather on an obsession with the institution of motherhood. In addition, the pervasive mistrust and desire to see the worst in others that exist in Morgan's Creek would never allow the unbridled worship of heroism that thrives in Oakridge. The people of Morgan's Creek are more vindictive and small-minded; those of Oakridge are simply well-meaning dullards whose foolish ideas come from an unwillingness to see things as they really are instead of from inherent nastiness. Both towns are the targets of Sturges's satire: Morgan's Creek for its sanctimonious and hypocritical moral attitude, and Oakridge for its eternal confidence in simple virtues such as heroism and motherhood.

The Sanctity of Motherhood

Mothers and themes of motherhood occur frequently in Preston Sturges's films. Some instances are central to the story (the good mother/ bad mother examples in *Remember the Night*), some are rather lurid (the sexual relationship between Tom Garner, Jr., and his stepmother in *The Power and the Glory*), and some are merely isolated jokes (the sign in a flophouse in *Sullivan's Travels* that reads, "Have you written home to mother?"). But in *Hail the Conquering Hero*, Sturges takes the American worship of motherhood to its logical extreme, creating a set of characters so obsessed with respecting mom that every moral question takes a backseat to this obsession. Virtually everything that happens to Woodrow and the town of Oakridge can be traced back to some action taken on behalf of Mrs. Truesmith, beginning, of course, with Bugsy, the Marine with the mother complex.

As Sergeant Heffelfinger explains early in the film, Bugsy is from a home for orphans and "never had any mother." After he got "a little shot up" in combat, his sorrow at not having a mother of his own turned into a perpetual concern with seeing that all mothers are treated well. Bugsy's fixation so dominates him that virtually anything brings the subject to his mind. When Sergeant Heffelfinger, in thanks for the beers that Woodrow bought for the Marines, offers to give their new friend General Yamatoho's tooth, Bugsy chimes in, "You could send it to your mother . . . if you got one." The fact that the tooth is a fake is apparently unimportant; it is the gesture alone that Bugsy sees as proper and respectful.

But once Bugsy hears what Woodrow has done to his mother—stringing her along with the story that he is still in uniform a year after his discharge—he immediately turns against the young man.

> *Bugsy*: You mean you ain't been home!?
> *Woodrow*: I wrote I was leaving for overseas.
> *Bugsy*: You shouldn't do that to your mother.
> *Woodrow*: I wrote a couple of letters to say I was all right, and asked a kid to mail them from overseas.
> *Bugsy*: Suppose he didn't get a chance to mail them! . . . That's a terrible thing to do to your mother. You ought to be ashamed of yourself.

As the sergeant and the other Marines get to know Woodrow, Bugsy borrows fifty cents from him and slips off to the phone booth to call Mrs. Truesmith with the message that her son is returning home from Guadalcanal, honorably discharged after being wounded. His explanation for the phone call is that now "she won't have to worry no more." What is especially important about Bugsy's move is that it is the first in a series of actions that will build on Woodrow's initial lie rather than reveal the truth. If Bugsy's primary interest were to put Mrs. Truesmith's mind at rest, he could just as easily have told her the real reason Woodrow is coming home — that he was discharged for medical problems. Instead Bugsy perpetuates Woodrow's deception — that he has remained in the Marines and has seen action overseas — and then puts a layer of fraud on top by claiming that Woodrow was discharged because he was wounded in combat. From this point on, Sergeant Heffelfinger and the Marines continue to compound the ruse, adding layer after layer of lies, until Woodrow's original ploy seems decidedly minor in comparison. And all of it, of course, is done in the name of protecting Mrs. Truesmith.

As the film progresses, Bugsy continues to act as the self-appointed guardian of Woodrow's mother and her feelings. When Woodrow balks at arriving in town wearing the Marine uniform with its counterfeit medals, Bugsy tells him, "You gotta think of your mother." He is always ready to berate Woodrow whenever he thinks that Woodrow shows callous disregard for his mother — particularly after Bugsy meets Mrs. Truesmith and finds in her the mother he never had. The surrogate mother–son relationship begins on the train to Oakridge, with Bugsy asking Woodrow sentimental questions such as "Is your Ma a good cook?" and "Does your Ma put up preserves?" Once he meets Mrs. Truesmith he tells her, "You can sure put me on your flag. I sure ain't got anybody else." In addition, the two characters are often linked with shots that show them looking at each other, standing near one another, or smiling at something the other one says.

So blinded is he in his devotion to Mrs. Truesmith that Bugsy never even considers the fact that anyone else might be hurt by the Marines' deception. When the town leaders are making political speeches outside the Truesmith house, Bugsy goes into the kitchen, where Woodrow is drinking the only alcohol he can get his hands on — cooking wine.

> *Bugsy*: Your Ma said not to drink any more of that stuff.
> *Woodrow*: Say, am I four years old or something?
> *Bugsy*: You behave yourself and do like your Ma tells you. You made her enough trouble.
> *Woodrow*: I made *her* trouble!? . . . You made *me* trouble. You and your mother complex!!
> *Bugsy*: Listen, Knucklehead, you take one more crack at your mother and I'll . . .

Woodrow Truesmith (Eddie Bracken, *center*) has to be forcibly persuaded to go along with the Marines' plan to bring him home as a conquering hero.

> [A few seconds later Mrs. Truesmith comes bustling into the room, hugging and kissing Woodrow as she enters, telling him how proud she is of him, and kissing him again as she leaves.]
> *Bugsy:* You see that look in her eyes?
> *Woodrow:* Yes, I saw it.
> *Bugsy:* That's what we're working for, see?

But Sturges does not confine his themes of motherhood to Bugsy. Songs that refer to mothers are heard throughout the movie, beginning in the first scene in the waterfront bar. After a band number that features a provocative dance by an attractive female singer, the mood changes drastically (and comically) as she launches into "Home to the Arms of Mother," complete with waiters chiming in on the chorus. Later, as Woodrow and the Marines arrive in Oakridge, the band prepares to play that very song, and during his welcoming address Mayor Noble solemnly quotes the title of the song as though on its own it speaks volumes. Later, at the church service honoring Woodrow, the hymn that everyone sings is "Home at Last," which also offers platitudes about motherhood and a mother's love.

The speech given by Dr. Upperman, the minister, during the service provides a good example of the idealized notion of motherhood that pervades Oakridge. Leading up to the news that the town has bought up Mrs. Truesmith's mortgage, the minister intones:

> Homecoming. What a beautiful word. Home to the arms of his mother, the widow of yet another hero, cut down in the bloom of young manhood.
>
> The arms of a mother who struggled through poverty and privation to raise her son rightly and courageously, that he might follow in the honorable footsteps of his father.
>
> The years were hard, not always was there work, and the winds of reality blew coldly against this frail woman protecting her infant son.
>
> She had one possession . . . her home, the little white house at the end of Oak Street. The home of heroes.
>
> She clung to it tenaciously but one day she reached the end of her rope and a mortgage was her only solution. Mortgages have a way of growing, like beautiful trees. This one increased, then increased again and still again till the widow owned very little of the house she loved so well. . .

As the entire congregation is moved to tears, Woodrow grows more and more appalled as the consequences of his well-meaning deception begin to dawn on him. He tries to protest, but the force of the paean to motherhood is just too powerful to overcome.

Even the gruff Sergeant Heffelfinger is swept up in the town's attachment to motherhood. Following the church service, when Woodrow expresses his concern to Heffelfinger about how the whole situation has escalated, the sergeant tries to convince him to go along.

> *Woodrow*: I was gonna hide in the Gents Room until. . .
> *Sergeant*: A Marine never hides in the Gents Room. That's what *semper fidelis* means: it means face the music.
> *Woodrow*: Yes, well, it doesn't happen to mean that at all. It means "Always Faithful."
> *Sergeant*: That's right. Faithful to your mother. . .
> *Woodrow*: It doesn't mean faithful to your mother. . .
> *Sergeant*: What's the matter with you? You're home, your mother is happy . . . did you see that look in her eyes? . . . I tell you, it'll all blow over. Everything is perfect, except for a couple of details.

Looking out for the feelings of Mom is an almost foolproof way of winning favor in Oakridge, as Woodrow himself soon finds out. When he is drafted to run for mayor, his random comment to the crowd—"I love my mother"—wins him thunderous applause and cheers. Like an out-of-control steamroller that runs over everything in its path, the town's obsession with motherhood in general and Mrs. Truesmith in particular overrides any other considerations.

That obsession reaches its peak with the climactic speech that Woodrow

delivers at the town hall. Coming clean for the first time about his deceptions, he also makes his motivation perfectly clear:

> [I stand before you] a coward because I postponed until now what I
> should have told you a year ago when I was discharged from the Marine
> Corps for medical unfitness ... a coward because I didn't want my
> mother to know. Well, it wasn't to save *her*; it was to save *me*....
>   I'm going to pack my things now so this will probably be my last chance
> to say good-bye to you. I know my mother will give you back the mort-
> gage, and I hope you won't hold it against her that her son didn't quite
> come through.

In very blunt terms Woodrow admits that he has lied to the people of Oakridge about his military record, disingenuously accepted their accolades,
and, worst of all for a town of mother worshipers, deceived his mother for
more than a year and embarrassed her on his return. The townspeople
would seem justified in turning their backs on Woodrow at the very least,
if not banishing him from their midst entirely. It is certainly what he ex-
pects and feels that he deserves after his speech at the hall.

     But Woodrow does not count on the one thing that he probably thinks
has gotten him into the most trouble: his attempt to spare his mother pain.
As Doc Bissell explains to Woodrow before he can leave town, "If to act
out a little lie to save one's mother humiliation [is] a fault ... in other
words, if tenderness toward and consideration of one's mother [is] a fault,
it [is] a fault any man might be proud of." It does not really matter what
Woodrow did, but because he did it *in what he thought was his mother's best
interest* he once again reaps praise and glory.

You Can Fool Some of the People All of the Time

     What ultimately saves Woodrow from embarrassment and banish-
ment from town is Oakridge's undying devotion to the ideal of motherhood and the townspeople's readiness to bend their perception of his
actions. They found it easy to think he was a valiant soldier because his
father was one; when they learn that he has been lying all along about his
military prowess, they still consider him a hero for taking such steps to protect his mom. This willingness of people to see what they want to see—or
perhaps need to see—in a situation is something that applies to more than
just the town's devotion to motherhood. The affliction pervades the entire
population of Oakridge and manifests itself in a variety of ways.

     The best illustration can be found in the town's mayor, Everett No-
ble. When he is working on his premature acceptance speech with his son
the two get into an argument about the proper use of words. "I am not running on a platform of correct grammar," Noble bellows. "I even let my

grammar slop over a little sometimes. . . . *Purposely.* . . . It gives that homey quality." Noble also repeatedly refers to himself as a civic leader who does not really want to be mayor but who simply responds to the demands of the people. "Heaven knows I did not seek this distinction, but since you force it upon me, what alternative have I...," he dictates for use in his speech. Later, when the campaign boss tells him that it is human nature for everyone to want to be mayor, Noble responds, "Everybody but me! With me it's just civic pride!" As transparent as Noble and his claims are, the fact is that the entire town has elected him time and time again over the bland but obviously genuine Doc Bissell. They choose to believe Noble's shallow assertions about his selfless commitment to Oakridge, and as Woodrow points out in his speech at town hall, only when a bigger phony comes along are the people willing to throw Noble out of office.

Woodrow too is susceptible to this kind of self-deception. In the film's first sequence, when he meets Heffelfinger and his unit in the bar, Woodrow recites the entire list of battles in which the Marines have participated. From the way in which Eddie Bracken plays the scene—solemnly intoning the names of campaigns while his eyes gaze toward heaven—and the way in which Sturges sets up the shot—slowly moving the camera in toward Bracken during his heartfelt litany—it is clear that Woodrow has a severe case of Marine worship. Not only could no actual group of men ever live up to Woodrow's idealized notions, but the Marines we come to know in Heffelfinger's unit are a far cry from any military ideal. They've gambled away all their money and would have nothing to eat and nowhere to go if not for Woodrow's generosity. When Woodrow learns firsthand just what the Marines are capable of doing—getting him into an awful lot of trouble—he still does not seem to understand that it is the foolishness of the townspeople, and not the actions of his friends, that has saved the day for him.*

Like Woodrow, the rest of the people of Oakridge choose to see what they want to in a situation, even if all evidence points to the contrary. A good example is the scene inside the Truesmith house as Judge Dennis, Doc Bissell, and the other town leaders tell Woodrow that he is being drafted to run for mayor. With no concrete proof of Woodrow's accomplishments other than the borrowed medals he was wearing when he returned, these men have convinced themselves that he is the person to turn the town around. "We need an honest man for mayor," Judge Dennis exclaims, "an honest man who will wake us up and tell us the truth about something he knows all about." Exactly what it is that Woodrow knows all about is unclear. Because he arrived wearing medals, however, it must

---

* *"I knew the Marines could do almost anything," an awestruck Woodrow says as his friends are leaving town, "but I never knew they could do anything like this."*

When the town leaders come to the Truesmith house, Woodrow (Eddie Bracken,
*front and center***) cannot imagine that they want anything but to run him out**
of Oakridge. What they really plan, though, is to ask him to run for mayor.

be something very important, for as Doc Bissell says, "If all good men wore
medals it wouldn't be so hard to tell the good from the bad."

Once Woodrow is introduced to the crowd gathered outside the house
the scene becomes even more absurd. Judge Dennis presents the new candidate by proclaiming, "I need say no more of the character of this young
man than that HE REFUSED TO WEAR HIS MEDALS!" The people
greet this line with wild cheers and applause, but as Woodrow begins to
speak it becomes apparent that they will respond in the same way to
anything he says. "Ladies and gentlemen . . . I . . . ah . . . wish I was dead,"
he begins, and the entire gathering laughs heartily. "You're making a big
mistake," Woodrow continues, which only elicits a greater roar. "I . . . ah
. . . love my mother very much," he stammers, and receives the greatest
ovation yet, topped only by the cheers that follow his screaming, "I really
don't deserve it!!"

The remainder of Woodrow's address consists primarily of half-
hearted protests that are ignored by the enthusiastic crowd. Still, everyone
sees him as a political genius. "He has a natural flair for politics," Judge
Dennis comments during the talk, which Dr. Upperman terms "as good

a political speech as I have heard since Bryan and the Crown of Thorns."
Even Mrs. Noble concurs, telling her husband, the master of pompous
oratory, "That boy made the loveliest speech." The specifics of what
Woodrow actually said—which do not amount to anything at all—are
completely irrelevant. Nothing he can say will dissuade the citizens of
Oakridge from seeing him as a hero.

It is that fact, of course, that ultimately saves Woodrow. "Politics is
a very peculiar thing," Doc Bissell tells him. "If they want you, they want
you. They don't need reasons anymore. They find their own reasons." And
Oakridge wants Woodrow Truesmith. He is their hero, partially because
he seems to fit in with the town's mother complex and partially because
they *need* to have a hero. The people of Oakridge worship heroes just as
they worship motherhood, and in both cases it is the ideal, not the reality,
that is most important.

Heroes and Their Deeds

In all the confusion that accompanies Woodrow's homecoming there
are only two people who seem to have any sense of perspective about what
is going on. The first is Mayor Noble, who is certainly not about to join
in the celebration for his political opponent and his son's romantic rival.
Even though he makes a point of saying that he believes that Woodrow *is*
a hero, he is the only resident of Oakridge who glimpses the reasons behind
the town's outpouring of emotion. As he explains to his campaign boss:

> I mean to say I have nothing against the boy personally. A hero is a fine
> thing . . . in its place. . . . I don't wish this young man anything but suc-
> cess in what he can do best. But what *can* he do best!? . . . That is our
> problem. I speak, not as your candidate for mayor, but as the most hum-
> ble voter. . . . I mean to say this problem is not local—it is national. In a
> few years, if this war goes on, heaven forbid, you won't be able to swing
> a cat without knocking down a couple of heroes. Now, are we to be
> governed by young men, *very* young men, however well-meaning and
> patriotic they may be, whose principal talent consists of hopping in and
> out of . . . foxholes and killing *hundreds* of enemies with one swoop of the
> sword, or are we going to be governed by respectable civic leaders of
> mature age who do not seek the appointment but accept it as a civic duty?

As much as Noble may be looking out for his own political future, he
also comes very close to pegging the mindset of his fellow citizens. Their
enchantment with the *idea* of a hero prevails over any objective assessment
of the person or the person's accomplishments. Noble correctly sees the
danger of having hundreds of heroes returning to Woodrow-like recep-
tions all across the country; the irony is that he fails to recognize that the

serious scrutiny he advocates for Woodrow would spell political doom for his own brand of hypocrisy as well.

The second person who perceives the reasons for Woodrow's acclaim is the man who orchestrates the entire affair, Sergeant Heffelfinger. Continually egging the crowds on and raising the stakes as Woodrow watches, he has obviously learned a thing or two about the allure of heroism over the years. "Look," he tells Woodrow, "I didn't expect this anymore than you did, but now that it's happened, let it happen. They want heroes? We got six of 'em ... all right, we throw in a seventh for good luck. Who's counting?"

To illustrate his point that people merely want to revel in the glory of heroism, not in the details, Sturges has Heffelfinger cite two examples for the disbelieving Woodrow. When the group is on the train heading for Oakridge, Woodrow at first refuses to wear the medal that the sergeant has pinned to his chest.

> What are you talking about? I don't even remember what I got it for. [He then points to a ribbon on the uniform of one of the other Marines.] You know what he got this for? Some Japs was roasting a pig across the stream and the breeze was blowing it all right over in his kisser. So he went over and got it. . . . Just a hog.

Later, when Woodrow again expresses concern over what might happen when people find out that he is not really a hero, Heffelfinger replies, "I been a hero, you could call it that, for twenty-five years and does anybody ever ask me what I *done*? If they did I could hardly tell them, I've told it so different, so many times." Because he understands what people *want* to hear and realizes that they *want* to share in some heroic glory, Sergeant Heffelfinger can turn the entire situation around following Woodrow's address at the town hall. The specifics of the heroism are not important; when Heffelfinger launches into his "what that kid just done took *real* courage" speech, he is quickly able to rally the citizens behind Woodrow, convincing them that their local boy is an even bigger hero than they had previously thought.

Sturges's most cynical comments on heroism appear not in Heffelfinger's or Noble's statements, however, but in references to General Zabriski. A statue of the general on horseback stands in the park, and as is the case with every local celebration, Woodrow's welcome-home festivities include a wreath-placing ceremony at the site. The scene at the statue is not included in the film, but in dialogue that appears in the script Sergeant Heffelfinger asks Libby's aunt just what General Zabriski did to merit such esteem. "Oh, nobody can remember," she replies. "But I think it was a battle or something."*

---

*The scene appears in the screenplay as published in Brian Henderson, ed., Five Screenplays by Preston Sturges.

What does appear in the film are two direct mentions of General Zabriski. Following the church service, the town leaders approach Woodrow
to discuss where to place the statue that they want to erect in his honor.
"Naturally General Zabriski has the choice spot, but then he's been there
so long," the chairman of the welcoming committee says, making it clear
that the general holds a sacred place in their hearts. Later that day, however, as Woodrow and the sergeant discuss his predicament, the truth
about the general comes out.

> *Sergeant*: By Tuesday [everything will] be forgotten.
> *Woodrow*: I hope you're right.
> *Sergeant*: I know I'm right. You take General Zabliski for instance...
> *Woodrow*: Zabriski.
> *Sergeant*: All right, where did *he* tend bar?
> *Woodrow*: That's a different case entirely. The town bought him from an
> ironworks that was going out of business. He just happened to be a
> bargain.
> *Sergeant*: Well, you're the only guy that knows it. All everybody else
> knows is he's a *hero*. He's got a statue in the park and the birds sit
> on it.

Whether or not Woodrow is really the only person in town who knows
about General Zabriski is unimportant. What matters is that the people of
Oakridge have no idea *what* the general did, yet they have no qualms about
honoring him as a true hero. The association with heroism is what matters,
not the details, and if the reality of the situation does not quite fit the heroic
mold there is always a little room for altering the perspective.

In *Hail the Conquering Hero*, Preston Sturges not only shows us how
modern-day heroes are created but also provides a clue as to what happens
to them after they have been invented. It is fairly easy to look into the
future of Oakridge and predict what will happen to the town and its hero.
Like General Zabriski, Woodrow Truesmith will probably remain a fixture
in the hearts of Oakridge citizens for the rest of his life, even if everyone
quickly forgets exactly what he did to garner his initial acclaim. He will be
elected mayor over and over again, just as Everett Noble was before him,
and he may even have a statue raised to him. The people will be proud to
think of Woodrow as someone very special, rather than as the conquering
hero who in fact conquered nothing at all.

THIRTEEN

The Sin of Harold Diddlebock

Written and Directed by Preston Sturges; Photography: Robert Pittack; Special Effects: John Fulton; Production Manager: Cliff Broughton; Technical Director: Curtis Courant; Edited by Thomas Neff; Art Direction: Robert Usher; Art Decoration: Victor A. Gangelin; Sound: Fred Lau; Music: Werner R. Heymann. Released by United Artists, 1947.

Cast: Harold Lloyd (Harold Diddlebock); Jimmy Conlin (Wormy); Raymond Walburn (E. J. Waggleberry); Frances Ramsden (Miss Otis); Rudy Vallee (Mr. Sargent); Edgar Kennedy (Bartender); Arline Judge (Manicurist); Franklin Pangborn (Formfit Franklin); Lionel Stander (Max); Margaret Hamilton (Flora, Harold's Sister); Jack Norton (James Smoke); Robert Dudley (Banker); Robert Greig (Coachman); Al Bridge (Circus Owner); Torben Meyer (Barber).

Synopsis: During a football game between Tate and Union State, Tate water boy Harold Diddlebock sits on the bench, as frustrated as the crowd at his team's inability to overcome its three-point deficit. As the clock winds down and more and more Tate players are taken from the field on stretchers, the coach has no choice but to put his water boy in the game. Harold's enthusiastic attempts to help his team initially meet with little success, but his ingenuity and determination finally pay off. On the last play of the game he chases a runner all the way downfield, tackles him and forces a fumble, then picks up the ball and runs nearly 100 yards back upfield to score the winning touchdown. The crowd goes wild, and one of the spectators—E. J. Waggleberry—is so excited that he follows Harold

146

into the locker room to offer the hero a job when he graduates from college.*

Remembering Waggleberry's pledge, Harold goes to the advertising firm's office as soon as he receives his diploma. Although Waggleberry seems to have little or no recollection of Harold, he keeps his promise and gives him a job—at the bottom of the company ladder in the bookkeeping department. Harold happily settles into his nook, but as the film moves ahead in time we see that he is still in the same place twenty-two years later, doing the same job but with none of the ambition he once had. One Tuesday morning Waggleberry fires Harold, criticizing him for his lack of thought and energy, which makes him a bottleneck in the company and a bad example to the younger employees. With a Swiss watch and nearly $3000 in company savings in his pocket, Harold cleans out his desk and prepares to leave the office for good. Before going he says good-bye to Miss Otis, the youngest of seven sisters who have worked at the firm over the years—every one of whom Harold has been in love with. Although he bought an engagement ring years ago, he explains to Miss Otis, circumstances always kept him from proposing to any of her sisters. Now he gives the ring to her, telling her that when she finds a man worthy of marrying they will not have to wait to save up money for a ring.

Out of a job and wandering through town, Harold meets Wormy, an unsuccessful horseplayer who hits him up for a loan. When Wormy hears Harold's troubles he claims to know the cure and takes his new friend to a bar for his first-ever drink. Seizing a golden opportunity, the bartender combines a staggering number of liquors to create an entirely new cocktail for the occasion—the Diddlebock. At first the drink does not seem to have too much effect, but before long Harold is braying like an animal and, in a drunken frenzy, insisting on being taken to a barber and a tailor for a complete overhaul of his image. While he is being fitted for an outrageously loud plaid suit, Max the bookie arrives in the shop to take bets on an upcoming race. Against Wormy's best advice, Harold puts $1000 on a thirty-to-one shot simply because the horse has the same name as his aunt. When the horse wins, Harold and Wormy embark on a nonstop round of drinking, dancing, gambling, and bestowing gifts on pretty girls.

When Harold finally wakes up on his living-room couch, it's Thursday morning and his stern-faced sister is hovering over him. He discovers that he has only a vague recollection of all the partying, no money in his

---

The entire football sequence is taken from Harold Lloyd's 1925 silent film The Freshman. Sturges trimmed slightly the footage that made up that movie's climactic game and added insert shots of Raymond Walburn as E. J. Waggleberry, apparently watching from the stands, as well as crowd noises and sound effects. Sturges's original material begins as Harold is carried into the locker room on the shoulders of his teammates, and Waggleberry follows with the offer of a job.

pockets, and no memory of the entire day of Wednesday. Things begin to come back to him somewhat when he gets dressed and goes outside, where he finds a hansom cab, horse, and driver that he apparently purchased in the preceding days. When Wormy shows up, Harold learns that in the midst of all the revelry he also acquired a circus—one that is in great debt, with hundreds of hungry animals waiting to be fed and scores of performers wanting to be paid. Since his gambling winnings are completely gone and he has no way of supporting the circus, Harold immediately tries to unload it. First he attempts to convince the previous owner to take the circus back, but the man refuses, saying he tried for too long to sell it. Then Harold and Wormy go to a home for hungry cats to get some food for the animals, only to be kicked out when they request several tons of meat. Without an easy answer to the problem, Harold is forced to do something that he has not done in years: think.

The plan that Harold devises is simple enough: he will find a banker who grew up in the Wisconsin town that is the winter home of the Ringling Brothers Circus. Such a person inevitably would have loved circuses as a child, and as a rich banker now would have both the means and the desire to own a circus. But when Harold and Wormy find such a person, they discover that someone has gotten to him first: he already owns a circus, which he is trying to get rid of, too. So Harold refines his idea, reasoning that as the most hated men in the country, bankers need to improve their image; what could be better than buying a circus and allowing children to be admitted free of charge? But merely asking for appointments with important bankers does not work, and Harold has to resort to some more creative thinking to get in the door. Wearing his wild plaid suit and led by Jackie the lion on a leash, he barges into the offices of the biggest bankers in New York. With Wormy right behind him plying the executives with Diddlebock cocktails, Harold explains his idea for improving the bankers' images. Fearful of doing anything but listening to the lunatic with his lion, the bankers all quietly pay attention, and everything goes smoothly until Jackie decides to step out an open window and onto the ledge of the building. Before long, Harold, Wormy, and Jackie are all dangling off the ledge and nearly drop to their deaths, but Jackie manages to guide them to safety. When they come down the trio are arrested with enormous fanfare—just as Harold was hoping. Locked safely in a jail cell, they wait for the bankers to arrive to bid against each other for the circus.

Much to Harold's distress, however, no one comes to the prison except Miss Otis, who bails them out. Puzzled about how his plan could have failed, Harold finally realizes that he has done nothing wrong at all—the newspapers simply gave the incorrect address of the jail. Racing to the published location they find just what Harold expected—sheer chaos as every banker in town wants a shot at buying Harold's circus. Fortified with a

Diddlebock cocktail, Harold watches as the bids go higher and higher, and just as Ringling Brothers promises to top any offer he passes out in the center of the confusion. When he comes to in his hansom cab Miss Otis tells him that not only did he receive $175,000 for his circus, but also, in recognition of his brilliant promotional scheme, E. J. Waggleberry has made him a partner in the advertising firm. Harold even discovers what he did on Wednesday—he finally made his way into the Otis family by marrying the youngest sister.

•

It would be hard to think of a more appropriate person around whom Preston Sturges would want to write a film than Harold Lloyd. Lloyd's amazing popularity in the silent years, with a string of box-office successes that ran two a year in the early and mid–1920s, was similar to that of Sturges in the early 1940s. Both men knew exactly what they wanted their films to look like and took complete creative control of each production.

Similar careers were not all that Sturges and Lloyd had in common, though. Sturges would have been attracted to Lloyd's bespectacled, average-looking character, who had become intertwined with the American Dream. Unlike the more universal characters of Chaplin and Keaton, Lloyd's character was a quintessentially American persona, an ambitious but generally naïve go-getter who completely bought into the notion that hard work equals success and that success equals money. Like the Horatio Alger novels of the late nineteenth and early twentieth centuries, Lloyd's films worked as clever pieces of American propaganda, convincing audiences of the 1920s that working hard, playing by the rules, believing in yourself, and never giving up really did work. As long as prosperity reigned, this unbridled faith in capitalism and the American Dream seemed completely justified, but once the stock market crashed and the Depression hit, the Lloyd character must have looked like a gullible fool taken in by a system that had clearly failed.

Although Lloyd retired from the screen in 1938, a victim of ever-diminishing audiences, the spirit of his character lived on—in a somewhat altered fashion—in the films of Preston Sturges. As seen through the director's far more cynical eyes, the hopeful go-getter became Jimmy Mac-Donald of *Christmas in July*, who succeeds by accident and in spite of his dumb ideas, or Tom Jeffers in *The Palm Beach Story*, whose plan for a suspended airport goes nowhere until his wife charms a wealthy tycoon. Sturges's own characters may have shared with Lloyd's the same dedication, ambition, and even belief in the system, and as in Lloyd's films they usually did succeed—but never because the system worked or because they played by the rules. Sheer luck, the foolishness of others, even dishonesty was more likely responsible.

It would have seemed entirely natural for Sturges, a writer and director who concentrated on themes of achievement and success in general,
to follow up on Lloyd's character twenty years later. That Sturges chose
to do so immediately after leaving Paramount, however, may tell us
something more about how Sturges viewed his *own* success. Despite the
critical acclaim he received for the films that he directed at his former
studio, Sturges felt strongly that he was not appreciated by the executives
who ran Paramount.

He had fought with them first over the making of *The Great Moment*,
then over its editing, and later engaged in a similar dispute over *Hail the
Conquering Hero*. When he left the studio to form an independent production company with Howard Hughes, *Harold Diddlebock* was the first film
he planned to direct. It is not difficult to imagine that the film's theme—a
creative and enthusiastic man beaten down by a stifling corporation—said
something very real to Sturges about his recent Hollywood experience.
Like Harold, cast out of the safety of the company and forced to think for
himself, Sturges was also venturing into untested waters—in his case, independent film production. And the film's ending, in which the former
employer acknowledges the outcast's brilliance by asking him back as a
partner, could easily be read as Sturges's hope for triumph and vindication
after he left Paramount.*

Whether Sturges felt a personal connection to *The Sin of Harold Diddlebock* is not as important as the fact that the film demonstrates the phoni-
ness of the American work ethic—a favorite Sturges theme. From the start
of the movie Sturges pits an unconventional, inspired approach to getting
ahead against the traditional by-the-rules method. For Sturges, the latter
approach includes following the dictum that hard work and years of toil
will equal success, but as so many of his characters invariably find out,
hard work has little to do with achievement.

Although Harold Lloyd's silent films were all about playing by the
rules and making it, Sturges was nevertheless able to find a Lloyd film that
supported his ideas. In the opening sequence from *The Freshman*, the Tate
squad is in real danger of losing as long as it follows a conventional game
plan. The coach refrains from putting the water boy in, even though he is
eager to play, because water boys are supposed to sit on the sidelines.
When the coach finally does give in to Harold's pleas the team turns itself
around.

---

*Even the silent football game lifted from another movie fits the pattern. In the original film,
Lloyd plays a water boy who is told he is actually on the team although no one but him has
any confidence in his abilities. But when he finally is given the chance he wins the game for his
school. It was much the same for Sturges at Paramount, where he toiled as a screenwriter for
years, all the while begging for the opportunity to be a director as well. When the skeptical executives finally gave in and allowed him to direct, Sturges proved to be a success.*

Harold's actions in the game also represent the triumph of an uncommon approach. When he first enters he plays energetically but by the book, and nearly ends up as just another Tate casualty. But after he takes matters into his own hands—no matter what he is *expected* to do—his team's fortunes begin to change. In the middle of a play he sees an opening in the line, grabs the ball out of the startled quarterback's hand, and dashes through for a substantial gain. A few plays later, as he picks up the punt he has just dropped and sees a crowd of Union State players bearing down on him, he goes into action again. Quickly pulling most of the lacing from the football, he drops the pigskin on the field, and as the entire squad of defenders dives for the loose ball, he jerks it back into his hands like a yo-yo. With nearly all the opponents lying on the ground beside him he is again able to gain considerable yardage.

Of course, there were differences between Lloyd's and Sturges's perspectives on achieving success. *The Freshman* ends in the best Harold Lloyd fashion: on the last play of the game Harold chases the opposing ball carrier downfield and forces him to fumble; Harold retrieves the ball and then races all the way back (avoiding what seem to be three teams' worth of defenders) to score the winning touchdown. It is doubtful that Sturges would have chosen so rousing a finish for one of his own films, especially if it relied so much on the hero's efforts rather than on luck or coincidence. Nevertheless, within *The Freshman*'s final sequence Sturges found the element—the rewards of unconventional conduct—that allowed him to develop Lloyd's character in his own unique fashion.

Living the Conventional Life

As soon as Sturges moves *Harold Diddlebock* out of the football locker room, he begins to outline the common, uninspired lifestyle that will keep his protagonist down for the next twenty-two years. Although he is "bursting with ideas," Harold takes his first step down the wrong path when he arrives at the office of E. J. Waggleberry looking for the job he was promised. In the two scenes that feature Waggleberry—one when Harold is hired and the other when he is fired—Sturges uses Waggleberry's company to prove that the American work ethic is a sham.

Although his memory of Harold's exploits is faint at best, Waggleberry nonetheless follows through on his assurance of a job. It quickly becomes clear why he can be so accommodating:

> We don't start people at the top, you understand. That would be too easy. We do it the American way.... We give them an opportunity to work up from the bottom. What satisfaction! What a feeling of accomplishment you will have, when you are able to look back from whatever rung of the

ladder your go-getiveness will have placed you on and say, "I, I did that!"
... You know nothing about the advertising business at all, I presume?
... Good! Then you won't have anything to unlearn. You'll be able to
start right in the basement, and your rise will be all the more spectacular!

Somewhat surprised at Waggleberry's offer of a lower-than-low job,
Harold tries to look at it in the best possible light, one that accepts at face
value the notion of rising brilliantly to the top. "Every man is the architect
of his own future," he tells Waggleberry, quoting one of the scores of prov-
erbs he has memorized, and then adds, "I'm full of ideas." But Waggleberry, who has no illusions about how success is achieved, is no more
interested in Harold's ideas than he is in Harold himself:

> Don't squirt them all out at once. The idea department is a little con-
> gested at the moment. ... It always is, for that matter. There never seems
> to be any shortage of ... oh, but that would only depress you. I'll tell you
> what I'm going to do for you—I'm going to find you a little nook in the
> ... ah ... bookkeeping department—a regular little niche. You might
> almost call it a cranny. The rest will depend on you.

To Waggleberry, Harold is just one more of the day-to-day workers,
the people who make it possible for his advertising firm to thrive. One after
another they are lured into minor, drudging jobs with the promise of being
able to work their way up to the level of the Waggleberrys of the world,
but they never make it much beyond some middle management tier, if that
far. Firms such as the one Harold goes to work for beat down any spirit,
initiative, or ideas that their young workers may have, leaving them to earn
a passable wage while they rationalize away their unfulfilled dreams.* As
if to drive this cynical point home with a final blow, Sturges has Waggleberry conclude his hiring of Harold with the following exchange.

> *Waggleberry*: How I envy you this chance you're receiving today. My
> father unfortunately left me the business ... just one of those things.
> You have no personal fortune, I hope?
> *Harold*: Well, no sir...
> *Waggleberry*: Great! And probably only the clothes you stand in!

When the scene flashes ahead twenty-two years, the former football
hero is a broken-down middle-aged man who's being called into the boss's
office to be given his walking papers. With Waggleberry's speech we begin
to realize just how the American work ethic has gone awry for Harold:

*For the perfect example of this situation see the discussion of Mr. Waterbury in Chapter Six,
Christmas in July.

I had great hopes for you, Diddlebock. If ever I saw a promising type of American youth, full of zing, full of zest, full of zowie, it was you. I remember that day I first saw you.... The bases were full, the crowd was breathless, you strutted up to the plate swinging three bats at once ... what? ... oh, no, it was hockey, wasn't it? Ice hockey, of course. You got the puck and ... it wasn't? Well, what does it matter anyway at this point?

Just as Waggleberry couldn't remember Harold the first time he saw the young man in his office ("I presume I offered you a job; I usually do when I get excited"), he once again is unsure just why he was impressed with him. Whether Harold excelled at baseball or hockey or football does not matter; what Waggleberry's speech shows is that he obviously has lots of other former star athletes working for him, none of whom he really knows or cares about. He never had any interest in hearing Harold's ideas, yet he places the blame for not making more of himself squarely on Harold's shoulders:

You have not only ceased to go forward, you have gone backward. You have not only stopped progressing, you have stopped thinking. You not only make the same mistakes year after year, you don't even change your apologies. You have become a bottleneck! You are the living proof of the low quality of work we demand of our employees, and a bad example to the younger employees, who figure that if you can get away with it they can, too, and they don't have to be any better than you are, which is zero.

Of course Harold is a bad example for the younger workers because he has been at the company long enough to realize that the carrot dangled in front of him for more than two decades will always be out of reach. The younger employees have not found that out yet, so they are still willing to slave away in the hopes that they might get somewhere. With a final platitude—"this is hurting me much more than it is you"—Waggleberry sends Harold back out into the world with little more than his company savings and his faded clichés.

The clichés are symbolic of the life that Harold has led up until his firing. On the day he begins his new job, Harold nails up a set of printed sayings, including "Success is just around the corner," beside his desk; as he removes them after being fired, the marks they have left on the wall emphasize the point that like Harold himself, they have done nothing but sit there for twenty-two years. A few scenes later, as Harold dejectedly makes his way out of the Waggleberry building for the last time, he unknowingly drops one of the signs. The camera pans down to it—"Success is just around the corner"—as it gets trampled under the feet of passersby.*

---

*When the shot occurs, the sign offers an ironic comment on Harold and the events of that day. What the viewer does not know yet is that it also serves as a prophecy of what is to come, for just around the corner Harold will meet Wormy.

The clichés also represent the hold that the success myth has over Harold. Even after he has been fired and finally understands that he has been duped by the system, Harold finds it is very difficult to give up these clichés. He is so reliant on them that he has one to counter any argument, as he demonstrates when Wormy tries to get him to take a drink.

> *Harold*: No, no. I tell you I have never in my whole life...
> *Wormy*: You're never too old to learn.
> *Harold*: You can't teach an old dog new tricks.
> *Wormy*: Every dog is entitled to one bite.
> *Harold*: Let sleeping dogs lie.
> *Wormy*: A barking dog never bites.
> *Harold*: He who sleepeth with dogs, riseth with fleas.
> *Wormy*: Now wait a minute. How about, A little wine for thy stomach?
> That's from the Good Book.... He who hesitates is lost?
> *Harold*: Lips that touch liquor shall never touch mine.
> *Wormy*: Eat, drink, and be merry?

Although Harold finally gives in and has a drink, the exchange with Wormy shows how dependent Harold has become on the words and thoughts that have been fed to him. His inability to think for himself is reflected in a number of other ways as well, from his sister's confirmation that he is a failure to his finding excuses not to act while six Otis sisters go on to marry others.

By substituting clichés for original thinking, Harold has allowed himself to be robbed of his creativity and kept in a meaningless job. He finally comes to realize this situation late in the movie as he wonders why he cannot come up with a way to get rid of his circus.

> *Harold*: I used to solve problems all the time when I was in college ... trigonometry, calculus... You know something? I don't think I've thought in years.
> *Wormy*: No kidding? I'm always thinking, always trying to figure an angle.
> *Harold*: That's because you have to. You haven't got security, you haven't got a job like I have. Like I *had*. Where you have to get up at the same time every day, eat the same breakfast, go to the office on the same car, work on the same ledger all day ... then go home the same way you came to the office, except backwards.... It doesn't take any thought to do all that, so you don't think anymore, like you stop taking exercise.... I was even in love with the same girl all my life, except in a different body.... You know something else? He may have been right to fire me. I'm just an old has-been.

By simply agreeing to enter the work arena and play by the established rules, Harold could never reach his ultimate goal—success. The game is set up to benefit not the players, but rather the bigwigs, such as Waggleberry, who are its custodians. Sturges is not saying that success cannot be achieved, but rather, as Harold Diddlebock finds out, that the surest way to get it is not by working hard and living honestly. It is going to take something far more unorthodox than that.

Living the Inspired Life

By the time Harold Diddlebock enters the tavern for his first alcoholic beverage, Preston Sturges has made it clear just how unimaginative his main character's life has been for twenty-two years. However, the shock of being fired and of having all his beliefs in the system shattered leads Harold to do a complete reversal. With the rest of the film Sturges shows us that playing against the accepted rules is far more likely to lead to success—or, at the very least, happiness—than is playing by Waggleberry's rules.

Even before Harold begins to turn his life around we see several examples of people who have avoided his downfall. The first is the group of men who worked for Waggleberry Advertising when E. J. Waggleberry's father ran the business. "My father fired everyone who got over fifty—man, woman, or child—it didn't matter to him!" Harold is told. "That was his motto, the cornerstone of his success!" But Waggleberry then admits, "I even participated in, or at least closed my eyes to, a small deception that some of the older employees practiced, when, because my father was extremely nearsighted, they dyed their hair and returned to work for us as their own sons." The inspired trick that these older employees came up with may have done nothing more than allow them to keep their less-than-thrilling jobs, but that is more than Harold was able to do.

Someone who has a more exciting career than that of the employees of Waggleberry Advertising is the bartender, and he certainly approaches his work with enthusiasm and inspiration. "You arouse the artist in me," he exclaims when he hears that Harold will be having his first drink ever. The bartender is so delighted at the rare opportunity before him that he takes great offense when Wormy suggests that he make a Texas Tornado for Harold:

> Oh, not for an occasion like this, Wormy. A Tornado's a perfectly reliable commercial drink, for conventions and hangovers and things like that, but this ... this is almost ... does the word "vestal"...? Maybe we ought to have organ music. I mean, opportunities like this come along all too rarely for a man with his heart in his work.

After asking Harold a series of seemingly irrelevant questions ("What year were you born?" "What kind of toothpaste do you use?"), the

The bartender (Edgar Kennedy, *right*) and Wormy (Jimmy Conlin) look on as Harold (Harold Lloyd, *left*) takes a sip of the drink that will change his life—the Diddlebock cocktail.

bartender somehow uses the answers as a guide to concocting the perfect drink for the occasion—the Diddlebock cocktail. Crafting it not only requires the kind of thought and creativity that Harold never used at Waggleberry Advertising, but it also gives the bartender a level of satisfaction that Harold never attained in his work.

For Harold, the Diddlebock cocktail is the catalyst that allows him to leave behind the restrictive mind-set that has prevented him from escaping his bookkeeping nook for all those years. He requests from a tailor a "courageous" new suit and winds up dressed in the loudest plaid suit and largest wide-brimmed hat that anyone has ever seen. The outfit will become an obvious symbol of Harold's growing ability to think for himself as well as of his increasingly brazen attitude. When he is wearing the outfit he seems able to conquer any problem; but when he rejects it he has trouble solving his dilemmas. For Sturges, that brashness is a prerequisite for success.

Once Harold is fortified with the Diddlebock cocktail and is wearing his new suit, he loses his inhibitions and his worries. When a bookie shows up at the tailor's shop, Harold carelessly puts down a $1000 bet on a thirty-to-one horse. That he elects to bet on a race at all is courageous for him, but choosing his horse by virtue of its name alone is an even riskier move.

His intuition pays off, but while his money is riding on the outcome he is not even the least bit concerned that he may lose it all. The win prompts him to bet on another horse in the same manner and set off on a day and night of reckless partying during which he is, according to his coachman, "most generous and high-spirited" with his money.

Harold's cavalier attitude toward money is another aspect of his shift away from playing by the rules. Like all good believers of the American work ethic, he has spent twenty-two years saving his money, but after being fired he starts to question the value of this philosophy. "It's just that I've been saving it for twenty years," he tells Wormy, "and I'm getting tired of it. It's what you call an impulse, like a man works all his life in a glass factory. . . . Well, one day he feels like picking up a hammer." And the further along he goes on the road to his new lifestyle, the more nonchalant Harold becomes about his money. "It's nothing but a symbol that costs next to nothing to print," he informs Wormy. "There's no shortage of it at any time!" Most tellingly, he answers questions about the wisdom of his wager by saying, "When the iron is hot, strike! Obey that impulse!"

Where obeying that impulse leads is to a wild few days that Harold later cannot remember. When he wakes up on his living-room couch, his initial tendency is to revert to the ways of the old Harold Diddlebock. He is repulsed by the plaid suit that he finds himself still wearing, as well as by the little bit of uninhibited behavior that his sister is able to tell him about. Wanting to return to his old self as soon as possible, he quickly changes back into one of his old, traditional suits. He barely makes his way outside, however, before he is confronted with the news that he owns a debt-ridden circus, and he immediately sets about ridding himself of the burdensome investment.

The first few attempts that Harold makes to solve his circus dilemma are based on fairly obvious ideas, and for that reason they fail. He tries to entice the former owner into buying the circus back at a reduced rate, but the owner refuses, telling Harold that he would like to be "nine thousand miles away from it, home in the arms of my mother." With the hundred-plus animals starving for food, Harold next solicits help from a charitable organization that feeds stray cats, but he is turned away when he asks for three tons of liver. Finally Harold comes up with the idea of finding a banker (all of whom are rich, he reasons) who grew up in the Wisconsin town that served as the winter headquarters for the Ringling Brothers Circus. Such a person, Harold deduces, would inevitably love circuses and would be thrilled at the prospect of purchasing one. Even this plan does not work, though: when Harold does find a banker with the appropriate background, he discovers that someone with the same idea has already sold the banker a circus.

What Harold really needs is an idea so inspired that no one else has

Clad in his "courageous" suit, Harold (Harold Lloyd, *second from left*) fields an avalanche of offers to buy his circus.

ever thought of it; as he tells Wormy, "There's nothing in this world as strong as a good idea." Working from Wormy's observation that everyone hates bankers, Harold carefully thinks aloud, debates with himself, and follows the argument to a logical conclusion:

> *How are bankers generally thought of?* Very poorly; they have a terrible image because they don't give people money, as they're supposed to do.
>
> *Would a banker buy the circus because he felt bad for the starving animals?* No; if he doesn't care about people, he certainly wouldn't care about animals.
>
> *Why would anyone buy a circus, then? Why did Harold?* Because he'd always planned to when he got rich, so that he could allow poor children to go in for free.
>
> *Would a banker buy Harold's circus for the same reason?* No, because he wouldn't care about children. But if he was concerned about changing his poor image, he would *definitely* see the appeal of it.

Having finally arrived at the solution to his problem, Harold is propelled into action, but one last element must fall into place. Like millions of other people with ideas, Harold and Wormy try to make an appointment with a bank president and are thrown out of the building. Only after his final inspiration—putting the "courageous" suit back on and bringing Jackie the lion along with him—is Harold able to get into the executives' offices and, with the help of some Diddlebock cocktails, present his proposal to the flabbergasted bankers. As he planned, Harold is arrested, his story is splashed all over the newspapers, and the bankers of New York come running to the jail to beg to buy his circus.

When Harold has recovered from all the excitement (and from his fortifying Diddlebock cocktails), success is finally his. He learns that he sold the circus for $175,000, and that his publicity stunt impressed E. J. Waggleberry so much that he is now a partner in the advertising firm that fired him just days before. His last and most satisfying discovery comes when Miss Otis tells him what he did on Wednesday:

> You mean you don't remember coming out to Flatbush in the middle of the night, with a full orchestra, and waking up the whole neighborhood while you told Mother that it was about time that you did something about one of her daughters, and then wrapping me in a long velvet cloak which turned out afterwards to be a window curtain and then galloping all the way back to New Jersey?

After failing to act for twenty-two years and allowing six sisters to slip through his fingers, Harold finally proves that he can be unconventional and inspired. In love, just as in his career, a few days of wild abandon yield better results than a whole lifetime of working hard and paying one's dues.

FOURTEEN

The Beautiful Blonde from Bashful Bend

Produced, Written, and Directed by Preston Sturges; Based on a story by Earl Felton; Photography: Harry Jackson; Special Photographic Effects: Fred Sersen; Edited by Robert Fritch; Art Direction: Lyle Wheeler and George W. Davis; Set Decoration: Thomas Little and Stuart Reiss; Sound: Eugene Grossman and Harry Leonard; Music: Cyril Mockridge; Vocal Direction: Ken Darby; Orchestral Arrangements: Herbert Spencer. Released by 20th Century–Fox, 1949.

Cast: Betty Grable (Winifred "Freddie" Jones); Cesar Romero (Blackie); Rudy Vallee (Charles Hingleman); Olga San Juan (Conchita); Sterling Holloway, Danny Jackson (The Basserman Boys); Hugh Herbert (Doctor); El Brendel (Mr. Jorgensen); Porter Hall (Judge O'Toole); Richard Hale (Mr. Basserman); Margaret Hamilton (Mrs. O'Toole); Al Bridge (The Sheriff of Bashful Bend); J. Farrell MacDonald (The Sheriff of Snake City).

Synopsis: On a small frontier homestead in the old days of the Wild West, an orphaned child named Winifred Jones is raised by her grandfather, who teaches her when she is still very young how to be a sharpshooter. The little girl, known to everyone as Freddie, grows up to be a beautiful saloon entertainer in the town of Bashful Bend, but never forgets her grandfather's lessons about looking out for herself. As she is performing one night she sees her boyfriend, Blackie, in the audience with another attractive woman. When the couple get up from their table and head in the direction of the rooms upstairs, it is more than Freddie can take. She finishes her song, races off in pursuit, and, bursting into a room, fires at her man. Unfortunately, the room happens to be occupied by Judge O'Toole, the local magistrate, and Freddie's bullet hits him right in the rear end. Quickly arrested and placed in jail, Freddie explains the situation to the sheriff, who agrees to take her back to the judge's room to try to smooth things over. Using her charms, she seems to be on the verge of convincing the judge to let her out of jail when Blackie and his paramour show up. Freddie and her boyfriend start quarreling, and as she takes another shot at Blackie her bullet ends up hitting O'Toole in the same spot again.

Freddie escapes in the confusion and manages, along with her friend Conchita, to hop aboard a train heading out of town. Because they had no time to pack, Conchita steals the baggage of a woman who died on the train, and Freddie is forced to assume her identity: Hilda Swandumper, schoolteacher. From the conductor Freddie learns that the town of Snake City is awaiting Hilda's arrival, and when they pull into the station they are greeted by a large crowd. Not everyone in Snake City welcomes the new schoolteacher, however. Mr. Basserman, the town troublemaker, and his two rebellious sons start a brawl that quickly gets out of hand and continues until Freddie surreptitiously fires a gunshot to restore order. That evening Charles Hingleman, the son of the head of the school board, takes Freddie for a tour of the town. As they spend time together, Charles begins to develop a romantic interest in the new teacher.

By the next morning, word has spread around Bashful Bend about a $1000 reward for Freddie's capture. When Blackie overhears the train conductor's description of Hilda Swandumper, he puts two and two together and sets off for Snake City. Meanwhile, on Freddie's first day of her new teaching career, she immediately runs into trouble with the Basserman boys. Wanting to put an end to their pranks, she sends the rest of the class outside for recess; then, using the gun Charles gave her for protection, she scares the boys by using their heads for target practice—missing by only inches each time. By the time the rest of the class returns, the Bassermans are willing allies in keeping the other students in line.

Before long, Blackie arrives in town and finds Conchita. When Freddie learns that Blackie has followed her to Snake City, she is convinced that he is after her for the reward. She arranges to meet him that night at the schoolhouse, then goes there early to hide Charles's gun and instruct the Basserman boys, who are waiting outside to help her. Before Blackie appears, Mr. Jorgensen, the U.S. marshal, arrives to make sure that Hilda is not the notorious Freddie Jones. After Freddie persuades him that she is not and gets rid of him, she discovers that Blackie has been hiding in the building the entire time. Despite his claims that he has simply come to Snake City to save her from prison, not to turn her in, Freddie does not believe him. Responding to a prearranged signal, the Basserman boys sneak up behind him and knock him out. They hide the body beneath the teacher's desk when they hear Charles approaching. When Blackie starts to come to, Freddie and Charles run away, and the Basserman boys are shot and killed in a fight with Blackie.

Back in town, Freddie, Charles, and the rest of the townspeople are trying to determine exactly what has happened when they are interrupted by Mr. Basserman, who is looking for revenge on the person who killed his sons. The scuffle that breaks out quickly turns into an all-out shooting war in the center of town. During the fighting, however, the Basserman boys show up completely unharmed—they only made believe they were dead to avoid being killed. Unaware that his sons are alive, Mr. Basserman keeps shooting, first taking Charles prisoner and then charging Blackie, who joined the fight on the Basserman side, with being a spy for the townspeople. When Basserman hoists both men outside a barn to hang them, Freddie goes into action. With the help of the two boys, she charges out to face Mr. Basserman and his men, severs Charles's and Blackie's nooses with one shot each, and, by proving that the boys are still alive, ends the gunfight.

Unfortunately, Freddie's sharpshooting display is all Mr. Jorgensen needs to convince him of her true identity. He takes her back to Bashful Bend, where she is forced to stand trial before Judge O'Toole. Although Blackie shows up once again with another woman, he speaks in Freddie's defense, claiming responsibility for the judge's injuries and asking him to marry the couple before she is convicted. Taken in by Freddie's vows to be a respectable wife and mother from now on, O'Toole agrees to perform the service and suspend her sentence. Before he does so, however, Freddie hears the flirtatious comments that Blackie's female companion is making, and in a jealous rage ends up firing a gun once again—right into the judge's rear end.

•

Of all the films that Preston Sturges directed in Hollywood, *The Beautiful Blonde from Bashful Bend* is his weakest. Told by 20th Century–Fox head Darryl Zanuck to create a Betty Grable vehicle and to adhere to certain conventions of Grable's films, Sturges did not have the creative freedom he had had with nearly all his other movies. He had to shoot the film in color (all his others were in black and white); he had to include a handful of musical numbers; and he had to display Betty's world-famous legs as much as possible. (His response to this last order was not only to put Betty in a dress slit to the thigh throughout the initial scenes, but also to have her lose the bottom of her dress during the final gunfight sequence; she ends up performing her sharpshooting wizardry and saving the day for Snake City in her frilly panties.) Sturges called the script, which he adapted from an Earl Felton story, "an unfortunate hodgepodge,"* and complained to Zanuck on more than one occasion about it. Even before

*Preston Sturges by Preston Sturges, *p. 308.*

he began shooting the film, Sturges realized that the restrictions placed on him would make it difficult for him to turn out a good movie; he told Zanuck, "The picture will . . . be a very minor effort in both your life and mine."*

Expected to produce a Betty Grable film rather than one of his own, Sturges clearly did not know how to proceed. As a director who excelled at making original and distinctive motion pictures, he must have found it demoralizing and frustrating to try to make a movie that was *like* other people's work. That the film pales in comparison to his Paramount work is not at all surprising; still, his filmmaking genius was so great that even in a mediocre effort like *The Beautiful Blonde* there are plenty of Sturgean touches.

The moments that do stand out most derive from the smaller character roles and players and from a number of lines of witty Sturges dialogue. Probably the single most memorable aspect of the movie is the comic performance of Hugh Herbert as the nearsighted doctor charged with removing the bullets from Judge O'Toole's behind. And while Al Bridge's Sheriff and Richard Hale's Mr. Basserman may not display the same combination of great writing, directing, and acting that made the Wienie King and Officer Kockenlocker so outstanding, they are still funny and effective— and undeniably cut from the same mold as their predecessors.

Even within the movie's constraints Sturges was able to inject some of his characteristic themes and viewpoints, beginning with the film's basic concept: a strong, independent woman attempts to pass herself off as something she is not in order to gain what she wants. This theme was not new to Sturges; Jean Harrington in *The Lady Eve* and Gerry Jeffers in *The Palm Beach Story* were the same type of protagonist.† In *The Beautiful Blonde*, Sturges once again structures his story around this idea and, as in *The Palm Beach Story*, intertwines it with the notion that women can use their sexual charms to control men.

It's All in the Presentation

Although the setting of the film is never made explicit, Bashful Bend and Snake City are presumably located somewhere in the American

---

*James Curtis, Between Flops, *p. 227. Curtis's book and Diane Jacobs's* Christmas in July *paint a complete and utterly depressing picture of Sturges's troubles during the writing and filming of* The Beautiful Blonde. *The highly independent Sturges had fallen so far from his glory years at Paramount that Zanuck would not even let him make minor casting decisions; in addition, according to Jacobs, the film was partially reshot and reedited without Sturges's participation (p. 387).*

†It is interesting to note that in all three of these films, which revolve around assertive female characters who manipulate men, the women are all known by nicknames that are exclusively or frequently men's names: Eugenia (Jean) Harrington, Geraldine (Gerry) Jeffers, and Winifred (Freddie) Jones.

Southwest (the train that runs between them is part of the Reno and Santa
Fe line) and the time period is sometime before the turn of the century.
And even though the still-untamed West can be a very rough place, it is
also obvious that the women of the region are expected to be fairly ladylike
and dependent on their men. For all her traditional female beauty, though,
Freddie Jones is anything but passive and weak. Growing up an orphan she
learned how to take care of herself better than any man could. Unfortunately, the men in the film cannot accept Freddie's independence and
toughness. She continually has to pose as something she is not—a demure,
subservient, helpless woman—in order to get what she wants or needs.

The most obvious example of Freddie's guise is seen when she passes
herself off as the prim and innocent Hilda Swandumper. But she assumes
that pose out of necessity, not calculation. On numerous other occasions
she chooses to put on an act in order to work her way out of a jam. When
Freddie first shoots Judge O'Toole, for example, she is locked in a jail cell
by the sheriff. She nearly bites his head off when he makes a suggestive
remark about her beauty and his proximity to her, but once she realizes
that she needs to get out of jail to see the judge, she begins flirting with the
sheriff and pretending to be interested in him. Taken in by her ploy, he
agrees to let her out of prison and to take her to the judge's hotel room.
There she finds the wounded judge (and his all-too-knowing wife) and
begins to flatter him, hoping he will drop the charges against her.

> *Freddie*: Oh, to know that you're alive, Your Honor, and not rotting away
> in some lonely grave.... I'm terribly, terribly sorry, Your Honor. If
> there's any man in the world I wouldn't have wanted to...
> *Mrs. O'Toole*: You stay away from my husband.
> *Freddie*: I'm not thinking of him as your husband, ma'am. You don't have
> to worry. I'm not thinking of him as a man at all. I'm thinking of him
> as a father, a forgiving father, to put his arms around me.... If you
> can only find it in your heart to forgive me ... to pretend this never
> happened.... I didn't mean it for you, Your Honor. I didn't mean
> it for anybody. I don't hardly know one end of a gun from
> another.... I don't hardly know how it got in my hand.... Look in
> my eyes, Your Honor. Think how they'll talk about you when you
> let me go. They'll say, "There's a man with a heart as big as a bull
> fiddle—even if he did get shot up a little." ... Tell the sheriff. Tell
> him to set me free. Don't hold the words back. And then when you're
> on your feet again, come up and point out the evil of my ways. I need
> your help. I need your guidance. I need a papa.... I'm the gentle
> type, Your Honor. I'm the home type. Look into my eyes ... look
> deep....

As with the sheriff, Freddie again wins a man over with her charms, but
only until Blackie and his girl show up and Freddie accidentally shoots the
judge a second time.

After she escapes ↘
more acceptable type of v
Conchita think they have n
less female routine; but when the conu...
tickets inside a valise, Freddie and Conchita drop ... _act like a_
they get to Snake City.* When she gets off the train, Fredd...ile-
crowd at the station that she brought her Indian girl with her because it
is dangerous for a young woman to be living on her own. And later she
gives Charles the impression that she does not know how to handle a gun
and is in need of his protection.†

Freddie also gives a plausible "dumb female" performance for Mr.
Jorgensen, the U.S. marshal, when he questions her in the schoolhouse
about her ability to handle a gun. Although she claims that she has never
held one before, the marshal insists that she try, and to prove her story, she
promptly points the gun at herself, then at Jorgensen, before firing it into
the floor. Reassured that she is not the escaped fugitive—either because he
is too foolish to see beyond her trick or because she does not fit the image
that he has been given—he gladly lets her go.

Freddie's last act of deception takes place at the very end of the movie,
when she is finally on trial for shooting Judge O'Toole. To avoid a jail
sentence she implores the judge to look at her and Blackie in a new light:

> I know it's hard for Your Honor to understand, because compared to
> people like Your Honor, we probably look like kind of terrible people, I
> mean, being gamblers and shills and singers and things like that. But way
> down deep we're just the same as everybody else. We dream of little white
> cottages, little white picket fences running around them . . . and with
> crickets chirping in the trees.

When the judge suggests adding children to complete the picture of
domesticity, Freddie agrees that she and Blackie would like to have lots
of them. Once again this complete reversal from the truth—the tough
sharpshooter and futigive portraying herself as a gentle, nurturing wife and

---

*Freddie's escape by taking a train out of town makes for an interesting comparison to Gerry's
flight in The Palm Beach Story. Both women get on the train without a ticket and need to
use their charms and their knowledge of men's expectations to stay on board. But while Sturges
plays out the situation brilliantly in Palm Beach, he takes the easy way out in The Beautiful
Blonde by having Freddie find tickets inside Hilda's luggage.

†Freddie's relationship with Charles is one of the elements that suffers because of Sturges's weak
screenplay. She seems to welcome his romantic attentions after finding out about his gold mine,
and one has the idea that she is pursuing him for his money. After the gunfight, however, she
suddenly decides that Blackie is a better man for her, but Sturges provides no real explanation
for the abrupt shift in her feelings. In The Palm Beach Story, Gerry just cannot bring herself
to stay with Hackensacker, even though it would be more profitable, but the resolution is far
more clear and satisfying than in The Beautiful Blonde.

"Hilda Swandumper" (Betty Grable, *second from left*) secretly fires off the shot that quells the disturbance at the Snake City train station.

mother—seems patently ridiculous, but it works. It is what the men want to hear women say, so even though Freddie has shot a U.S. judge twice and fled from the law while under arrest, O'Toole is perfectly willing to let her go free. The judge's change of heart not only proves that, like Gerry Jeffers, Freddie can use her feminine charms to get what she wants, but also that in Bashful Bend and Snake City, the law is about as fair and effective as it is in Dan McGinty's graft-ridden city.

The Futility of the Law

Early in the film, when we catch our first glimpse of Freddie sitting in her jail cell, the sheriff of Bashful Bend chastises her for shooting Judge O'Toole. "This is a law-abiding town," he tells her, "not the Wild West." The statement makes sense at the time—you cannot just go around shooting judges and expect to get away with it. But as the movie progresses we see that the law and those appointed to enforce it are nowhere near as powerful or respected as the sheriff might think. For all the talk about obeying the law and all the people who are supposed to be authority figures, there is very little order or adequate rule to be found anywhere.

Sturges establishes the ineffectiveness of the law in the opening scene, when Winifred Jones, about five years old, is being taught by her grand-father to shoot a gun. Although she is doing quite well, the little girl is more interested in playing with her doll; her grandfather makes it clear, though, why she *must* learn to be a great shot:

> You leave that dolly be and learn your lessons, Winifred. Load up that gun, 'cause this is a rough country, little lady.... Being a good shot ain't gonna get you into trouble, it'll keep you outta trouble. You ain't got a pappy or a mammy, and I'm getting old.... There's no telling where I'm gonna be when you start to blossom out into the flower of young womanhood.... Then that there shooting iron's got to be your mammy and your pappy and your big brother.

With the possible exception of Blackie, Grandpa seems to be the only male in the film who understands just how ineffectual society's laws and rules actually are. He sees it as his responsibility to teach Freddie how to take care of herself, because nothing—not a law book, not the unwritten rules of civility, and especially not a man—can be relied on to protect her or anyone else.

Once Freddie grows up we see that her grandfather was absolutely right. In Bashful Bend, the sheriff is utterly incompetent: not only does he allow Freddie to leave her jail cell while she is under arrest, but he is also unable to quell the chaos that erupts in the judge's hotel room. Convinced that Freddie is sincere as she delivers her conciliatory speech to Judge O'Toole, the sheriff is so unprepared once the fighting breaks out that he is incapable of either restraining Freddie or preventing her escape from the hotel room and from the entire town.

And the lawmen in Snake City are not any more qualified than those in Bashful Bend. At the train station, the troublemaking Basserman family begins taunting the new schoolteacher, calling her derogatory names. The other men of the town, including Sheriff Sweetzer and Mr. Jorgensen, the U.S. marshal, attempt to defend the fair woman's honor by first verbally and then physically trying to put Mr. Basserman in his place. In the pro-cess, though, they nearly allow Mr. Hingleman to be killed, and the situa-tion is brought under control only when Freddie secretly snatches the sheriff's gun from his holster and fires off one perfectly aimed shot. She cleverly attributes the shot to the ancient and nearly infirm Sheriff Sweet-zer—a ludicrous assertion that is wholeheartedly accepted by the people, who *want* to believe that the local authority deserves the credit.

The fighting at the train station is not the first trouble caused by the Bassermans, though. Judging by the comments of several residents, the Basserman boys have been up to their pranks for quite a long time. Yet within hours of arriving in town, Freddie has no problem putting them in their place and actually eliciting their support—something none of Snake

City's leaders have been able to do. Nor have they been able to stop the boys' father, Gus, from being the town nuisance; it would be foolish to expect Sheriff Sweetzer and Mr. Jorgensen—who cannot even tell that Hilda might not be what she claims—to subdue his unlawful tendencies.

But the real proof of the incompetence of the Snake City government comes during the climactic gunfight. Although the sequence appears to be little more than a set of sight gags revolving around shooting, Sturges makes it clear that none of the town's leaders are having any success against the Bassermans. The only thing that brings the fighting to a halt is Freddie's marksmanship and the return of the Basserman boys.

The gunfight scene also highlights another, albeit minor, theme of the film—the inability of men to do what they think they can do. None of the men is as accurate a shot as Freddie; Charles, for example, is completely inept with a gun. The women in the movie prove to be the most effective fighters from the moment Mr. Basserman and his gang initiate the fight in the Hingleman kitchen. While Mr. Jorgensen and the other men of Snake City are struggling just to get their guns out of their holsters, the women are already driving the gang out of the house by throwing pots and pans at them (seeing the success of this tactic, the men quickly abandon their firearms and join in). Similarly, once the battle is in full swing, most of the shots that actually hit Basserman's men are fired by Conchita, Freddie, and some of the other women. Throughout the film the women make it clear how little respect they have for men and their supposed abilities: Freddie once remarks, "I don't care what you do to a man, but a girl!..." while Conchita complains, "The more you do for these tramps, the more you get it in the end." Just as in *The Palm Beach Story*, the men who pride themselves on being protectors of innocent, helpless women are actually the ones who are most at the mercy of the women themselves.

In the end, Preston Sturges was correct to disparage *The Beautiful Blonde from Bashful Bend* as a hodgepodge and a minor work. Finding Sturgean themes in it is not difficult, but finding *well-developed* Sturgean themes is, as the film seems ripe with unexploited possibilities. For example, Snake City could easily have been the setting for satirical observations on small-town life of the kind put forth in *The Miracle of Morgan's Creek* or *Hail the Conquering Hero*; the notion of a town that cannot protect its citizens from corruption and lawlessness could have been fashioned into a cynical political statement as in *The Great McGinty*; and the thought that we honor strength and self-sufficiency in theory but often feel threatened by it in reality could have been turned into a commentary on human nature, as in *The Great Moment*. But Sturges was not able to develop the potential in this material. It is a shame that the man who created such distinctive and stimulating films from the early 1930s through the mid–1940s ended his Hollywood career on such a chaotic note.

FIFTEEN

Conclusion

The previous chapters in this book have closely analyzed the way in which Preston Sturges dealt with some aspects of life in America. For the most part the fourteen films were examined on their own, with few comparisons drawn between them. Many of the themes reappeared from film to film, but several subjects were unique to a particular film or were handled slightly differently in each movie. It is easy to make connections between *The Miracle of Morgan's Creek* and *Hail the Conquering Hero*, for example, as both share the same cynical outlook on human nature; on the other hand, trying to find similarities between the tender love story of *Remember the Night* and Sturges's caustic view of human relationships in other movies is nearly impossible.

Sturges's career is not a gigantic jigsaw puzzle in which every piece has to fit perfectly. Like any writer/director in the studio system, he was assigned projects that he did not want to be involved with, and had changes imposed on him even for those films he chose to make. But although a handful of his movies may seem in setting and tone to be anything but Preston Sturges films, there remains a surprisingly consistent viewpoint in his sixteen years of moviemaking. In the films discussed in this book, which include all but three of Sturges's major works, he deals in some form or another with life in the United States and specifically with those elements that are mythologized as the basis of our unique and implicitly superior way of life. As we examine his treatment of life in America—focusing on the topics of families, honesty and success, and democracy and justice—it becomes clear that Sturges saw little reason for our devotion to these glorified ideals.

The Strength of Family Life

When Preston Sturges was making films, the stability of the family was still the crucial and unquestioned foundation of American life. A loving, nurturing family was one of the keys to getting a young person started on the road to success and happiness. From the parents and siblings of one's

169

youth to the spouse and children of one's adulthood, families were, and
to a large extent still are, supposed to provide support throughout a person's life. For Sturges, however, they rarely conform to such an ideal. In
film after film he presents family units that not only offer little comfort for
the children, siblings, or parents involved, but that actually hold their
members back from achieving personal or professional happiness. The exact nature of the relationship, whether between husband and wife, father
and daughter, or mother and son, does not seem to matter much; chances
are that it is in some way unsound.

The source of instability for many of these families can be found in
the marriages at their core. Few of the unions that Sturges portrays are
happy and supportive (the bickering Nobles from *Hail the Conquering Hero*
are the perfect example), while the attitudes of those characters consider-
ing wedlock are often decidedly unconventional. The marriage that is
probably seen in the most traditional—and positive—light is that of Tom
and Sally Garner in *The Power and the Glory*. As a young couple they are
obviously in love and fiercely devoted to each other: Tom gives up the job
he likes to satisfy Sally's wish that he get an education and advance his
career, while Sally takes on a demanding job to pay for Tom's schooling.
As Tom becomes more and more successful, however, the special relationship he had with Sally begins to deteriorate. Sturges makes a direct connection between Tom's professional climb and the demise of his marriage:
just before committing suicide, Sally tells her husband that it was his career
that tore them apart. Sturges further drives his point home by contrasting
Tom and Sally's failed marriage with the loving relationship between
Henry and his wife. Although Tom may have lived out the American
Dream, he has also been robbed of the personal happiness that the unsuccessful Henry has enjoyed.

In *Christmas in July*, Sturges also presents a struggling couple who
found happiness together—Jimmy MacDonald's mother and his late
father—but they were not able to enjoy even the modest life that Henry
and his wife shared. The amount of money they needed just to get by was
so great that Mr. MacDonald literally worked himself to death earning it.
Seeing what happened to a marriage, even a satisfying one, that was not
blessed with wealth, Jimmy MacDonald vows not to marry his girlfriend
until he has the means to assure them of a happy *and* long-lived union. It
is not that he is not serious about his love for Betty; if anything, he is too
serious. He understands the unfortunate reality that if he cannot become
a success it is better for him not to say, "I do."

While Jimmy may treat matrimony as a very serious commitment,
many of Sturges's characters take a far more capricious view. In *Easy Living*, Mrs. Ball walks out on her husband, declaring her intention to divorce
him, but races back to his side pledging her love and devotion within less

than twenty-four hours. And she is provoked not by a major conflict or a proven indiscretion: she leaves the house in a rage when Mr. Ball confiscates one of the many furs that fill her closets, and she decides to divorce him after reading a gossip column item linking her husband to a young woman. Once she hears of the stock market crisis that is threatening his fortune, she returns to his arms, proclaiming her willingness to do anything for him, including scrubbing floors.

Compared with the beliefs of the women in *The Palm Beach Story*, however, Mrs. Ball's idea of marriage looks nothing short of conservative. Gerry Jeffers makes no excuses for the fact that her prime motivation is materialism. Although she still has feelings for her husband, Tom, she is perfectly willing to divorce him, marry a rich man, and continue to include her "brother" Tom in her life. And Gerry is not alone in her cavalier view of marriage. With numerous husbands already behind her and many more planned for the future, Maude treats matrimony like some type of sport. She sees nothing wrong with being married to one man, keeping another, and making serious moves on a third all at the same time. And while Maude's brother, Snoodles, may look scornfully on his sister's marriage games, he has a similarly unorthodox opinion of the institution: he wants to set up a mock marriage—with children rented for the occasion—to see whether Gerry would make an appropriate wife. Sturges then concludes this skewed portrait of wedlock with an ending demonstrating that the only requirement for a spouse is that he or she look right.

That very concept—of marrying someone just for outward appearances—shows up again in *The Great McGinty* as one of the central components of the story. At first Dan McGinty takes Catherine for his wife simply so that he can be a more appealing mayoral candidate; but even when the couple grow to love each other, Sturges is far from endorsing the traditional idea of marriage. Although the relationship may civilize McGinty, turning him from a wild bachelor into a devoted father and loving husband, it also changes him in a far more costly way. As he falls in love with Catherine, he starts acting according to her values of altruism and betrays himself by going against his true nature. His marriage makes him happy for a while, but in the end it gets him run out of the country and costs him all the money and power he has obtained.

In addition to those in *The Palm Beach Story*, Sturges's most outrageous assaults on the institution of marriage can be found in *Sullivan's Travels* and *The Miracle of Morgan's Creek*. Early on in *Sullivan's Travels*, we learn that John L. Sullivan is married but does not even live with the spouse he refers to as "the Panther Woman." Sully's business manager suggested the marriage as a hedge against taxes, but instead of saving Sully money it has brought him nothing but aggravation and a hole in his checkbook. The only escape Sully has from the union is to die—or at least to appear to die, a feat he actually pulls off. Finally, it would be hard to mock marriage more than Sturges does in the ninety-eight minutes of *The Miracle of Morgan's Creek*. From the soldier who marries Trudy using an assumed name and a curtain ring for a band, to the "appointment" of Norval Jones as Trudy's legal husband, the entire film treats wedlock with none of the respect that the people of Morgan's Creek—and of America— like to think they accord it.

But if marriage does not fare very well in Sturges's films, family life surely rates no better. With only a few exceptions, all of Sturges's families to one degree or another fail to conform to society's often idealized view of the home. Even in the films that do depict loving families, there is usually some relationship or situation that undercuts the portrayal. In *The Power and the Glory*, Tom and Sally are so happy together that there seems to be no reason why they would not provide a stable upbringing for their young son; but as Tom attains success in his career he draws away from Sally as well as from Tom Jr. By the time Tom Jr. is of college age, he is a lazy and disrespectful son, his parents are close to divorce, and the groundwork has been laid for the eventual suicides of Tom and Sally. Even *Remember the Night*, which presents Sturges's most positive family by far in the warm and caring Sargents, contains his bleakest family relationship: the irreversible rift between Lee and her spiteful mother.

The contrast between a happy family and an unhappy one can also be seen in *The Great McGinty*, but in this case the two examples are found within the same household. Once the marriage of convenience between McGinty and Catherine turns into a genuine, loving relationship, he becomes a model father to her youngsters, devoting plenty of time to them and their well-being and winning their respect and affection. Unfortunately, although Sturges does not stress the point, McGinty's departure at the end of the film can only spell unhappiness for the children (as it does for Catherine). McGinty may have provided enough money for their upbringing and education, but he deprives them of his presence, just as their real father did.

Even though not all of Sturges's families break up because of divorce, suicide, or desertion, it is rare to find one that is complete. *Diamond Jim*, *Remember the Night*, *Christmas in July*, *The Miracle of Morgan's Creek*, *Hail the Conquering Hero*, and *The Beautiful Blonde from Bashful Bend* all feature characters who are missing one or both parents, and particularly in the more serious films, the loss has profound effects on the protagonists. Jim Brady is so devoted to his late mother that he will not touch a drop of liquor—except for one decisive moment—because she asked him not to; he also spends his entire life trying to find the deep, sincere love that he lost on the day she died. And while John Sargent in *Remember the Night* has a mother whose immeasurable love can overcome the absence of a father, Lee Leander's life has been much the poorer because the mother who raised her remains unforgiving and hateful.

The Leanders may qualify as the most impaired family in Sturges's films, but plenty of others are not far behind. The Kockenlocker daughters in *The Miracle of Morgan's Creek* are always taunting their father and lying to him, while he threatens them with violence. The contempt between members of the Ball family in *Easy Living* and between the Pikes in *The Lady Eve* is less extreme, but both families quarrel constantly. In both households the sons waste the family money on activities that their parents do not understand, while the fathers seem to have little knowledge of and little concern for what their wives and children are doing.

Perhaps Sturges's most unusual family, the Harrington clan in *The Lady Eve*, is distinguished not by simple hatred and derision, which are at least common in many sets of relatives, but rather by *unfamilylike* behavior. Jean and her father, the Colonel, are so unlike a supposedly normal American family that it can be difficult at times to determine whether or not they are actually related. It is hard to imagine a daughter telling her father that she is dying to fix him up with a rich old woman because she is tired of having to do "all the dirty work." Nor does it seem possible that a loving father—even if he is a con man—would seriously try to take a man at cards just after learning that the man is about to become his son-in-law. The absurdity of the relationship reaches its peak when father and daughter use the prospective son-in-law as a pawn in their game of one-upmanship.

From serious films, such as *The Power and the Glory*, to comedies, such as *The Miracle of Morgan's Creek*, Preston Sturges repeatedly ridicules and tears down one of the primary building blocks of American mythology, the sanctity of the family. Except in rare instances, Sturges's families are not the loving, supportive units we like to think they are; rather, they are at best annoying and slightly distracting and at worst capable of sabotaging a family member's march toward success.

Integrity and Success

If Preston Sturges's characters cannot look to their families for support, it would seem logical for them to rely on themselves and their own efforts. According to the American Dream, the guaranteed road to success is paved with hard work, perseverance, honesty, and a commitment to bettering oneself (usually through education). As if to prove this notion, Sturges presents us with John Sargent in *Remember the Night*, who has attained his position in the district attorney's office by studying hard, working extra jobs at night, and refusing to let anything stand in the way of his becoming a success.

However, John Sargent is about the only Preston Sturges character who can make such a claim. The people we see in Sturges's films generally fall into one of two groups: they follow through on their end of the bargain and wind up disappointed, or they do not even bother to try yet become successful in spite of themselves. Tom Garner from *The Power and the Glory* falls in the first category. Initially content to remain a lowly track-walker, the illiterate Tom is pushed by his wife to improve himself and make his way up the ladder of success. After working day and night—quite literally—to get an education, he slowly ascends through the ranks until he becomes the president of a railroad. Although Tom ultimately gains wealth and position, he does so at the expense of his personal life. For him the promise that riches can provide happiness proves a disastrous lie.

In Tom Garner's case, the hard work he put into his schooling pays off in the form of professional advancement. More often in Sturges's films education has nothing to do with life in the real world. In *Diamond Jim*, the uneducated Jim Brady does not need diplomas or degrees to succeed; shrewdness alone is enough. But in some Sturges films education goes beyond being merely unnecessary and becomes positively constraining. For John Ball, Jr., in *Easy Living*, a college degree seems to get in the way of securing or keeping a job. Not only is he unable to find any position in the want ads for which he is qualified, but he is incapable of holding a job at the Automat for more than one day. Harold Diddlebock has a similarly ineffectual college education in his background. While he may be able to think creatively on the football field and win the big game for his school, once he is ready to get a job everything he has absorbed in school does no more than keep him in the same position for twenty-two years. He finally succeeds only when he throws aside every rule that he has "learned" to follow and acts on impulse and imagination.

In two films Sturges shows how irrelevant formal education is by contrasting naïve characters who have college degrees with much wiser people who are not so educated. In *The Lady Eve*, the topflight education that Charles Pike received may have made him an expert on snakes and Amazon jungles, but it certainly has not helped him to get along in a world full of devious, dishonest people. Muggsy Murgatroyd has been appointed by Charles's family to be his constant companion because they realize that this uneducated and vulgar ruffian has all the skills necessary to see that Charles is not taken advantage of. In the same way, John L. Sullivan of *Sullivan's Travels* can boast of having attended impressive schools, yet he is too dense to see that his simplistic plan to find out about trouble will only get him into lots of it. It takes the insight of someone like his butler to understand that the problem of poverty cannot be solved with a mere movie, as Sully hopes. The butler has gained his wisdom not by sitting in classrooms or believing in myths that clearly do not work, but rather by living near the bottom of society and keenly observing the conditions around him.

The notion that education is so valuable is implicit in the promise that hard work and honesty will inevitably lead to success, but as Sturges shows, that promise is false. With the exceptions of Tom Garner (who pays a very high price) and John Sargent, no Sturges characters find success by virtue of their own endeavors. America is far from being a land of opportunity, for as Dr. Jackson tells Morton in *The Great Moment*, poor boys should stay behind the plow rather than try to study medicine. From Mary Smith in *Easy Living*, who has just a few pennies saved, to Tom Jeffers in *The Palm Beach Story*, who has to hide from his landlord because he cannot pay the rent, Sturges's characters find the only reward of hard work to be failure—or even, as Jimmy MacDonald's father learns, an early death.

When success does come calling, it is usually by sheer chance. Some people, such as Charles Pike, John Ball, Jr., and John D. Hackensacker, have the good fortune to be born to a rich family; surely none of these men could ever make money on their own. For others, a bizarre stroke of luck brings them riches. Mary Smith literally has success, in the form of a fur coat, fall on her head, and Jimmy MacDonald finally succeeds not because his slogan is any good, but rather because his coworkers play a prank on him that sets into motion an elaborate series of events. Tom Jeffers ends up getting his airport built, but only because his wife happened to step on the face of one of the richest bachelors in the world, who happened to fall in love with her. Such coincidences make for happy endings, but they also suggest a much bleaker thought: for all the lucky fools who have had success fall in their laps, there must be millions of others who have worked just as hard and need money just as badly but who simply were not in the right place at the right time.

The other element that darkens Sturges's view of success is the part that self-interest, or even dishonesty, can play in aiding one's ascent to the top. The perfect example is W. T. G. Morton of *The Great Moment*, an ordinary dentist who wants to find a way to relieve his patients' pain. Although the weaknesses of the film make Morton's motives a bit unclear at times, it is certain that once he discovers the secret of ether he wants to keep it to himself in order to ensure a monopoly on painless dentistry. As long as he is concerned only with the success of his own practice, his offices are overflowing and the money keeps rolling in. Once he decides to use ether to help others, however, his business begins to fall apart, people turn against him, and he ends up losing his practice and all his money—simply because he tried to do something good for someone.

Sturges takes the role of self-interest one step further in some of his other films, where those people who deceive and cheat others have the most success. The Harringtons and Sir Alfred in *The Lady Eve* not only make a career of conning people, but they lead a much more exciting life than they would if they were honest. Dan McGinty does much the same in his political career. The longer he remains allied with the corrupt politicians, the higher he rises in the political machine. Only when he attempts to do something for others—when he tries to rid his state of child labor and tenements—does he lose the money and position he attained.

Even Woodrow Truesmith and his Marine friends, who should represent the ultimate form of self-sacrifice, learn that deception can pay off. If Woodrow had returned to town after being discharged for hay fever, he would have been treated like any other person in Oakridge; but because he comes back pretending to have been wounded in action, he benefits from the townspeople's desperate need for someone to idolize. Even after admitting his hoax, Woodrow ends up a respected citizen, a man of distinction and honor. Like Dan McGinty and the Harringtons and Gerry Jeffers, he finds the kind of success through dishonesty that eludes those hardworking people who naïvely wait for their reward to come.

Justice and Democracy

With no loving families to support them and no assurance that their hard work will get them anywhere, all Sturges's characters can do is hope that the American system will provide them with a square deal. But in Sturges's films the things that are supposed to ensure equality and fair government—juries of one's peers, democratic elections, and so on—fail just as often as the other elements of the American myth do. The notions that good guys will always win, that the most qualified people will be elected to government, and that the justice system will decide fairly in the vast majority of cases could not be further from the truth.

The strength of a democracy rests with one assumption that is rarely stated: that the people who make up the democratic masses will think carefully and judge wisely on all issues before them. As indicated in the discussions of individual films, however, Preston Sturges's America is filled with people who are easily swayed and misled by anything from brazen lies to unsubstantiated rumors. In *Diamond Jim*, the leading money men of the late 1800s panic at a drop in the price of railroad stocks and foolishly jump to the conclusion that railroads will no longer be important in American industry. Despite Jim Brady's exhortations, they sell all their stock and throw Diamond Jim—as well as thousands of other investors— into financial ruin.

Just as the intellectual and business elite are susceptible, average citizens are no more thoughtful or savvy about the decisions they make. Many of Sturges's films contain numerous examples of unthinking, exploitable mobs. In *Easy Living*, the price of steel plummets when thousands of people dump their stock at once, on the basis of one spurious piece of information; later, a far more calculated but just as phony tip causes them all to turn around and buy back the stock, sending the price right back up in a matter of hours. In *The Great Moment*, the public that hails W. T. G. Morton as a benefactor of humankind viciously turns on him when the press whips them into a frenzy by portraying him as greedy and inhumane. And in *The Miracle of Morgan's Creek*, the townspeople are all willing to condemn "immoral" conduct until it is in their interest to do otherwise — then they accept Trudy and Norval just as eagerly as if they had been model citizens all along.

If this is what the average people in Sturges's America are like, it is easy to see why they would choose political leaders who are almost without exception self-serving, corrupt, or simply incompetent. Although Everett Noble in *Hail the Conquering Hero* is obviously more concerned with retaining his office and promoting his chair company than with looking out for his constituents, he is elected again and again, always over the more thoughtful but less flashy Doc Bissell. The entire political process depicted in *Hail the Conquering Hero* makes a mockery of our supposed ideal of citizen participation and the merits of democracy. From the drafting of Woodrow as a mayoral candidate for no *real* reason to Noble's comments about the danger of letting people have too much freedom to elect their leaders, Sturges shows us how incapable the system is of choosing competent people to govern. The inhabitants of Oakridge are happy to go along with a fraudulent system, though, because they are clearly not as interested in good government as they are in getting a good show.

In *The Great McGinty*, however, the people do not have any real say in the election of their officials. The candidates campaign and promise the voters everything they want to hear, but with all the winners essentially predetermined by a corrupt system, the city (or state) is at the mercy of The Boss. Every party is under his control and every vote that matters is his to buy. The difference between Dan McGinty and Everett Noble is that McGinty and The Boss give the people just enough to make them think they are getting something good. Millions of dollars are poured into public works projects that do provide jobs and facilities for the people, even if kickbacks are also lining the pockets of the politicians. The citizens are happy to accept the dominance of The Boss and his political machine because they actually have something to show for it.

When it comes to the law — perhaps the greatest symbol of the superiority of American government — Sturges shows us that it is far from equitable, and about as reliable as families and hard work. Beginning with the lowest rung on the ladder, law enforcement officers, the legal system is incapable of outsmarting almost anyone. *The Beautiful Blonde from Bashful Bend* contains a fairly typical group of sheriffs and marshals, all of whom are powerless not only to prevent prison escapes and quell fights, but also simply to figure out that Hilda Swandumper is not who she claims to be. Similarly incompetent officials can be found in *Remember the Night* (the hayseed judge), *Sullivan's Travels* (the police officer who arrests Sully for stealing his own car), and *The Miracle of Morgan's Creek* (the entire group of screaming officials who want to arrest Norval for anything they can think of, as well as Officer Kockenlocker).

More importantly, Sturges depicts the entire criminal justice system as faulty and capable of being exploited for specific purposes. In *The Great McGinty*, the political machine has such tight control over things that the laws have become essentially meaningless—at least for party members. The force of the law can be held at bay when McGinty is in The Boss's good graces, or unleashed on him in a minute when he tries to cross the machine. Even when The Boss and McGinty are languishing in jail, the machine has enough power to sneak a loyal accomplice into the prison, under the guise of being a new guard, where he breaks the two "criminals" out of their cells.

The Boss and McGinty also display their ability to manipulate the law during their brief appearances in *The Miracle of Morgan's Creek*. At the film's end, when it is apparent that Norval has committed all kinds of crimes and that Trudy does not have a legitimate father for her children, the man elected to uphold the laws of the state leaps into action. McGinty retroactively marries Norval and Trudy and makes Norval a longtime guard in the state militia, while arranging for Norval's other offenses— such as bank robbery—to be removed from the books.

The manipulation of the legal system is much more subtle in *Remember the Night*, as John Sargent is chosen to prosecute cases against women because he usually wins convictions. Aware that jurors are predisposed to feel sorry for female defendants, John knows how to handle the proceedings and ensure that the women are not acquitted. When it comes to Lee Leander's trial for robbery, we see just how good John is at his work. Whether his actions are moral or not, the very fact that he is *able* to get the trial recessed when it appears that Lee will be acquitted, or bully her so that she is assured of being found not guilty, does not say much for the integrity of the system. (Lee's attorney demonstrates a similar but far less sophisticated talent for swaying a jury. The reaction he gets to his outrageous claim that Lee was hypnotized by the dazzling bracelet is not that much different from what he is describing: the jurors are mesmerized.)

Perhaps Sturges's most cynical view of the legal system, though, is found in those instances in which different people receive different treatment under the law. He develops this idea in a humorous context in *The Beautiful Blonde from Bashful Bend*, when Judge O'Toole is all set to drop the charges against Freddie just because she is attractive and has told him a heart-warming but clearly fanciful tale about her desire to settle down to a quiet, married life. But *Sullivan's Travels* reveals the tragic side of an unfair legal system, as Sully gets around the crimes he committed simply because he holds an important place in society, while others without his wealth and position are treated much more harshly.

•

Throughout the analysis of fourteen of Preston Sturges's most important films and in the paragraphs here that draw together ideas from the entirety of his Hollywood career, this book has attempted to demonstrate that Sturges's picture of life in America was amazingly consistent, especially for a studio writer/director who was cranking out entertainment in order to make a living. The vision of America that Sturges placed on movie screens did not exactly conform to the country's own image of itself, particularly during the early 1940s when World War II gave people a heightened belief in the superiority of American democracy. To Sturges, the ideas that America instilled in its people appeared to be more myth than reality: that the nation is dedicated to providing its citizens with a good life; that success equals money and status, and that the opportunity to achieve success is equally available to everyone through hard work, desire, and honesty; and that all Americans are guaranteed equal justice under the law and competent government through the democratic process. As a satirist and a cynic, Sturges took great pleasure in poking fun not so much at those ideas, but rather at the way in which Americans made fools of themselves for taking the ideas too seriously.

If Sturges did not think America actually ran according to its professed ideals, what did he perceive to be the motivating force behind the actions of its people? One possible answer to that question can be found by observing the role that image and pretense play in his movies, as his characters use the precepts of the American myths to fool others—or even themselves—in order to get what they want. In film after film, Sturges returned to one idea: that style—in the form of self-promotion, advertising, or simply the acclaim accorded people who only *appear* to be worthy—will almost always triumph over substance. In some films, such as *Hail the Conquering Hero*, the importance of image constitutes the major theme, but more often this idea is developed in a background incident or character or as just one part of the larger satire. Tracing and analyzing the many facets of this theme could easily furnish the material for another book, but some of the more obvious examples include the following:

Diamond Jim. A master of the art of self-promotion, Jim Brady gains his first important railroad job with A. E. Moore & Company by presenting himself in a way designed to impress the employer, even if it is unorthodox and largely misleading. Later he learns to enhance his public image through his predilection for diamonds and an ostentatious lifestyle. Finally, he is an early exploiter of media hype, as he attempts to sell the railroad world on his new steel cars through an elaborate, death-defying stunt, one of Sturges's examples of the power of advertising.

Easy Living. Louis Louis cannot attract customers to his hotel in spite of the hard work he has put into it and the luxurious accommodations he is offering. Just days away from foreclosure, however, he comes upon a salacious (and patently false) piece of gossip, which he uses to create the impression that his hotel is where important people prefer to carry on their affairs. As a result, in a matter of hours he achieves the kind of success that eluded him when he simply tried to provide good service.

The Great McGinty. Dan McGinty's entire political career is built on the triumph of image over reality. He is promoted as an alternative to the incumbent mayor (who is also controlled by The Boss), is hailed throughout as being on the side of the people, and even takes a wife just so that they can be photographed together. The citizens are perfectly content to accept the truth of the image, for The Boss and his political machine know how to manipulate them and their psychological needs. Even at the end of McGinty's career, when the people presumably turn against him because of his corrupt practices, they are only responding to the picture of the governor that The Boss has decided to expose.

Christmas in July. With its focus on advertising companies and their slogans, this film is one of Sturges's most pointed looks at America's obsession with images. From the one-room apartment that appears to have four rooms to everyone's belief that Jimmy is talented simply because other people have said so, the entire movie overflows with examples of fanfare winning out over content. No one at Maxford House or at the Baxter company ever mentions one word about actually offering customers the best coffee they can buy; instead the executives try to find clever slogans that will make people think that one brand is better.

Sullivan's Travels. Although Sully is sincere about experiencing firsthand the life that poor, troubled people live in America, the studio heads finally agree to his plan only because they see it as a great publicity stunt. Insisting on sending photographers, publicists, and other studio people along with Sully, the executives turn the initial part of his journey into what one of them calls "the greatest expedition of modern times, almost the greatest sacrifice ever made by human man." As a result, when Sully is rescued from the labor camp and tells the studio heads that he is not going to make his "social document," he immediately hears, "But it's had more publicity than the Johnstown flood! What are we going to do with all that publicity?"

The Palm Beach Story. Like *Christmas in July*, this film contains numerous examples of image versus substance. Gerry's entire undertaking is predicated on the idea—correctly so, as it turns out—that she can use her appearance alone to procure a trip to Florida, a rich husband, and the funding for Tom's airport. Maude sizes up potential husbands on a purely superficial basis; she wants to marry goodlooking men before she knows anything about their personality or character, which would likely ruin her infatuation with them. And even at the film's end, all that seems to matter to Maude and Snoodles is that Gerry's and Tom's siblings *look* right; that they might be different types of people never enters their minds.

The Great Moment. W. T. G. Morton may be providing a valuable service to his patients after he discovers ether, but it is advertising—specifically the offer to give customers double their money back if they feel any pain—that propels him to fame and fortune. When he later finds himself unjustly saddled with the reputation of being a greedy, uncaring dentist who would let people suffer in pain, he cannot do anything to convince the newspapers and the people that he is nothing like that. And the young girl whose leg is being amputated nearly has to undergo surgery without any anesthetic simply because the doctors of the Massachusetts Medical Society fear that their professional image will suffer if they back a discovery made by a mere dentist.

The Miracle of Morgan's Creek. From the *Bugle*'s editorial on military marriages to the scornful reaction to Woodrow and Trudy's late-night date, the people of Morgan's Creek seem overly concerned with promoting strong values in their town. In reality, as long as the image of righteousness is in place the practice of it is irrelevant. When the town becomes the focus of international attention and a symbol of family life, the citizens are more than satisfied with the knowledge that Norval and Trudy meet all the outward requirements of being married.

Hail the Conquering Hero. Like *The Great McGinty*, this film deals with image making in the political arena. The way in which Oakridge chooses its mayoral candidates—Everett Noble and Woodrow True-smith—shows that there is nothing more important than making voters *think* that someone is suited for the office. The speech that Noble continually practices consists of words that are empty, just like the deeds the town hails Woodrow for performing. But as Woodrow finds when he admits his pretense only to be acclaimed even more, all you have to do is pass the General Zabriski test—look right for the part—in order to be accorded respect.

The Sin of Harold Diddlebock. Once again Sturges creates a story that revolves around advertising, both in its setting (Harold works for an advertising firm) and in its plot (he has to come up with a way to sell his circus). The plan Harold devises is, like Jim Brady's train wreck, a brilliant promotional stunt. It counts on the unwitting but inevitable involvement of the mass media (the newspapers publicize Harold as "an escaped lunatic") and on the knowledge that bankers are willing to make only cosmetic, not substantive, changes to improve their poor image. Harold's scheme works because, just like his suit, it does not have to have any real merit; it only has to be loud and outrageous enough to grab everyone's attention.

The Beautiful Blonde from Bashful Bend. As in *The Palm Beach Story*, Sturges again examines the way images and expectations are intertwined with gender, this time in the character of Freddie Jones. As a strong, self-sufficient woman, Freddie encounters nothing but trouble, but once she presents herself as innocent and helpless she is able to secure whatever she sets her sights on. Twice she persuades Judge O'Toole to drop the charges against her, and in Snake City she nearly catches herself a rich but wimpy miner who is fully convinced that Freddie needs him to look after her.

In these and other films, Sturges portrays a society that, as much as we might like to think otherwise, is dominated by flash and sparkle. From the vantage point of the 1990s, such an observation does not seem extraordinary, but it means that Sturges saw fifty years ago where our society was heading. It is difficult to imagine that the depiction of politics in *The Great McGinty* was not influenced by Watergate and the Iran–Contra scandal, or that the satire of moral hypocrisy in *The Miracle of Morgan's Creek* was not a reaction to the religious right and the televangelists of the 1980s. But Sturges's ability to foresee how mass media and advertising would turn America into a country dominated by and devoted to images proves that he had a keen understanding of the society in which he lived.

Many things have happened in America in the nearly fifty years since Preston Sturges ceased to be an active filmmaker, and one cannot help but think that most of them would have set his mind spinning with ideas. Watergate and the savings and loan scandal; newspapers that publish pictures but no news; Ronald Reagan's presidency of images and Madonna's career of images—all would have fit in perfectly in the celluloid world that Sturges created. That he is not here to give us his insights on these events, and to poke fun at us for the way we have reacted to them, is our great loss, for while his satire may not have taught us to act more sensibly, at least it would have given us a really good laugh.

Filmography

The Big Pond

Produced by Monta Bell; Directed by Hobart Henley; Based on the play by George Middleton and A. E. Thomas; Dialogue Director: Bertram Harrison; Scenario: Robert Presnell and Garrett Fort; Dialogue: Preston Sturges; Photography: George Folsey; Edited by Emma Hill; Sound: Ernest Zatorsky; Musical Arranger: John W. Green. Released by Paramount, 1930.

Cast: Maurice Chevalier (Pierre Mirande); Claudette Colbert (Barbara Billings); George Barbier (Mr. Billings); Marion Ballou (Mrs. Billings); Andree Corday (Toinette); Frank Lyon (Ronnie); Nat Pendleton (Pat O'Day); Elaine Koch (Jennie).

Fast and Loose

Directed by Fred Newmeyer; Based on the play *The Best People* by David Gray and Avery Hopwood; Dialogue Director: Bertram Harrison; Screenplay by Doris Anderson and Jack Kirkland; Dialogue: Preston Sturges; Photography: William Steiner; Sound: C. A. Tuthill. Released by Paramount, 1930.

Cast: Frank Morgan (Bronson Lenox); Miriam Hopkins (Marion Lenox); Carole Lombard (Alice O'Neil); Charles Starrett (Henry Morgan); Henry Wadsworth (Bertie Lenox); Winifred Harris (Carrie Lenox); Herbert Yost (George Grafton); David Hutcheson (Lord Rockingham); Ilka Chase (Millie Montgomery); Herschel Mayall (Judge Summers).

The Power and the Glory

See Chapter One.

Thirty Day Princess

Produced by B. P. Schulberg; Directed by Marion Gering; Based on the story by Clarence Budington Kelland; Adaptation by Sam Hellman and Edwin Justus Mayer; Screenplay by Preston Sturges and Frank Partos; Assistant Director: Art Jacobson; Photography: Leon Shamroy; Edited by June Loring; Art Direction: Hans Dreier; Sound: J. A. Goodrich. Released by Paramount, 1934.

Cast: Sylvia Sidney (Princess Catterina/Nancy Lane); Cary Grant (Porter Madison III); Edward Arnold (Richard Gresham); Henry Stephenson (King Anatol); Vince Barnet (Count); Edgar Norton (Baron); Robert McWade (Managing Editor); George Baxter (Spottswood); Ray Walker (Mr. Kirk); Lucien Littlefield (Parker); Marguerite Namara (Lady-in-Waiting); Eleanor Wesselhoeft (Mrs. Schmidt).

We Live Again

Produced by Samuel Goldwyn; Directed by Rouben Mamoulian; Based on the novel *Resurrection* by Leo Tolstoy; Adaptation by Maxwell Anderson and Leonard Praskins; Screenplay by Preston Sturges; Assistant Director: Robert Lee; Photography: Gregg Toland; Edited by Otho Lovering; Art Direction: Richard Day; Production Design: Sergei Sudeikin; Sound: Frank Mahler; Musical Director: Alfred Newman. Released by United Artists, 1934.

Cast: Anna Sten (Katusha Maslova); Fredric March (Prince Dmitri Nekhlyudov); Jane Baxter (Missy Kortchagin); C. Aubrey Smith (Prince Kortchagin); Ethel Griffies (Aunt Marie); Gwendolyn Logan (Aunt Sophia); Jessie Ralph (Matrona Pavlovna); Sam Jaffe (Simonson); Cecil Cunningham (Theodosia); Jesse Arnold (Korablova); Fritzi Ridgeway (The Red Head); Morgan Wallace (The Colonel).

The Good Fairy

Directed by William Wyler; Associate Producer: Henry Henigson; Based on the play by Ferenc Molnar; Screenplay by Preston Sturges; Assistant Director: Archie Buchanan; Photography: Norbert Bodine; Edited by Daniel Mandell; Art Direction: Charles D. Hall; Sound: Joe Lapin. Released by Universal, 1935.

Cast: Margaret Sullavan (Luisa Ginglebusher); Herbert Marshall (Dr. Max Sporum); Frank Morgan (Konrad); Reginald Owen (Detlaff); Alan Hale (Schlapkohl); Beulah Bondi (Dr. Schultz); Eric Blore (Dr. Motz); Hugh O'Connell (Telephone Man); Cesar Romero (Joe); Luis Alberni (The Barber); Torben Meyer (Head Waiter); Al Bridge (Doorman); Frank Moran and Matt McHugh (Moving Men).

Diamond Jim

See Chapter Two.

The Gay Deception

Produced by Jesse L. Lasky; Directed by William Wyler; Screenplay by Stephen Avery and Don Hartman; Additional Dialogue: Arthur Richman; Assistant Director: Al Schaumer; Photography: Joseph Valentine; Art Direction: Max Parker; Sound: S. C. Chapman; Musical Direction: Louis de Francesco; Song "Paris in the Evening" by Preston Sturges and Ted Snyder. Released by 20th Century–Fox, 1935.

Cast: Francis Lederer (Sandro); Frances Dee (Mirabel); Benita Hume (Miss Channing); Alan Mowbray (Lord Clewe); Akim Tamiroff (Spellek); Lennox

Pawle (Consul General); Adele St. Maur (Lucille); Ferdinand Gottschalk (Mr. Squires); Richard Carle (Mr. Spitzer); Robert Greig (Adolph); Luis Alberni (Ernest); Lionel Stander (Gettel); Al Bridge (Jail Attendant); Jack Mulhall (Bank Teller); Torben Meyer (Waiter).

One Rainy Afternoon

Produced by Jesse L. Lasky; Directed by Rowland V. Lee; Based on the screenplay *Monsieur Sans Gene* by Slovenskee Liga Pressburger and Rene Pujol; Screenplay by Stephen Avery; Additional Dialogue: Maurice Hanline; Photography: Peverell Marley and Merritt Gerstad; Edited by Margaret Clancy; Art Direction: Richard Day; Sound: Paul Neal; Musical Direction: Alfred Newman; Musical Score: Ralph Irwin; Song "Secret Rendezvous" by Preston Sturges and Ralph Irwin. Released by United Artists, 1936.

Cast: Francis Lederer (Philippe Martin); Ida Lupino (Monique Pelerin); Hugh Herbert (Toto); Roland Young (Maillot); Erik Rhodes (Count Alfredo); Joseph Cawthorn (M. Pelerin); Countess Liev de Maigret (Yvonne); Georgia Caine (Cecile); Richard Carle (Minister of Justice); Angie Norton (Hortense).

Hotel Haywire

Produced by Paul Jones; Directed by George Archainbaud; Screenplay by Preston Sturges; Assistant Director: Stanley Goldsmith; Photography: Henry Sharp; Edited by Arthur Schmidt; Art Direction: Hans Dreier and Robert Odell; Set Decoration: A. E. Freudeman; Musical Direction: Boris Morros. Released by Paramount, 1937.

Cast: Leo Carrillo (Dr. Zodiac Z. Zippe); Lynne Overman (Dr. Parkhouse); Mary Carlisle (Phyllis); Benny Baker (Bertie Sterns); Spring Byington (Mrs. Parkhouse); George Barbier (I. Ketts); Porter Hall (Judge Newhall); Collette Lyons (Genevieve Sterns); John Patterson (Frank Ketts); Lucien Littlefield (Elmer); Chester Conklin (O'Shea); Franklin Pangborn (Fuller Brush Salesman).

Easy Living

See Chapter Three.

Port of Seven Seas

Produced by Henry Henigson; Directed by James Whale; Based on the play *Fanny* by Marcel Pagnol; Screenplay by Preston Sturges; Assistant Director: Joseph McDonough; Photography: Karl Freund; Montage: Slavko Vorkapich; Edited by Frederick Y. Smith; Art Direction: Cedric Gibbons, Gabriel Scognamillo, and Edwin B. Willis; Sound Recording: Douglas Shearer; Musical Score: Franz Waxman. Released by Metro-Goldwyn-Mayer, 1938.

Cast: Wallace Beery (Cesar); Frank Morgan (Panisse); Maureen O'Sullivan (Madelon); John Beal (Marius); Jessie Ralph (Honorine); Cora Witherspoon (Claudine); Etienne Girardot (Brueneau); E. Allyn Warren (Captain Escartefigue); Robert Spindola (Boy); Doris Lloyd (Customer).

If I Were King

Produced and Directed by Frank Lloyd; Based on the play by Justin Huntly McCarthy; Screenplay by Preston Sturges; Assistant Director: William Tummel; Photography: Theodore Sparkuhl; Special Effects Photography: Gordon Jennings; Edited by Hugh Bennett; Art Direction: Hans Dreier and John Goodman; Set Decoration: A. E. Freudeman; Sound: Harold C. Lewis and John Cope; Musical Direction: Boris Morros; Musical Score: Richard Hageman. Released by Paramount, 1938.

Cast: Ronald Colman (Francois Villon); Basil Rathbone (Louis XI); Frances Dee (Katherine de Vaucelles); Ellen Drew (Huguette); C. V. France (Father Villon); Henry Wilcoxon (Captain of the Watch); Heather Thatcher (The Queen); Stanley Ridges (Rene de Montigny); Bruce Lester (Noel le Jolys); Walter Kingsford (Tristan l'Hermite); Alma Lloyd (Colette); Sidney Toler (Robin Turgis).

Never Say Die

Produced by Paul Jones; Directed by Elliot Nugent; Based on the play by William H. Post; Screenplay by Don Hartman, Frank Butler, and Preston Sturges; Assistant Director: Harold Schwartz; Photography: Leo Tover; Special Effects Photography: Farciot Edouart; Edited by James Smith; Art Direction: Hans Dreier and Ernst Fegte; Set Decoration: A. E. Freudeman; Sound: William Wisdom and Walter Oberst; Musical Direction: Boris Morros. Released by Paramount, 1939.

Cast: Bob Hope (John Kidley); Martha Raye (Mickey Hawkins); Ernest Cossart (Jeepers); Paul Harvey (Jasper Hawkins); Andy Devine (Henry Munch); Siegfried Rumann (Poppa Ingleborg); Alan Mowbray (Prince Smirnow); Gale Sondergaard (Juno); Frances Arms (Mama Ingleborg); Ivan Simpson (Kretsky); Monty Woolley (Dr. Schmidt); Foy Van Dolson (Kretsky's Bodyguard); Donald Haines (Julius); Gustav von Seyffertitz (Chemist).

Remember the Night

See Chapter Four.

The Great McGinty

See Chapter Five.

Christmas in July

See Chapter Six.

The Lady Eve

See Chapter Seven.

Sullivan's Travels

See Chapter Eight.

The Palm Beach Story

See Chapter Nine.

The Great Moment

See Chapter Ten.

I Married a Witch

Produced by Preston Sturges; Directed by Rene Clair; Based on the novel *The Passionate Witch* by Thorne Smith; Screenplay by Robert Pirosh and Marc Connelly; Assistant Director: Art Black; Photography: Ted Tetzlaff; Special Effects Photography: Gordon Jennings; Edited by Eda Warren; Art Direction: Hans Dreier and Ernst Fegte; Set Decoration: George Sawley; Sound: Harry Mills and Richard Olson; Musical Score: Roy Webb. Released by United Artists, 1942.

Cast: Fredric March (Wallace Wooley); Veronica Lake (Jennifer); Robert Benchley (Dr. Dudley White); Susan Hayward (Estelle Masterson); Cecil Kellaway (Daniel); Elizabeth Patterson (Margaret); Robert Warwick (J. B. Masterson); Eily Malyon (Tabitha); Robert Greig (Town Crier); Aldrich Bowker (Justice of the Peace); Emory Parnell (Allen); Charles Moore (Rufus); Al Bridge (Prison Guard); Chester Conklin (Bartender).

Star Spangled Rhythm

Directed by George Marshall; Associate Producer: Joe Sistrom; Screenplay by Harry Tugend; Sketches by George Kaufman, Arthur Ross and Fred Saidy, and Melvin Frank and Norman Panama; Assistant Director: Art Black; Photography: Leo Tover and Theodore Sparkuhl; Edited by Paul Weatherwax; Art Direction: Hans Dreier and Ernst Fegte; Musical Direction: Robert Emmet Dolan. Released by Paramount, 1942.

Cast: Victor Moore (Pop Webster); Betty Hutton (Polly Judson); Eddie Bracken (Jimmy Webster); Walter Abel (B. G. DeSoto); Anne Revere (Sarah); Cass Daley (Mimi); and as themselves: Bing Crosby, Bob Hope, Fred MacMurray, Ray Milland, Dorothy Lamour, Paulette Goddard, Dick Powell, Veronica Lake, Alan Ladd, Ernest Truex, Cecil B. DeMille, and Preston Sturges.

The Miracle of Morgan's Creek

See Chapter Eleven.

Hail the Conquering Hero

See Chapter Twelve.

The Sin of Harold Diddlebock

See Chapter Thirteen.

Unfaithfully Yours

Produced and Directed by Preston Sturges; Screenplay by Preston Sturges; Assistant Director: Gaston Glass; Photography: Victor Milner; Special Effects Photography: Fred Sersen; Edited by Robert Fritch; Art Direction: Lyle Wheeler and Joseph C. Wright; Set Decoration: Thomas Little and Paul S. Fox; Sound: Arthur L. Kirback and Roger Heman; Musical Direction: Alfred Newman. Released by 20th Century–Fox, 1948.

Cast: Rex Harrison (Sir Alfred de Carter); Linda Darnell (Daphne de Carter); Barbara Lawrence (Barbara); Rudy Vallee (August); Kurt Kreuger (Anthony); Lionel Stander (Hugo); Edgar Kennedy (Sweeney); Al Bridge (House Detective); Julius Tannen (Tailor); Torben Meyer (Dr. Schultz); Robert Greig (Jules); Georgia Caine (Dowager); Isabel Jewell (Telephone Operator); Marion Marshall (Telephone Operator); J. Farrell MacDonald (Doorman); Frank Moran (Fire Chief).

The Beautiful Blonde from Bashful Bend

See Chapter Fourteen.

Letters from My Windmill

Produced by Jean Martinelli; Directed by Marcel Pagnol; Based on the stories "The Three Low Masses," "The Elixir of Father Gaucher," and "The Secret of Master Cornille" by Alphonse Daudet; Screenplay by Marcel Pagnol; English Subtitles by Preston Sturges; Photography: Willy Faktorovitch; Edited by Monique Lacombe; Art Direction: Robert Giordani and Jean Mandaroux; Sound: Marcel Royne; Musical Score: Henri Tomasi. Released by Tohan Pictures, 1955.

Cast: Henri Vilbert (Dom Balaguere); Daxely (Garrigou/The Devil); Yvonne Gamy (The Old Woman); Keller (The Marquis); Rene Sarvil (The Chef); Rellys (Father Gaucher); Robert Vattier (The Abbot); Christian Lude (Father Sylvestre); Fernand Sardou (M. Charnigue); Edouard Delmont (Master Cornille); Roger Crouset (Alphonse Daudet); Pierrette Bruno (Vivette).

The French They Are a Funny Race

Produced by Alain Poire and Paul Wagner; Directed by Preston Sturges; Based on the book *The Notebooks of Major Thompson* by Pierre Daninos; Screenplay by Preston Sturges; Assistant Directors: Pierre Kast and Francis Caillaud; Photography: Maurice Barry, Christian Matras, and Jean Lallier; Edited by Raymond Lanny; Art Direction: Serge Pimenoff, Robert Andre, Robert Guisgand, and Claude Moesching; Sound: Jene Rieul; Musical Score: Georges Van Parys. Released by Continental Distributing, 1957.

Cast: Jack Buchanan (Major Thompson); Martine Carol (Martine Thompson); Noel-Noel (M. Taupin); Totti Truman Taylor (Miss Ffyth); Catherine Boyl (Ursula); Andre Luguet (M. Fusillard); Genevieve Brunet (Mlle. Sylvette).

Paris Holiday

Produced by Bob Hope; Directed by Gerd Oswald; Associate Producer: Cecil Foster Kemp; Based on a story by Bob Hope; Screenplay by Edmund Beloin and Dean Riesner; Assistant Director: Paul Feyder; Photography: Roger Hubert; Edited by Ellsworth Hoagland; Sound: Frances Scheid and Robert Biart; Musical Score: Joseph J. Lilley. Released by United Artists, 1958.

Cast: Bob Hope (Robert Leslie Hunter); Fernandel (Fernydel); Anita Ekberg (Zara); Martha Hyer (Ann McCall); Andre Morell (American Ambassador); Preston Sturges (Serge Vitry); Jean Murat (Judge); Maurice Teynac (Doctor Bernais); Irene Tunc (Shipboard Lovely); Roger Treville (Golfer Patient); Yves Brainville (Inspector Dupont).

Selected Bibliography

Ackerman, Dan. "The Structure of the Preston Sturges Film." *Cinema Texas* 10, no. 3 (Spring 1976): 78–82.

Bogdanovich, Peter. "Screenwriters and Preston Sturges." In *Pieces of Time*. New York: Arbor House, 1973.

Budd, Michael. "Notes on Preston Sturges and America." *Film Society Review* 3 (1987): 22–26.

Corliss, Richard. "The Author/Auteurs: Preston Sturges." In *Talking Pictures: Screenwriters in the American Cinema*. Woodstock, N.Y.: Overlook Press, 1974.

Curtis, James. *Between Flops: A Biography of Preston Sturges*. New York: Harcourt Brace Jovanovich, 1982.

Cywinski, Ray. *Preston Sturges: A Guide to References and Resources*. Boston: G. K. Hall, 1984.

Denby, David. "Adam and Eve on a Luxury Liner." *Premiere*, October 1991, 20, 108.

Dickos, Andrew. *Intrepid Laughter: Preston Sturges and the Movies*. Metuchen, N.J.: Scarecrow Press, 1985.

Durgnat, Raymond. "The New Sarcasm." In *The Crazy Mirror*. New York: Horizon Press, 1969.

————. "Subversion in the Fields." *Films and Filming* 12, no. 3 (December 1965): 42–48.

Ericsson, Peter. "Preston Sturges." *Sequences*, no. 7 (Summer 1948): 22–29.

Farber, Manny, and W. S. Poster. "Preston Sturges: Success in the Movies." In *Negative Space*, by Manny Farber. New York: Praeger Publishers, 1971.

Gassner, John, and Dudley Nichols, eds. *The Best Film Plays of 1943–1944*. New York: Crown, 1945.

Hamilton, Ian. *Writers in Hollywood*. New York: Harper and Row, 1990.

Harvey, James. *Romantic Comedy in Hollywood*. New York: Knopf, 1987.

Henderson, Brian, ed. *Five Screenplays by Preston Sturges*. Berkeley: University of California Press, 1985.

Jacobs, Diane. *Christmas in July: The Life and Art of Preston Sturges*. Berkeley: University of California Press, 1992.

Kael, Pauline. "Raising Kane." In *The Citizen Kane Book*, by Pauline Kael, Herman Mankiewicz, and Orson Welles. Boston: Little, Brown and Company, 1971.

Kracauer, Siegfried. "Preston Sturges or Laughter Betrayed." *Films in Review* 1, no. 1 (February 1950): 11–13, 43–47.

Levy, Emanuel. "The 1940s: Ambivalence and Cynicism." In *Small-Town America in Film*. New York: Continuum, 1991.

Preston Sturges by Preston Sturges. Adapted and edited by Sandy Sturges. New York: Simon and Schuster, 1990.

Rabinovitz, Lauren. "Easy Living." *Cinema Texas* 13, no. 1 (September 26, 1977): 79–85.

Reitz, Carolyn. "The Miracle of Morgan's Creek." *Cinema Texas* 8, no. 45 (April 7, 1975): 1–5.

Rubinstein, E. "Hollywood Travels: Sturges and Sullivan." *Sight and Sound* 47, no. 1 (Winter 1978): 50–52.

Rubinstein, Elliot. "The Home Fires: Aspects of Sturges's Wartime Comedy." *Quarterly Review of Film Studies* 7, no. 2 (Spring 1982): 131–41.

Sarris, Andrew. "Preston Sturges: The Man Who Made Comedy Cry." *Village Voice*, November 24, 1975, 135–36.

————. "Preston Sturges in the Thirties." *Film Comment* 6, no. 4 (Winter 1970): 80–85.

Spoto, Donald. *Madcap: The Life of Preston Sturges*. Boston: Little, Brown and Company, 1990.

Ursini, James. *The Fabulous Life and Times of Preston Sturges, an American Dreamer*. New York: Curtis Books, 1973.

Index